REDMOND: A LIFE UNDONE

REDMOND:
A LIFE UNDONE

CHRIS DOOLEY ∾

Gill & Macmillan

Gill & Macmillan
Hume Avenue
Park West
Dublin 12
www.gillmacmillanbooks.ie

978 07171 6582 7

Print origination by O'K Graphic Design, Dublin
Indexed by Cliff Murphy
Printed and bound by ScandBook AB, Sweden

This book is typeset in 11.5/15 pt Minion.

The paper used in this book comes from the wood pulp of managed forests. For every tree felled, at least one tree is planted, thereby renewing natural resources.

A CIP catalogue record for this book is available from the British Library.

5 4 3 2 1

For my partner, Mary, and my mother, Bridget,
and in memory of my late father, Jack

ACKNOWLEDGEMENTS

The idea for this book arose in conversation over a pint in the International Bar four years ago with my friend Colm Keena, which was prompted by a column about John Redmond written by our colleague Stephen Collins in *The Irish Times* the previous weekend. Colm and I were reflecting on how comparatively little attention is given to Redmond's campaign for Home Rule in the years leading up to the Easter Rising of 1916, when set against the information readily available about the Rising and its aftermath. After we discussed how much we'd like to read a good book about the pre-Rising years, I resolved to try to write that book myself. I start then by thanking Colm (and Stephen) for the idea.

Much of the research for the book was conducted in the reading and manuscript rooms of the National Library, in Dublin, which are wonderful spaces in which to work. I thank all the staff there for their invaluable assistance, in particular Mary Broderick, who took a particular interest in my project, and Keith Murphy, who helped source the charming photographs of John Redmond, and his wife Amy, at home in Aughavanagh. Thanks are also due to the staffs of Trinity College Library, Dublin, and the Parliamentary Archives in London.

A big thanks to my agent, Faith O'Grady, whose enthusiasm for the book and dedication to it from day one was a source of great encouragement. Working with the team at Gill & Macmillan has been a huge pleasure and thanks are due to all for their courtesy, patience and professionalism. Conor Nagle, in particular, helped steer the project through and was always there with a helpful word of advice when it was needed.

A special thanks to Claire Tighe, parliamentary assistant at the SDLP's Westminster office, for her illuminating and entertaining tour of the Houses of Parliament, which provided many insights into the physical environment in which John Redmond spent much of his working life, as well as underlining the richness of Ireland's contribution to British parliamentary politics. Thanks also to my colleague Mark Hennessy for making the tour possible.

Stephen Collins provided much support and encouragement when the book was in its early stages of preparation, and I'm also grateful to Diarmaid Ferriter, professor of modern Irish history at UCD, for reading some draft chapters and providing very helpful feedback.

I also thank my editor at *The Irish Times*, Kevin O'Sullivan, deputy editor, Denis Staunton, and former deputy foreign editor, Evelyn Bracken, for their support in a variety of ways, which made it possible for me to complete this work.

A heartfelt thanks also to my friends Chris Macey and Alan Byrne, who each undertook a close reading of the text and came up with more suggestions for improvements than I would care to admit to; suffice it to say the book is immeasurably better because of their input, though any deficiencies that remain are of course my sole responsibility.

And the greatest thanks to my partner, Mary Boland, for support in more ways than I have space to enumerate, not least her stoic endurance as I returned daily from the National Library, breathless with news of the astonishing events of a hundred years ago. Having a first class writer and editor in my life was an advantage I availed of to the full and Mary's painstaking work brought about countless improvements to the text. Without her practical and moral support this book would never have seen the light of day.

CONTENTS

'The life of a politician, especially of an Irish politician, is one long series of postponements and compromises and disappointments and disillustions.'

JOHN REDMOND, House of Commons, 21 May 1917

PROLOGUE

Sunday, 31 March 1912. O'Connell Street in Dublin has never seen anything like this. Since mid-morning, when the 64 special trains bringing people from all over the country began to arrive in the capital, its main thoroughfare has been filling from end to end. By early afternoon the street is so tightly packed that you could, as one observer put it, walk from one end to the other on the shoulders of the people.

Many of those present have marched into the city centre to the martial airs of pipers' bands leading the way from the train stations at Kingsbridge, Amiens Street, Broadstone, Harcourt Street and Westland Row. Thousands of others have arrived on the city's various tram lines.

The atmosphere is one of excitement, good cheer and expectancy, not just for the tumultuous day ahead, which will not be forgotten by anyone present, but for the great transformation in Ireland's fortunes that is about to come. A new Home Rule Bill is to be introduced by the British government within days and, after decades of struggle by Irish MPs in the House of Commons, and numerous setbacks, Ireland is once again to have its independence.

For the first time since the Act of Union came into effect in 1801, when London assumed direct control of Irish affairs, Dublin is to have its own parliament and Ireland is to be – in the words of Thomas Davis's song, which will get many vigorous airings today – 'A Nation Once Again'.

Four speakers' platforms have been specially erected for the occasion, each colourfully decked out and with a canvas backdrop making the bold assertion 'Ireland A Nation', echoing Davis's now near 70-year-old refrain. The same three words are emblazoned on a white scroll spanning the vast width of the thoroughfare at its northern end near the Parnell monument.

House fronts along the street are bright with flags and banners fluttering in the light breeze, many of them bearing the simply expressed demand of all those present, estimated to number between 100,000 and 150,000: 'We Want Home Rule'.

The occasion is a boon for city centre businesses. Some pubs have closed for fear of being unable to manage the crowds, but hotels and restaurants have taken on extra staff for the day and street vendors are doing a spectacularly lively trade, particularly in Home Rule badges and green walking canes. The 'Home Rule oranges' are also going down well. 'On Saturday they were ordinary oranges, of course,' the following day's *Irish Independent* will wryly observe.

The only discordant note is struck by the small, brave bands of suffragettes, who attempt to walk through the throngs carrying sandwich boards with inscriptions such as 'Down With Government Coercion', 'Irish Women Want The Vote' and 'Self-Government means Government by Men and Women'. They are generally regarded as an amusing and harmless diversion, though in one unsavoury incident outside the Mansion House – where a reception is being held for the day's keynote speakers – policemen intervene after a group of the women have their sandwich boards torn from them and smashed. The *Independent*, reporting that some of the suffragettes lost their hats and had their hair dishevelled, finds the incident 'exciting, though partly amusing'.

As the time for the speeches approaches, Sackville Street, as it is still officially known – though 'O'Connell Street' is already in common usage – can no longer hold the still-swelling crowds, who now stretch all the way across O'Connell Bridge and into Westmoreland Street and D'Olier Street. Thousands of others spill into the side street.

Those closest to the 'students' platform' erected in the shadow of the Daniel O'Connell statue at the south end of the street will give their loudest cheers to young Michael Davitt, son of the great land rights campaigner of the same name who died six years ago in 1906. At a second platform, by the Father Mathew statue, veteran nationalist MP from Dublin John Dillon will make the principal speech. His Belfast-based colleague in the Irish Parliamentary Party, Joe Devlin, will lead the speakers at the platform sited at the junction with Middle Abbey Street.

The early comers, however, have gathered at the 'No. 1 platform', the main stage, erected close to the recently unveiled monument to the revered nationalist leader Charles Stewart Parnell. There, the man who was chiefly responsible for having that monument erected and who has done most to maintain Parnell's legacy since his mentor's fall from grace and premature death three decades previously, is to be the keynote speaker. And there are few better public speakers around than John Redmond.

Although not given to undue expressions of emotion, the MP for Waterford can be forgiven for feeling exultant. A member of the House of Commons since 1881 and undisputed leader of the Irish nationalist movement for the past 12 years, Redmond has devoted his political career to the cause of self-government for Ireland. And now his life's work is about to come to fruition. His achievement in bringing Home Rule within touching distance, through a combination of political acumen and perseverance, has made him the most popular politician in Ireland and one of the most respected by all parties in the British parliament.

At 1.50 p.m. Redmond and his wife Amy leave the Mansion House to begin their short journey to O'Connell Street, via St Stephen's Green, Grafton Street, College Green and Westmoreland Street. The pair, accompanied by Lord Mayor of Dublin Lorcan Sherlock, are in the first of a procession of horse-drawn carriages that is greeted by ever-louder cheers from the masses as it gets closer to its destination. The cavalcade is led by two bands and accompanied by a group of hurley-wielding members of the GAA, as well as representatives, clad in green and white, of the Irish National Foresters, a benefit society that supports the nationalist cause.

The procession that follows includes long lines of members of the United Irish League, the Ancient Order of Hibernians and the National Foresters, marching in branches and accompanied by some 170 pipers' bands and brass bands. The weather is almost summer-like, the morning's ominous black clouds having given way to bright afternoon sunshine.

Prolonged cheers greet the arrival of Redmond's carriage at the platform at 2.20 p.m. The crowd is so dense that many of those who have tickets to join him on the stage – mainly members of Dublin Corporation – have trouble getting access. Nevertheless, proceedings begin 15 minutes ahead of schedule when, at 2.45 p.m., baritone J.C. Browner steps to the front of the stage to begin a rendition of 'A Nation Once Again'. The tens of thousands gathered there take up the chorus with enthusiasm:

> A nation once again
> A nation once again
> And Ireland, long a province, be
> A nation once again!

When the singing finishes, the crowd cheers. And then cheers again. Then the Lord Mayor steps forward to introduce the star turn. Have they confidence in John Redmond, he asks, to loud roars of approval. Do they trust 'his wisdom, his sagacity, his patriotism'? The response is more loud cheers in the affirmative.

When Redmond takes the stage, he has to wait for the cheering to subside before he can begin. All the roadblocks, frustrations and setbacks he has encountered in his long pursuit of his goal can only add to the sweetness of the moment. All the striving for recognition that marked the early years of his political career, such as when Parnell overlooked him for the Wexford seat held by his late father, is now surely an inconsequential memory. His short stint in jail over his support for an evicted tenant farmer probably seems amusing from where he is standing now. Standing before his people, on the cusp of this crowning achievement, Redmond might also be forgiven for thinking that his place in history among the great Irish leaders is secure.

Ever the pragmatic politician, he is more likely thinking about the negotiations with the British government on the contents of the Home Rule Bill that have been taking place behind the scenes. Nevertheless, he cannot resist drawing a parallel between his own position and that of another great orator, Daniel O'Connell. 'This gathering, its vastness, its good order, its enthusiasm and its unity are unparalleled in the modern history of Ireland. In point of numbers it recalls the monster meetings of O'Connell, but never, at the best of his days, did he assemble a gathering so representative of all Ireland as this meeting today,' he declares.

Every class is represented here, landlords and tenants, labourers and artisans, the professions of Ireland, Irish commerce, Irish learning and art, Irish literature, are all represented at this meeting [cheers]. In fact it is no exaggeration to say that this meeting *is* Ireland [cheers].

But Redmond knows that not all of Ireland is represented at this assembly. In the north-east, Protestants loyal to the British crown have organised themselves to resist Home Rule by whatever means necessary. Six months earlier, a hundred thousand of them gathered at a rally in Craigavon to hear their new leader, Sir Edward Carson, tell them: 'We will yet defeat the most nefarious conspiracy that has ever been hatched against a free people.' Since then, amid increasing tension, steps have been taken to set up a provisional government for Ulster in the event of Home Rule being enacted. The newly established Ulster Volunteer Force (UVF) has begun military drilling. It is not yet fully armed, but before long it will be. And it has the full backing of Britain's opposition Conservative Party.

It is against this background that Redmond makes a fresh appeal in his speech, which at just under 20 minutes is unusually short, to the northern unionists. Referring to the 'one gap in our ranks, one body of our fellow countrymen [who] are absent today', he asks his audience: 'What have I to say to them today? I say that for them in this hour of triumph for Ireland a nation we have not one word of reproach nor one trace of bitter feeling.' The crowd cheers in response.

'We have one feeling only in our hearts, and that is an earnest longing for the arrival of the day of reconciliation.' After someone shouts 'Hear, hear', Redmond continues: 'I say to these fellow countrymen of ours, they may repudiate Ireland – Ireland will never repudiate them, and we today look forward with absolute confidence, in the certainty of the near approach of that day when they will form a powerful and respected portion of a self-governed Irish nation, that they will have an opportunity of reviving once more the glories of their own ancestors, the Protestant patriots of Grattan's parliament.' Once more, the cheers go up.

They continue and increase in volume as Redmond goes on to make a confident declaration: 'Believe me, Home Rule is winning. We will have a parliament sitting in College Green sooner than the most sanguine and enthusiastic man in this crowd believes.'

With the finishing line so close and the political wind so strongly at his back, surely nobody now, not even Edward Carson and his putative army, can wreck John Redmond's dream of delivering self-governance to Ireland, and doing so by entirely peaceful and constitutional means.

~

A few hundred yards from where Redmond is speaking, another man takes the stage. His speech, from Joe Devlin's platform at the junction of O'Connell Street and Middle Abbey Street, gets no attention in the following day's national newspapers. This may be because he is too little known or is considered of no importance. It probably doesn't help that he delivers some of his speech in Irish.

Patrick Pearse, the headmaster of St Enda's School in Rathfarnham, tells his listeners that there are many present who desire more than Home Rule within the British Empire, which is what is currently on offer – they would destroy the empire if they could. But he accepts that Home Rule would be for the good of Ireland, which would be stronger with it than without it.

'Let us unite and win a good Act from the British,' he exhorts the crowd. 'I think it can be done. But if we are tricked this time, there is a party in Ireland, and I am one of them, that will advise the Gael to have no counsel or dealings with the Gall [the foreigner] for ever again, but to answer them henceforward with the strong hand and the sword's edge. Let the Gall understand that if we are cheated once more there will be red war in Ireland.'

These are not views to which John Redmond would subscribe. But if he is told of Pearse's speech, it is unlikely to concern him. He knows there is little appetite in Ireland for the extreme views held by a small minority of men such as Patrick Pearse.

Chapter 1 ∿

THE DICTATOR FROM DUBLIN

That is a policy which Ireland cannot and will not uphold.

Herbert Pike Pease, Liberal Unionist MP for Darlington, is battling to avert a catastrophe. A member of the House of Commons for more than a decade, the Cambridge-educated 42-year-old is fighting his third general election. But he has never contested one as important as this, and it is unlikely he ever will. It is January 1910, and Britain is in the grip of a constitutional crisis. How it is resolved will not only chart the future course of British politics, it will also determine the fate of the Irish Parliamentary Party's decades-long fight to secure Home Rule.

Pike Pease's election poster leaves no room for doubt about the potential calamities confronting his country, boldly declaring:

THE BRITISH EMPIRE has flourished and its people have lived happily under its ANCIENT CONSTITUTION.
THE RUIN OF THE EMPIRE AND ITS PEOPLE is now threatened by a CONFEDERATION of LIBERALS, RADICALS, SOCIALISTS and IRISH HOME RULERS.

After that stark warning, a rallying cry:

Citizens of the Empire Up and Defend your Inheritance

followed by the exhortation:

SUPPORT THE UNIONIST PARTY – which stands for a SOUND AND WELL-BALANCED CONSTITUTION.

Out with the Wreckers AND PROMOTERS OF DISUNION
Vote for Pike Pease, the Unionist candidate.

The chief radical and wrecker in Pike Pease's mind is undoubtedly the Chancellor of the Exchequer, David Lloyd George, whose 'people's budget' of the previous year has unleashed nothing less than class warfare. The Chancellor's plan to impose a 'super tax' on the wealthy and to introduce new taxes on estates to help pay for his 'war on poverty', in the form of pension and welfare payments, has been blocked by the House of Lords.

It's not the first time the Tory-dominated upper house has vetoed Liberal Party legislation, but never before has it had the temerity to throw out a budget passed by the House of Commons. The Liberals, in government now for four years and long since fed up with the partisan approach adopted by the Lords, have called an early election to seek a mandate from the British people to alter the balance of power between the two houses of parliament.

So the choice now facing voters is not simply between the Liberal Party and its Conservative and Liberal Unionist opponents, it is a choice between sweeping out the old order or maintaining Herbert Pike Pease's 'sound and well balanced constitution'.

In all of this, John Redmond and the Irish Parliamentary Party, which he leads, are far from disinterested observers. No party has a greater stake than the Irish nationalists in seeing the removal of the Lords veto, which was used to stop a Home Rule Bill in its tracks in 1893 after Charles Stewart Parnell had brought the issue of Irish self-rule to the forefront of British politics. Now Parnell's disciple Redmond, who has succeeded the master as leader-in-waiting of the Irish nation, is set to play a key role in the unfolding political drama.

For the Irish Parliamentary Party, the election campaign has begun well. In a keynote address at the Royal Albert Hall on 10 December, Prime Minister Herbert Asquith left no one in doubt about the Liberals' determination to curb the House of Lords' powers. Indeed, he and his fellow Liberal ministers would not hold office, he said, unless they had secured the necessary safeguards to ensure that 'the party of progress' could govern effectively. To that end, the absolute veto of the House of Lords would have to go.

Referring in the same speech to Ireland as 'the one undeniable failure of British statesmanship', he pledged Liberal Party support for 'a system of full self-government [in Ireland] in regard to purely Irish affairs'. In other words, Ireland is to have its long-sought Home Rule parliament should the Liberals be re-elected.

Few in Ireland saw the announcement coming, given the Liberal Party's previous abandonment of the Home Rule policy promoted by its late leader William Gladstone. As a result of that, the Liberals' standing among Irish people is low. And Lloyd George's 'people's budget' is no more popular in Ireland than it is in his party. It includes a proposed tax on whiskey that has provoked bitter opposition because of its potential damage to the distillery industry, one of Ireland's few economic success stories.

Asquith's sudden conversion to Home Rule, however, came as no surprise to John Redmond, who had been negotiating quietly for such a declaration from the prime minister and had been informed of it in advance. Redmond's approach had been a simple one: he had told the Liberal Party that if it did not make Home Rule for Ireland a part of its election manifesto, the Irish Parliamentary Party – or Irish Party, as it is widely known – would urge its supporters in Britain to vote against the Liberal candidates. He had even warned the party in writing that a failure by Asquith to declare in favour of Home Rule in his 10 December speech would be 'fatal'.

~

The election results in a stalemate, with the Liberals returning to the House of Commons with 274 seats – just two more than the Conservatives and their Liberal Unionist allies, who finish in second place despite having won a greater share of the popular vote.

For Herbert Pike Pease, the result is a personal disaster. He loses his seat to Ignatius Lincoln, a Hungarian con artist, born Ignácz Trebitsch, who will go on to serve time in prison for fraud and to add 'German spy' and 'Buddhist monk' to his colourful cv. John Redmond, though, can celebrate an unqualified victory. In spite of opposition at home from William O'Brien's All-for-Ireland League, which takes eight seats in Cork, the Irish Party emerges with 72 seats and now holds the balance of power in the Commons. With the Liberals committed to introducing Home Rule and removing the House of Lords veto, Redmond now has a clear path to achieving his lifelong goal – the re-establishment of a Dublin parliament to rule over Irish affairs.

His first task is to ensure that the inconclusive outcome of the election does not cause Asquith to waver in his determination to – in the words of another Liberal Cabinet member, Winston Churchill – 'smash up the veto'.

The unconvincing election result has led to speculation that Asquith is indeed about to waver, by postponing a confrontation with the House of Lords – and the Conservative opposition – in favour of getting Lloyd George's budget passed by agreement. This is a menacing scenario for Redmond and the Irish Party. If the budget is passed and the Lords veto remains in place, Home Rule will remain as out of reach as ever.

In a speech in the Gresham Hotel in Dublin on 10 February, before the new parliament has convened, Redmond spells out what he expects from the British prime minister. As he rises to address a large crowd of supporters and fellow Irish Party MPs in the hotel's Aberdeen Hall, there is an air of riotous celebration over the outcome of the election, and he must wait for the cheers and a rousing rendition of 'For He's a Jolly Good Fellow' to subside before he can begin. After some swipes at the 'factionists' – namely William O'Brien and his colleagues – who competed against the Irish Party for the nationalist vote, he turns to the serious business at hand.

Having reminded his audience of Asquith's pledge that neither he nor his Cabinet colleagues would ever take office again without an assurance that they could curb the veto of the House of Lords, Redmond, as quoted in the following day's *Irish Times*, goes on: 'I have always regarded Mr Asquith as a man of his word,' to which somebody responds 'hear, hear'.

> His word sometimes has not gone as far as I would wish it to go, but I have never had the slightest reason to believe that he would not stand by his word as it was given. I say it is inconceivable that in this matter he should now waver in his purpose or palter with his pledges.
> [A voice: 'Don't let him!']

To do so would, in my humble judgement, and I speak with great diffidence, would be to wreck the Liberal Party [cheers], to drive them for the next 20 years into the wilderness. I will not insult him by suggesting he has any such intention [cheers].

He asks if it is seriously suggested that the House of Commons, 'having won a victory at the polls against the Lords, should send the budget back to the Lords with a request that under the existing system of the Constitution they would be kind enough by favour to pass the budget into law'.

Now, I venture to say that to do so would be to give the whole case against the Lords away ['hear, hear' and loud applause]. To do so would be to allow this great constitutional crisis that has arisen, the greatest for 200 years, to fritter out ['hear, hear']. To do so would mean to slack down the fires of enthusiasm among the democrats of England ['hear, hear']. To do so would be to disgust every real democrat in Great Britain ['hear, hear'] and let me say that to do so would be to break openly and unashamedly the clear and explicit pledges on the faith of which, at any rate, Ireland gave her support to the government at the last election [applause].

When parliament reconvenes, Redmond's concerns are vindicated. On 21 February, the King's Speech setting out the government's agenda for the upcoming session of parliament is one of the shortest on record. There is, in effect, only one item on the government's agenda – the House of Lords veto. But the wording used is ambiguous. King Edward speaks of forthcoming proposals to 'define the relations between the houses of parliament' so as to secure the 'undivided authority' of the House of Commons over finance and its 'predominance' in legislation.

Whatever this means in practice, and nobody is sure, it hardly amounts to an all-out assault on the House of Lords and its powers.

When Asquith stands up in the Commons to respond to the King's Speech, he gives Redmond and his followers further cause for alarm. Until this moment it has been widely understood that the prime minister has secured a commitment from the king that, if it proves necessary, Edward will exercise his royal prerogative to flood the House of Lords with a sufficient number of new Liberal peers to ensure a bill abolishing the veto is passed by the upper house.

But now Asquith insists he has received no guarantees of any kind from the king and that it is his duty to keep the sovereign out of politics as far as possible. He goes on to talk about the necessity of passing the budget rejected last year by the Lords, and of some urgent measures needed to ensure Britain continues to meet its financial obligations.

For a moment, it appears that the political crisis that has paralysed the country since the Lords' rejection of Lloyd George's budget has finally eased. Asquith has pulled back from the brink and is now taking a much softer line on the veto than he did in his fiery Albert Hall speech. That illusion is immediately shattered, however, by Redmond. Speaking directly after the prime minister, his response to Asquith gives the political establishment an unexpected jolt.

He first explodes the notion that Irish Party support for the Liberal government can be taken for granted. 'Your British politics do not concern us, except so far as they impinge on the fortunes of our country,' he tells the house.

> We therefore necessarily belong to no English party, and I take leave to say to those who have been so glibly including us in calculating majorities in this house that they have no title or warrant to do so, and that our votes will in this parliament, as in past parliaments, be directed by one sole consideration – by what we regard to be the interest for the time being of Ireland.

He then reminds Asquith of his pledge in the Albert Hall not to assume office unless he could be certain of removing the House of Lords veto – a pledge repeated by several Cabinet ministers during the election campaign. If the widely held interpretation of his Albert Hall speech – that the prime minister had a guarantee of support from the king if necessary – was incorrect, Asquith has had plenty of time to contradict it, but he hasn't done so.

Now it seems, says Redmond, that the Irish MPs are being asked to vote for the budget and end the financial crisis, work through the 'humdrum' details of parliament, and wait for a veto bill that will pass through the Commons only to be inevitably kicked out by the Lords. That, he concludes, 'is a policy which Ireland cannot and will not uphold'.

When Redmond sits down, the Commons is enfolded in what one newspaper the next day will describe as a 'dramatic silence'. Nobody rises to speak after him, and within minutes the debate is adjourned to allow all parties time to reflect.

A renewed political crisis of several weeks' duration ensues as the Liberal government scrambles for a way out of its predicament. Without Irish Party support, it does not have a workable majority in the House of Commons and will be unable to get its budget through the lower house, never mind the Lords. Redmond, however, must proceed with care. His party holds the balance of power, but it needs the Liberals to stay in government, as there is no prospect of the Conservatives introducing Home Rule.

Nevertheless, at a meeting on 24 February with the government Chief Whip, Alexander Murray (known by his title, the Master of Elibank), Redmond says that unless the government moves 'at once' to abolish the House of Lords veto, the Irish Party will consistently oppose it in the House of Commons.

During the following days and weeks, Redmond continues to put pressure on the government to act on the veto issue. The potential immediate fall of the government is averted on 28 February when Asquith secures approval from MPs to postpone all Commons business for the next 24 days other than the financial measures necessary to keep the state afloat. He promises that as soon as that period is up, on 24 March, he will bring forward resolutions on relations between the two houses of parliament. These will include proposals to exclude the Lords 'altogether from the domain of finance' and to limit its power of veto in other areas.

This is not enough for Redmond, who in response says that the prime minister has neglected to say what will happen if his veto proposals are rejected by the House of Lords. Will he then go to the king and ask him to exercise the royal prerogative, in other words to create enough new Liberal peers to ensure that the veto is abolished?

'I ask him, first of all, that this obscurity shall be cleared up,' Redmond adds.

> I ask, is it the intention of the right honourable gentleman, when his resolution is suspended or rejected by the Lords, to ask for guarantees, and, if they are refused, does he propose to continue – contradistinction to what he said in his Albert Hall speech – does he propose to continue responsible for the government of the country?

Lloyd George tells Redmond, in the same debate, that there is no question of the government shirking its pledges on the veto issue. But he insists that it cannot ask the king for guarantees until its proposals on the matter have been passed by the House of Commons and the Lords has been given a chance to consider them.

Privately, Lloyd George also tells Redmond that he is prepared to offer concessions on the budget, including movement on the whiskey tax, in order to secure the Irish nationalists' support for it. Redmond, however, sticks fast to his policy, now coined as 'no veto, no budget'. Unless the government moves on the veto, there will be no 'people's budget'.

Finally, in early April, the Cabinet relents and gives in to Redmond's demands. First, on 29 March, Asquith tells the Commons that he proposes to remove entirely the House of Lords veto in relation to financial matters and to limit its power in relation to other bills so that it may delay them, but not reject them.

Redmond supports the proposals, but sees no prospect of them getting through the House of Lords unless Asquith delivers on his pledge to resign from office in the absence of a guarantee from the king that he will use the royal prerogative if necessary to see the resolutions through. The first of the two veto resolutions is passed by the Commons on 7 April and then, a week later, comes the breakthrough. Following a vote in favour of the second veto resolution – proposing to replace the House of Lords' absolute veto with a power to delay bills only – a sombre Asquith stands to tell the house he wishes to make a statement.

It's 11 p.m., but the chamber is full following the vote that has just taken place, and Redmond is among those in his seat as the prime minister says what the Irish leader has been pressing him to say for the past several months.

> If the Lords fail to accept our policy [on removing the veto], or decline to consider it as it is formally presented to the house, we shall feel it our duty immediately to tender advice to the Crown as to the steps which will have to be taken if that policy is to receive statutory effect in this parliament.
>
> What the precise terms of that advice will be – [an MP interrupts: 'Ask Redmond!'] – I think one might expect courtesy when I am anxious, as the head of the government, to make a serious statement of public policy – what the precise terms of that advice will be it will, of course, not be right for me to say now; but if we do not find ourselves in a position to ensure that statutory effect shall be given to that policy in this parliament, we shall then either resign our offices or recommend the dissolution of parliament.

The interjection from the unnamed MP is evidence of the dominant position Redmond has attained in British politics, as is the scornful response to Asquith's announcement by the leader of the opposition, Arthur Balfour. The statement just made by the prime minister, he says, is obviously the result of a deal done with another group in the house, a clear reference to the Irish Party.

> As I understand, the honourable and learned member for Waterford [John Redmond] and his friends have agreed to swallow the budget, their aversion of which they have not concealed, which is a growing aversion, as the feeling in Ireland makes more and more manifest …
>
> The Irish Party are going to accept a budget they dislike, and are going to accept it because they think that that policy conduces to that larger object they have in view, namely, Home Rule for Ireland. They are going to get what they do not want in the shape of the budget, but I am not sure that they are going to get what they do want. [Several MPs: 'Wait and see!']

As a consequence of the breakthrough, Redmond and his party do indeed 'swallow the budget', which now passes quickly through both houses of parliament. For Redmond, accepting an unpopular budget is a fair price to pay in return for a major step forward in his pursuit of Home Rule. His tactics are seen to have won the day, to the deep vexation of the Tory press. The *Daily Mail* labels him 'the dictator from Dublin', while the London *Times* complains that Redmond is now the country's 'real master'.

John Redmond has been the undisputed leader of the Irish Party for a decade now, but his standing has never been so high – at home or abroad. Within weeks, however, British politics is convulsed yet again, this time by a development that threatens to undo all the progress he has made.

Chapter 2 ～

ASQUITH'S COUP D'ÉTAT

By Home Rule I mean what Parnell meant, what Gladstone meant.

On Saturday, 7 May 1910, Britain wakes to an unseasonably chilly day and what *The Times* newspaper describes as 'overpowering' news: 'King Edward VII is no more.'
Few are unmoved by the sudden death of the popular monarch known to all as Bertie. Britons of all classes liked their wayward, philandering, gambling, party-going, cigar-smoking, pheasant-shooting king, whose nine years on the throne were a welcome relief after the stifling 63-year reign of his mother, Queen Victoria. But his demise is not only a cause of shock and genuine sorrow among the masses; it also transforms the political situation to the detriment of the Irish nationalist cause.

It's not that King Edward was a supporter of Home Rule. He was outraged, indeed, at the notion that he might be asked to inundate the House of Lords with new Liberal peers in order to ensure the passage of a bill limiting the powers of the upper house. He strongly held the view that before he could even consider such a step, a further general election would be required to ascertain the views of the people on the matter. And he had conveyed this opinion to the prime minister, Herbert Asquith.

The king was fuming, then, when he received a letter from Asquith in April advising him that the government intended to press ahead, during the current parliament, with its plan to address the veto issue. Asquith told the monarch that, if the House of Lords failed to co-operate in its own disempowerment, the government would 'tender advice to the Crown' on the necessary steps to be taken.

'It is simply disgusting,' Edward wrote to his private secretary, Lord Knollys, on 16 April. It was plain, he said, that Asquith was going to ask him 'to swamp the H[ouse] of Lords by a quantity of peers ... I positively decline doing this – besides I have previously been given to understand that I should *not* be called upon to agree to this preposterous measure. Certainly the PM and many of his colleagues assured me so – but now they are in the hands of Redmond & Co they do not seem to be their own master.'

Despite his refusal to commit to creating the new peers as demanded by the government, and his obvious hostility to John Redmond and the Irish cause, the king's death just a few weeks later is a double setback for the Home Rule movement. First, it dissolves some of the bitterness between the government and opposition as the two sides unite in mourning the dead king, thereby stimulating a new spirit of compromise. This is a troubling vista for Redmond, who is convinced that there is no middle ground to be found on the issue of the House of Lords veto. If the veto doesn't go, there will be no Home Rule.

The other difficulty created by the king's death is that it weakens Asquith's hand. The prime minister was reluctant to press King Edward to use the royal prerogative to create the additional Liberal peers needed to ensure a veto bill is passed. He committed to doing so only after being harried at every turn by Redmond, and it is surely unthinkable that he could try to force such a radical manoeuvre on Edward's inexperienced successor, George V.

After all of his efforts since the election to keep the government focused on the removal of the veto, Redmond has reason to fear that everything is suddenly back in play. And sure enough, there is soon talk of a conference of the party leaders to be called by the new king in an effort to find common ground.

Redmond repairs for a break to his home at Aughavanagh, an old military barracks once used by Charles Stewart Parnell as a shooting lodge. It is in this secluded residence in the Wicklow Mountains that the Irish leader likes to spend his rest time, in the company of his family. Ten years after the premature death of his first wife, Johanna, the mother of his three children, Redmond married Ada Beesley, an Englishwoman thirteen years his junior, in London in 1899. He calls her Amy; she calls him Jack. While at Aughavanagh, he lives the life of an archetypal country gent, walking, hunting and fishing for leisure, and occasionally entertaining guests.

For Redmond, it is an ideal location at which to take time out from the House of Commons for reflection and to recharge his batteries before returning to face the demands of parliamentary politics. His critics, and even some supporters, believe this lifestyle leaves him cut off both physically and emotionally from the people he represents.

While at Aughavanagh in early June, he receives a letter from T.P. O'Connor, the Irish Party's Liverpool MP, who has news of the government's thinking. O'Connor – the only Irish nationalist representing a constituency outside Ireland – has just been out to dinner with Chancellor of the Exchequer David Lloyd George and government Chief Whip Alexander Murray. The outlook is not good from the Irish Party's perspective. Lloyd George told O'Connor that he believed a conference between the party leaders was now inevitable, as it would be 'disastrous' for the Liberal Party to refuse an invitation to talks from the king.

Irish Party deputy leader John Dillon is copied in on O'Connor's letter and is alarmed by its contents, describing them to Redmond as 'as bad as well could be'. He writes back to O'Connor with instructions – subject to Redmond's approval – that he tell Lloyd George that the Irish leadership favours 'bringing on' the crisis over the veto by the middle of July at the latest, and sees no reason for postponing matters.

On 6 June, two days after his first letter, O'Connor reports on a further meeting with senior members of the government. This time Lloyd George was accompanied by Home Secretary Winston Churchill and Irish Secretary Augustine Birrell. The Cabinet, O'Connor has been informed, has met that day but taken no decision on how to proceed. All three ministers have assured him, however, that there is no question of the Liberals surrendering their principles on the veto in the event of a conference with the Tories. They believe the conference will involve nothing more than an informal, non-binding exchange of views between Asquith and Conservative Party leader Arthur Balfour. 'Birrell laughed outright at the idea of any wavering,' O'Connor concludes: 'so did they all.'

Redmond, however, is anything but reassured. He remains convinced that the only way to curtail the powers of the House of Lords is for the government to confront the upper house head on, and as early as possible. Writing back to O'Connor on 8 June, he says that he regards the prospect now before them as 'extremely serious', and that any compromise by Asquith on the veto issue would be regarded as 'a betrayal' by the Irish Party. 'I really think,' he concludes, 'lest there should be any misunderstandings, that you ought to read this letter to Mr Lloyd George.'

Redmond's protestations and advice have no effect, and a constitutional conference of the party leaders – to which he is not invited – duly begins deliberations. Having apparently had the government in his hands just two months previously, events have suddenly spun beyond his control.

To the consternation of Redmond and his colleagues, the talks between the Liberals and Conservatives/Unionists turn into something far more durable than a mere exchange of views between Asquith and Balfour. At the end of July, Asquith tells the House of Commons that the parties are making progress and intend to continue the talks. Eventually, however, the Irish question proves to be the sticking point, with the Liberals refusing a Conservative demand that Home Rule be excluded from any deal to limit the Lords' veto, and in November the talks collapse.

Redmond is on the Atlantic when he learns of the breakdown, on the way home from a successful fundraising tour of the eastern United States with Joe Devlin, the Belfast MP who, as head of the Ancient of Order of Hibernians, is the Irish Parliamentary Party's organiser in chief. If ever the party needs to ensure it has a supportive crowd for a rally, Devlin is the man to make sure it gets one. T.P. O'Connor has been to Canada for the same purpose, and between them the two missions raise $100,000 – about £20,000 – for the Irish nationalist cause.

A stalemate has now been reached on the House of Lords veto issue and another general election is called. As the campaign rages through late November and into December, Redmond is dubbed the 'dollar dictator' by the Conservative opposition, who are infuriated at the sight of an Irish nationalist politician holding such a powerful position in British politics, and worried too about the money at the Irish Party's disposal following the successful fundraising tours of the USA and Canada.

Redmond is now the Conservatives' bogeyman and each day's newspapers bring new reports of his having been denounced the previous evening on some Tory campaign platform or other. Lord Lansdowne, Henry Petty-Fitzmaurice, owner of a vast estate in south-west Ireland and leader of the Conservatives in the House of Lords, tells a crowd of nine thousand supporters in Portsmouth on 30 November of the dire consequences to flow from the Liberals' determination to make Home Rule its first priority if returned to office. 'If the Liberals come in,' he thunders, 'all these great questions of Poor Law reform, of unemployment, and of other great social and ameliorative measures will have to stand to one side while Mr Redmond is being served first.' The London *Times* devotes half a page to the speech the following day.

Redmond, too, is making headlines as he campaigns energetically in both Ireland and Britain. In a speech on a Liberal Party platform to an audience of six thousand in Walsall on 2 December, also reported in *The Times*, he sets out what his party stands for:

> By Home Rule I mean what Parnell meant, what Gladstone meant. I mean this, and this only, that there shall be created by statute of the imperial [Westminster] parliament, a parliament of Ireland elected by the Irish people, charged solely to the duty of managing purely Irish affairs, with an executive responsible to it for the administration of those affairs, subject, as every Home Rule parliament within the empire is today, to the supremacy of the imperial parliament.

The occasion underlines the extent to which Redmond has come to be viewed by Liberal supporters not only as a champion of Home Rule, but also as a great campaigner for constitutional reform. To cheers from his listeners, Redmond tells them that he comes as a friend of 'the democracy of Great Britain' to aid them in 'ending once and for all the most intolerable tyranny ever endured by an educated and enfranchised people'.

The whole world, he says, is laughing at the English hereditary system of government. The vote of one man, whose ancestors – by whatever 'dirty or disgraceful means' – obtained a peerage, the vote of one such man, be he 'imbecilic' or 'utterly unfitted by character for the company of decent men', is more powerful today than the votes of fifteen thousand electors, he tells his audience.

But lest anyone think that he is repositioning himself as a crusader for democratic reform in Britain, Redmond adds that he must be 'candid' in this matter. Home Rulers, he says, are 'not entirely unselfish'. The abolition of the veto of the House of Lords, which means the opening of the way to all the great reforms on which all their hearts are set, means the abolition of the last obstacle in the way of Home Rule.

The election produces almost exactly the same result as that of the previous one in January. This time the Liberal Party emerges with 272 seats, matching the combined total secured by the Conservatives and Liberal Unionists. This is a drop in three seats for the governing party and one for the Conservatives/Unionists. Labour wins 42 seats, while the Irish Party now has 74 seats, up from 71 in January. Adding in independents, including William O'Brien's Cork-based All-for-Ireland League, the new parliament will have 84 Irish nationalist MPs.

Asquith interprets the result as a mandate for political reform and on 21 February 1911, just three weeks into the life of the new parliament, he introduces a bill in the House of Commons providing for the House of Lords' veto over legislation to be replaced by a power to delay bills only, by up to two years. The Parliament Bill is bitterly opposed by the opposition and the debate over it rages for several months.

When the Lords sends the bill back to the Commons with amendments, Asquith makes a highly controversial – but decisive – move. On 20 July he writes to Balfour, the Conservative leader, to tell him that if necessary the government will advise King George to exercise the royal prerogative to ensure that the bill is passed by the Lords without significant changes, and that the king has already agreed to act accordingly.

This threat finally to proceed with the drastic plan to overwhelm the House of Lords with Liberal peers in order to secure the passage of the Parliament Bill and, worse, the news that the king is on board to implement it, causes uproar. In a leader article in its edition of 21 July – in which it publishes the prime minister's letter to Balfour – The Times denounces Asquith's 'coup d'état' and again bemoans the fact that the Irish nationalists appear to be running the show. 'Nemesis waits him, secure of her prey, when he attempts to satisfy the impossible demands of his Irish masters,' the article concludes.

An *Irish Times* article on the same day also describes Asquith's move as a 'coup d'état', implemented at the behest of his 'Nationalist and Socialist taskmasters', and it too concludes with a melodramatic warning for the prime minister: 'They that take the sword shall perish by the sword.'

Bedlam ensues when the House of Commons next sits, on 24 July. Rising to join the debate on the Parliament Bill, the prime minister is shouted down by the opposition and repeated cries of 'traitor!' fill the air. The reality, however, is that Asquith – and John Redmond – have won the day. Faced with the choice of passing the bill as it stands, or having the make-up of the House of Lords radically altered through the creation of a new set of Liberal peers, Lord Lansdowne advises his Unionist colleagues to accept the bill. Many decline to acquiesce and the outcome remains in doubt until the last moment, but on 10 August the House of Lords duly falls on its sword, voting the bill through by 131 votes to 114.

Eight days later the Parliament Act receives the royal assent and with that the primary obstacle to Home Rule for Ireland is removed. From this point on, the House of Lords may delay a Home Rule Bill by up to two years, but it will be powerless after that to stop it from becoming law. On 22 August, parliament breaks for its autumn recess, enabling Redmond to devote his energies to the completion of a long-standing project – the erection of a monument in Dublin to his late leader and role model, Charles Stewart Parnell.

From the day John Redmond entered politics as MP for New Ross three decades previously, aged 24, Parnell was his guiding light. By the time of Redmond's election in February 1881, the obstructionist tactics deployed by Parnell and some of his colleagues had already made them the most despised men in the House of Commons.

Redmond would never forget Parnell's composure in these most adverse of circumstances. Rising to speak in the Commons, the MP for Meath (and later Cork) would be greeted with – as Redmond puts it – 'howls of execration', sometimes resulting in him standing serenely for up to half an hour before he could utter a word.

When the Irish Party split in December 1890 after Gladstone's Liberals threatened to withdraw co-operation with it because of its leader's extra-marital relationship with Katharine O'Shea, Redmond emerged from the shadows to become Parnell's ablest defender. He argued that in selling their leader for the sake of maintaining an alliance with an English party, the Irish MPs would also be selling their independence.

He failed to bring most of his colleagues with him, however, and after Parnell's death the following year at the age of 45, and then a general election in 1892, Redmond found himself at the head of a small band of just nine Parnellite MPs. But he thrived in the leadership role. After Gladstone's second Home Rule Bill was rejected by the House of Lords in 1893, Redmond's Parnellites distinguished themselves from the larger anti-Parnellite group by supporting positive measures for Ireland, even if they fell short of the ultimate goal of an Irish parliament.

This was to be the key difference between the rival Irish parties over the next decade. When the Tories returned to power in 1896 with a more enlightened policy towards Ireland than it had previously had, it was famously denounced by the anti-Parnellites' leader John Dillon as 'killing Home Rule with kindness'. But Redmond embraced the new approach and worked with the government to secure as many concessions as he could. His approach enabled him to influence the major advances of the decade, including the creation of an Irish Department of Agriculture and the establishment of county councils under the Local Government Act of 1898, which ended control of local government by the landlord class.

When the Parnellite and anti-Parnellite factions reunited in February 1900, Redmond was elected leader, finding himself back where Parnell had been a decade before, at the head of a unified Irish nationalist party in the House of Commons. Now, 11 years later, he is on the brink of completing Parnell's work.

The project to erect a fitting monument to the late nationalist leader – instigated by Redmond – is being overseen by a voluntary body set up in 1898. It has taken 13 years of planning and fundraising to bring it to fruition before the day finally arrives on Sunday, 1 October 1911.

The unveiling of the monument – a bronze statue of Parnell by the New York-based Irish-born sculptor Augustus Saint-Gaudens, atop a granite pillar – is the occasion for what the *Irish Independent* the next day will describe as a 'gigantic Irish demonstration'. The proceedings begin with a parade over three miles long in which more than fifty bands and numerous bodies – including local authorities, the Irish National Foresters, the GAA, business groups and trade unions – participate. A 'ladies' section' is headed by Countess Markievicz. A young Dublin poet, Joseph Plunkett, records the occasion in his personal diary: 'Tremendous crowd. Saw John Redmond.'

In scenes that would be repeated at a major rally for Home Rule a few months later, Redmond has to wait for the vociferous cheering to subside before he can begin his oration. He opens by reminding his audience that it is 20 years to the week since the death of their 'mighty leader'. It seems a long time to wait for a monument to the Chief, he says, but on the other hand, this event could not be taking place at a more fitting moment. The national cause is at last back at the point to which Parnell had led it before 'the catastrophe' of his demise.

'Fellow countrymen,' he continues, 'the promised land is before our eyes, and we are all about to enter it, and, as the spirit of Parnell watches us today, let us think of him. What would be our feelings if Parnell was amongst us? What would be his feelings if he could come and take part in our triumph?'

Loud cheering, punctuated by cries of 'bravo Redmond!', rises through the Dublin city air, as the many thousands present celebrate what does, truly, feel like a long-awaited moment of triumph for the nationalist movement.

Elsewhere in Ireland, however, large crowds are also beginning to gather, to hear the inspirational speeches of another man. Northern loyalists, alarmed by the recent political developments, have united behind a new leader, a former colleague of John Redmond's on the Leinster law circuit. But this past association counts for nothing. Edward Carson has vowed that Redmond's talk of triumph will soon prove premature.

Chapter 3

INTRODUCING EDWARD CARSON

We will yet defeat the most nefarious conspiracy that has ever been hatched against a free people.

On a Saturday afternoon in the autumn of 1911, the Protestant people of Ulster are introduced to their new leader, a 57-year-old lawyer from Dublin. The impact is electrifying, and it sets the province on a path from which there will be no turning back.

Sir Edward Carson's first encounter with his new followers takes place on 23 September – eight days before the unveiling by John Redmond of the Parnell monument in Dublin – at a massive demonstration at Craigavon, on the outskirts of Belfast. If the rest of Ireland and Britain are not yet fully alive to the profound sense of anger and betrayal felt by Ulster unionists at the prospect of Home Rule for Ireland, this event ought to shake them from their complacency.

The meeting, on the estate of Unionist MP Sir James Craig, has been called to allow the people of Ulster to welcome Carson – who remains a remote figure in the province despite being leader of the Ulster Unionists for 19 months now – and to hear what advice he has to offer about the campaign ahead. The unionists are in a novel and difficult place; the decision of the House of Lords to vote through the Parliament Act and thereby co-operate in the abolition of its own veto over legislation has made the passage of a Home Rule Bill appear inevitable. So the unionists know that simply opposing the measure in the House of Commons, where they are in a minority, will not be enough; if the Liberal government, supported by the Irish nationalists, sticks to its policy on Home Rule, the unionists will be powerless to stop it.

So the question for Edward Carson in Craigavon is not merely: How do the unionists oppose Home Rule? It is: What should they do after it has been enacted against their wishes? In what the *Irish Times* will describe in its report on Monday as 'the greatest anti-Home Rule demonstration that ever Ulster has seen', more than a hundred thousand people turn up to hear Carson's answer.

Most of the men present, representing unionist clubs and Orange lodges throughout the province and beyond, arrive in orderly procession from Belfast city centre, marching four abreast through streets decked out in red, white and blue and lined with cheering crowds. The parade takes some three hours to complete and it is 4.45 p.m., an hour and fifteen minutes later than scheduled, before the vast assemblage is complete and the speeches can begin.

The setting and circumstances are ideal. The lawn at Craigavon, a spacious country house on a hill above the Belfast–Holywood road, with a view of Belfast Lough, slopes steeply towards the road below, forming a natural amphitheatre and giving the entire audience a clear view of the speakers' platform at the crest of the hill. On the stage, the veteran Liberal Unionist Thomas Andrews moves a resolution welcoming Carson and pledging to stand by him 'in whatever action he may take and through any danger he may have to face'.

Andrews then warms up the crowd with a declaration that draws roars of approval:

> We will never, never bow the knee to the disloyal factions led by Mr John Redmond. We will never submit to be governed by rebels who acknowledge no law but the laws of the Land League and illegal societies.

When Carson steps forward to speak at 5.25 p.m., the resolution of welcome and support having been duly passed and other introductory speeches concluded, the enormous crowd responds with loud cheers, the waving of white handkerchiefs, and a vigorous rendition of 'For He's a Jolly Good Fellow'. The festive mood quickly subsides, however, as Carson tells his audience, with typical earnestness and seriousness of purpose, that this is 'a momentous moment' in his life, and probably also in theirs.

I only say, openly and honestly, I thank you. I know full well what this meeting means; I know full well what the resolution you have just passed means; I know what all these addresses mean; I know the responsibility you are putting on me today. In your presence I cheerfully accept it, grave as it is.

This draws cheers from his audience, but Carson continues:

And I now enter into a compact with you and every one of you, and, with the help of God, you and I joined together – I giving you the best I can and you giving me all your strength behind me – we will yet defeat the most nefarious conspiracy that has ever been hatched against a free people.

Further cheers greet his every statement, as Carson goes on to tell the crowd he knows that the resolution they have just passed has an even wider meaning.

It shows me that you realise the gravity of the situation that is before us, and it shows me that you are here to express your determination to see this fight out to a finish.

Even 'Mr Redmond', Carson adds, admits that Ireland has never been as prosperous as it is now. Unparalleled advances have been made in recent years, thanks to measures introduced by various Unionist governments before the Liberals came to power, and because Ireland is still a member of 'a great United Kingdom'.

Yet this is the moment that the government are about to choose to plunge Ireland once more into desperate political chaos, and once more to distract men's minds from the common measures which they might take together for the benefit of the country, and bring about that hatred of class against class and religion against religion which every one of us would like to see abolished in the interests of our common land [cheers].

For the government, Carson adds, Home Rule is a question of party politics, of 'mere party trickery', of one side getting the better of the other. It is a means of keeping itself in office with the help of nationalist votes. What the government does not realise, he tells his audience, is 'that to you and me it is a question of gambling with our civil and religious liberty'. But, as the cheers grow ever louder, he insists they are not going to let this happen.

> We fought this battle twice before in a straight fight, and we won. We are going to fight it again, and we are going to win. Yes, but make no mistake. We are going to fight with men who are prepared to play with loaded dice. They are prepared to destroy their own Constitution so that they may pass Home Rule, and they are prepared to destroy the very elements of constitutional government by withdrawing this question from the electorate, who on two previous occasions refused to be a party to it.

Carson and his colleagues claim that the Liberal government has no mandate to introduce Home Rule because, following Asquith's pledge to introduce it in his Albert Hall speech at the outset of the last election, Liberal ministers subsequently avoided the subject for the remainder of the campaign. And when Home Rule had been explicitly put before the electorate in Gladstone's time, they had twice rejected it.

The Ulster Unionist leader has more to say, and the vast crowd can't get enough of this masterly performance. After someone shouts, 'We will not have Redmond for king anyway', Carson paints a bleak picture of what life would be like under a nationalist parliament in Dublin. The government, he says, would be picked by men 'who have as black a record as ever was behind the citizens of any country'.

> Your old civil service will be gone; the police, the protectors, will be taken away. Religious education will be in the hands of the nationalist party, and therefore they can compel you to direct the education just as they please and, in point of fact, I should not wonder if one of the first acts was to try and make you all speak that Irish which none of themselves can understand [laughter].

In point of fact, to put it shortly, every act of government that affects the daily lives of every one of you, and every one of our citizens, will be at the mercy of the administration set up under Home Rule, and you will have no appeal save to a parliament in College Green ['Never!']. I know what that parliament will be ['We do!']. You know what your place and your share in it will be, and all I can say is that any man that trusts for justice from them, God have mercy upon him [laughter and cheers].

Placing the loyalists of Ulster under the jurisdiction of a Home Rule parliament would be a tyranny to which they could never submit, Carson adds.

After all, our demand is a very simple one. We ask for no privileges, but we are determined that no one shall have privileges over us ['Never!' and cheers]. We ask for no special rights, but we say that we claim the same rights from the same government as every other part of the United Kingdom [cheers]. We ask for nothing more, we will take nothing less [cheers]. It is our inalienable right as citizens of the British empire, and heaven help the men who try to take it from us [cheers].

With his audience now in a state of high excitement and eager for the battle ahead, Carson poses a rhetorical question: What possible advantage can they derive from Home Rule?

Do you gain financial advantage by dissolving partnership with the exchequer of the richest country in the world? ['No!'] Do you gain greater civil freedom in abandoning a government which has been an example of liberty to every foreign nation? ['No!'] Do you gain greater religious freedom? ['No!']

Thrilled by his bold and confident speech, the loyalists of Ulster no longer regard Edward Carson as a stranger. This southern Irishman with a Dublin accent, who played hurling as a student in Trinity College, now has all of Protestant Ulster behind him, and they are pledged to go wherever he chooses to lead, whatever the cost.

That Carson should find himself in this position is probably as much of a surprise to himself as it is to anybody else. As he nears the end of a successful political and legal career, he has most likely already exceeded the ambitions he held when, as a young law graduate of Trinity, he earned his living vindicating the rights of tenant farmers in the Irish courts.

In a career founded on extreme hard work and ambition rather than any noted intellectual brilliance, he has been involved in some of the most celebrated trials of the age, most notably when his defence of the Marquess of Queensberry in the libel action taken by Oscar Wilde – an old Trinity acquaintance – precipitated the writer's downfall and disgrace. He has served as Solicitor General for Ireland and later for England, earning himself a knighthood in the process. And he has continued to have a lucrative legal practice.

Unsurprisingly, then, when the 19 Irish Unionist MPs – 16 of whom represented Ulster constituencies – found themselves without a leader after the January 1910 election, Carson did not seek the post, and was reluctant to accept it when it was offered. The Ulster MPs had turned to a southerner to lead them because – as Ulster Unionist Council member Ronald McNeill would later explain – they knew they had nobody within their ranks with the parliamentary or oratorical skills of John Redmond.

Carson was being asked, at this late stage in his career, to take on the task not only of commanding a small band of MPs in the House of Commons but of leading the loyalist population of Ulster through the crisis posed by the apparently unstoppable momentum towards Home Rule. On 21 February, several days after receiving the invitation to lead them, he relayed his decision to the Ulster MPs: he would take on the job.

It would take some time, however, before he would make his mark. As the constitutional crisis over the House of Lords veto continued through 1910, the Ulster loyalists saw little of their new chief. But he did make a stirring speech in Belfast in December, during the second general election of the year, in which he described Home Rule as an 'outrage on common sense' and 'a fraud on the people'.

The following month, January 1911, Carson was back in Belfast to chair a meeting of the 400-strong Ulster Unionist Council, the representative body for loyalists throughout the province. A motion was passed asserting that the result of the December general election, which had seen the Liberals remain in power with the support of the Irish Party, did not amount to a mandate for Home Rule.

After that, Carson continued to lead the Ulster Unionists largely from London, but anyone who questioned the strength of his conviction that Home Rule would be a calamity for Ireland – north and south – would have had their doubts erased by his contribution to a debate on the issue in the House of Commons on 15 February.

Demonstrating that his opposition to Home Rule was at once visceral and practical, Carson also dropped a hint of the extreme tactics soon to be adopted by him and his followers in their campaign against its introduction:

> I admit, and I freely admit, that upon the question of Home Rule for Ireland, I am bitter. I say I loathe the idea because, in my belief, it would be of no possible advantage to my country, and in my belief it would be to the absolute detriment of my country. If you believe that I am sincere in that you will agree that I have a right to oppose this proposition in every possible way that is open to me.

Carson's absence from Ulster continued for some months yet. He was not present for the 12 July celebrations, the most intense in many years as the spectre of Home Rule grew ever larger.

~

On this Saturday evening in Craigavon, however, an unbreakable bond has been forged between the Dubliner and the Ulster loyalists. But he has yet to tell them what they have really come to hear: If they are powerless to prevent Home Rule, how are they to respond to its implementation?

Their preferred option would be to put their case to the people in another election, Carson tells his audience, but the prime minister has said they will not be allowed to do so. 'Very well. By that determination he drives you in the ultimate result to rely upon your own strength, and we must follow all that out to its logical conclusion [cheers].' In the event of a Home Rule Bill being passed, the Ulster Unionists must be ready to govern the districts over which they have control.

> We must be prepared – and time is precious in these things – the morning Home Rule passes, ourselves to become responsible for the government of the Protestant province of Ulster [cheers]. We ask your liberty at the meeting of the Ulster Unionist Council to be held on Monday to there discuss the matter, and to set to work, to take care, so that at no time and at no intervening space shall we lack a government in Ulster which shall be a government either by an imperial parliament or by ourselves [cheers].
>
> I am told that we will be put down by Mr Redmond's 'strong arm' ['Never!' and booing] backed by British forces ['Never!] ... I think I have read a good deal of history. I know that force has been used for conquest; I know that force has been used to compel retention to a government against the will of the people, but a precedent has yet to be created to drive out by force loyal and contented citizens from a community to which by birth they belong [cheers]. And the day that a British government sets its soldiers to drive you and me out of the community of the United Kingdom, that day will be the end of the British empire [cheers].

He concludes with a rallying cry that draws prolonged cheers:

> We are out once more upon a great campaign against betrayal – a betrayal of the foulest and most humiliating character. Let every man take that betrayal to his own heart. Talk of it in your offices to one another; talk of it in your workshops to one another; talk of it at your firesides, and teach your children of it so that it may sink deep into your hearts, as to what it is proposed to do, and ask yourselves this one question: 'What have I done, what has Protestant Ulster done; what have the loyal men of the north done that they should be put upon the defensive in this act of foul conspiracy?'
>
> And as that comes home to each and every one of you, let your action be guided in future by this, that it is never a man's part to

submit to betrayal, and if you do a man's part in resisting it you
will at least have done your duty, and you will be able with a clear
conscience to face in history those who come after you.

Meeting two days later, the Ulster Unionist Council wastes no time
in giving effect to Carson's call to begin preparing the establishment
of a provisional government of the province. It sets up a five-man
commission to draw up, in consultation with Carson, the constitution
of the new government, to come into effect on the day a Home Rule
Bill is passed.

Nationalist Ireland greets with disdain this news of a putative
government for the north, with no army to back it. In a leader article
on Monday, 25 September, the *Freeman's Journal* dismisses Carson's
Craigavon speech as typical of the 'blatherskite' in which it has been
the Ulster Unionists' custom to indulge. The reality, however, is that
Carson and his supporters have taken an irrevocable step of the most
far-reaching significance; by moving to set up a provisional government
for Ulster they have committed themselves not only to opposing the
introduction of Home Rule but to defying the authority of the British
state should it attempt to impose it.

If Carson was relatively unknown to the people of Ulster before
the Craigavon demonstration, he is now a celebrity. Large crowds of
well-wishers turn out to greet him at every station a few days after
the Ulster Unionist Council meeting when he and his Galway-born
wife, Annette, take a train journey to Portrush, where he is to address
a further demonstration. The pair are met at their destination by
cheering crowds and a band. In an impromptu speech Carson tells
his followers that to hand them over to 'Mr Redmond and his disloyal
crew would be an outrage'.

The unionists' campaign against Home Rule is now fully under
way, and just over three months later, in early January 1912, it enters
another phase. An application is made to two magistrates by the Belfast
Grand Orange Lodge for leave to begin military drilling of members.
Permission is granted, giving legal cover to the drills that have been
sporadically taking place since the Craigavon rally in September.

Soon, tens of thousands of members of Orange lodges and unionist clubs throughout the province can be seen marching in formation and practising military drills, armed – but only for now – with dummy wooden 'rifles'. And it is not just the men of Ulster who are preparing for battle ahead. Although still deprived of the right to vote in elections, the loyalist women of the province have established the Ulster Women's Unionist Council and by the beginning of 1912, less than a year after its formation, it has between forty thousand and fifty thousand members. At a meeting in a packed Ulster Hall on 18 January, the women's council adopts a motion declaring support for 'our husbands, our brothers, and our sons, in whatever steps they may be forced to take in defending our liberties against the tyranny of Home Rule'.

The Ulster Hall is a venue of almost sacred importance to Ulster unionists. It is the setting where 25 years previously, in 1886, Lord Randolph Churchill delivered his famous speech in defence of the union, urging his excited audience not to forget their 'watchword' of nearly 200 years: 'No surrender!' Shortly afterwards, he issued his famous rallying cry: 'Ulster will fight, and Ulster will be right.'

There is consternation, then, when it is announced that Winston Churchill is to come to the same Ulster Hall, to stand on the stage graced by his father a generation earlier, to make a speech in favour of Home Rule. To compound the outrage, he plans to share the platform with the nationalist leaders John Redmond and Joe Devlin.

This combined act of political apostasy and filial impiety – as one unionist will later describe it – is too much for the loyalists of Ulster to bear. Their anger is heightened by the fact that the invitation to Churchill has been issued by Lord (William) Pirrie, chairman of the Harland and Wolff shipbuilding company and leader of the Ulster Liberal Association, whom loyalists accuse of deserting unionism at a moment when liberalism was gaining the upper hand. And there is nobody, as Edward Carson will frequently make clear, that an Ulster loyalist despises more than a 'turncoat'. To compound matters, notes a correspondent for *The Times* on 18 January, it has been suggested that Pirrie's Liberal Association would have insufficient members 'to fill a tramcar', although the writer accepts that this is an exaggeration.

Carson and his followers quickly determine that this threatened breach of a stronghold of Ulster unionism by such a gallery of rogues as Pirrie, Churchill and Redmond will not go unchallenged.

Chapter 4 ∾

MR CHURCHILL COMES TO BELFAST

Why should Ireland not have her chance?

The opening lines of the short report in the *Freeman's Journal* give no hint of the storm of controversy to come. 'The Press Association Belfast correspondent was yesterday officially informed that Mr Churchill and Mr Redmond will visit Belfast on 8th of February, and will address a Home Rule gathering in the Ulster Hall. It is expected that Mr Churchill will make an important announcement regarding the Home Rule question.'

Even unionist papers such as the *Irish Times* and the London *Times* appear sanguine about the latest development. In identical reports in their editions of 5 January 1912, they refer to the 'exceptional interest' attaching to Churchill's planned visit to Belfast and recall his father's 'memorable speech' in the city a quarter of a century earlier. But there is no talk of apostasy or filial impiety.

The unexpected announcement, nonetheless, presents unionists with a dilemma. If the First Lord of the Admiralty – the position Churchill now holds in the Liberal government – is allowed to sweep into town to make a speech in support of Home Rule in the heartland of Ulster loyalism, in front of a nationalist audience and in the company of the Irish Party leadership, he will undoubtedly damage the unionists' cause. All the hard talk about Ulster resistance come what may will be seen as just that: hard talk.

Churchill has a reputation as a plain speaker and in public has been forthright in his support of the government's Home Rule policy. In a speech to his constituents in Dundee in October, he said the government intended to introduce a Home Rule Bill in the next session of parliament and press it forward with all its strength, adding: 'We must not attach too much importance to these frothings of Sir Edward Carson.' The idea that anybody – never mind Randolph Churchill's son – might be allowed the use of the Ulster Hall stage to issue such insults against their leader is something the Ulster Unionists cannot countenance.

They equally know, however, that if they attempt to prevent the meeting from going ahead they will be accused of shutting down free speech and could lose valuable support in Britain as a consequence. They are also conscious that the Ulster Hall does not belong to them; it is the property of Belfast Corporation. If they try to bar others from using the venue, won't they be guilty of the very kind of political oppression they claim to be resisting?

On 16 January, the standing committee of the Ulster Unionist Council meets to consider its options. After a long debate, it unanimously passes a resolution, proposed by James Craig, which causes a sensation when published in the following day's newspapers:

> That the Standing Committee of the Ulster Unionist Council observes with astonishment the deliberate challenge thrown down by Mr Winston Churchill, Mr John Redmond, Mr Joseph Devlin, and Lord Pirrie in announcing their intention to hold a Home Rule meeting in the centre of the loyal city of Belfast, and resolves to take steps to prevent its being held.

The nationalist press is outraged by the decision, but also exultant because of what it sees as an own goal by the Ulstermen. Conservatives in Britain, the *Freeman's Journal* reports on 17 January, privately believe that their unionist colleagues in the north of Ireland have made a 'political blunder of the first magnitude'. The Ulster Unionist Council's 'amazing' decision, claims the *Irish Independent*, has caused deep embarrassment to its friends in London. Even the *Irish Times* has misgivings, stating in an editorial that 'on general grounds' the council's decision is an attack on freedom of speech that 'cannot be justified'. But the article goes on to say that the unionists are right to resist the 'bold and clever plan' hatched by Churchill and his nationalist allies to misrepresent Ulster's position to the British public.

For the next several weeks the controversy rages, with neither side showing any intention of backing down, despite mounting concern that a violent confrontation will be inevitable should the meeting go ahead. Rumours circulate that armed plainclothes policemen are already on the ground in Belfast to familiarise themselves with the city in advance of Churchill's visit. There is talk of members of the Ancient Order of Hibernians, of which Joe Devlin is Grand Master, travelling to the event in large numbers from Newry and elsewhere to be present in support of their nationalist brethren. Calls for the authorities in Dublin Castle to 'proclaim' the meeting and thereby force its cancellation go unheeded, as do demands for Belfast Corporation to withdraw the use of the Ulster Hall on public safety grounds.

Speculation mounts as to how the unionists intend to carry out their plan to stop the meeting taking place, and after it meets on 23 January, the Ulster Unionist Council declines to comment. But on the same day Belfast Corporation receives an application from the council for the letting of the Ulster Hall on 6 and 7 February. It is already booked for the 6th, for a concert by the Belfast Philharmonic Society. But the council is told that the hall is available on the 7th – the day before the Churchill rally.

The unionists' tactics are now clear: they plan to take up residence in the Ulster Hall on 7 February and remain there for as long as it takes to prevent the Churchill meeting going ahead. Although no statement has been made to that effect, reports *The Times* on 24 January, 'there appears to be little doubt ... that the building will be occupied by an audience on the evening of the 8th hostile to Home Rule and very unwilling to hear the son of Lord Randolph Churchill attempting to discount the cherished beliefs which his father upheld in the same hall.'

Recognising that a farcical as well as dangerous confrontation is now in prospect, Churchill defuses the situation by writing to Lord Londonderry, a leading figure on the Ulster Unionist Council, to say that while he still intends to speak in Belfast on 8 February, the actual venue is 'not a point of any importance' to him. He is therefore prepared to accede to the unionists' wish for him not to hold the meeting at the Ulster Hall. 'There will thus be no necessity for your friends to endure the hardships of a vigil, or sustain the anxieties of a siege,' he adds, with typical sarcasm-tinged humour. In his reply, Londonderry assures Churchill that the council has no intention of interfering with any meeting he might arrange 'outside the districts which passionately resent your action', although he pointedly adds that the unionists can accept no responsibility for anything that might occur during Churchill's visit.

The crisis has been averted, but the drama is only beginning. At 7.30 a.m. on a cold and wet Thursday, 8 February, Churchill and his wife, Clementine, disembark from the ferry at Larne to be greeted by a hostile crowd which loudly boos the pair before breaking into renditions of 'Rule, Britannia!' and 'God Save the King'. Anti-Home Rule placards and union flags adorn the walls of the quayside. The Churchills, looking pale after a rough ferry crossing from Stranraer, smile at the demonstrators as they board the train for Belfast, before someone draws the blinds of their carriage, denying the couple a view of the orange 'No Home Rule' bills posted all along the route of their journey.

Another large and angry crowd awaits Churchill at the station in Belfast, but he responds to every roar of abuse with a smile and a raising of his hat, before he and Clementine climb aboard Lord Pirrie's motor car and head off at speed to the Grand Central Hotel on Royal Avenue. There the couple plan to rest before Churchill delivers his speech in a marquee at the Belfast Celtic football ground in the nationalist area of the city.

As protesters gather outside in the rain, there is a moment of light relief when – as the *Irish Independent* will describe it the next day – 'a gentleman somewhat of the appearance of the First Lord of the Admiralty' leaves the hotel and approaches a taxi cab. A 'wild yell of groans' gives way to laughter when the crowd realises its mistake.

By the time the Churchills emerge from the hotel, shortly before 1 p.m., and enter a waiting motor car, at least ten thousand people have assembled to vent their anger. 'They were mainly men, and to a man they were Unionists,' *The Times* will report the next day. Both the Churchills are dressed in black, but Clementine, who is visibly enjoying the excitement, is flamboyant in a fur turban with a spray of black feathers in front, a velvet dress with a silk collar, and large diamond earrings.

Amid loud jeers and heckles, the crowd surges around the Churchills' car and – in spite of a heavy police presence – lifts it off its wheels on one side. For a moment it looks as if the car might be overturned with Churchill and his wife inside, but the police intervene to drive the crowd back.

Nevertheless, as the procession of six cars – with five following the vehicle occupied by the Churchills – slowly wends its way through the excited throng, many men get their heads in close to Churchill and issue what *The Times* reporter, observing from one of the cars in the rear, describes as 'fearful menaces and imprecations'. The First Lord of the Admiralty never flinches, and his wife looks equally unperturbed, even when balls of flour and sulphur, and a large piece of bread, are flung towards their vehicle.

As the motorcade inches its way through the business quarter of the city, if Churchill cared to look upwards he might spot some familiar faces observing the spectacle from an upstairs window. Edward Carson, Lord Londonderry, James Craig and other unionist leaders have gathered at the Ulster Club to keep close watch on the proceedings. When Churchill passes below, Carson steps on to the club's balcony to get a closer view. Catching sight of their leader, the protesters cheer and break into further renditions of 'Rule, Britannia!' and 'God Save the King'. There are loud calls for a speech from Carson, but he ignores them, preferring to watch the commotion in silence.

Minutes later, the scene changes dramatically as the hostile unionist crowd melts away, to be replaced by an equally boisterous multitude that also engulfs the motorcade. But Churchill's ears are now ringing with the sound of lusty cheers, rather than boos and hisses. The motorcade has passed into nationalist Belfast, and thousands of people have lined the Falls Road to welcome him. The grotesque effigies of Churchill and Redmond on display moments earlier are no longer to be seen; now it's the turn of Carson and Lord Londonderry to receive such treatment. There is laughter at the sight of a birdcage, with two crows inside, bearing the inscription 'Ulster Provisional Government'.

Police order the removal of a pair of effigies, suspended from a building on ropes, labelled 'Carson and Londonderry, turncoats'. The injunction goes unheeded, however, so officers form a human ladder and pull the figures down. Another Carson effigy bears the inscription: 'Died in the last ditch'. Irish, papal and American flags are prominently displayed, and several streamers span the thoroughfare.

Large numbers of workers, including black-shawled young women from the local mills, have come out to join in the welcome, while others shout support from the windows of houses, schools and clubs. So keen is the enthusiastic crowd to get close to Churchill to shake his hand that a member of his party – the Liberal MP Hamar Greenwood, later to be chief secretary in Ireland in the notorious era of the Black and Tans – has to stand on the running board of Churchill's car to try to hold the people back.

On the way to the football ground, where a capacity crowd of nearly eight thousand is waiting in the marquee to hear Churchill's speech, his car passes a horse-drawn carriage in which John Redmond, his brother and fellow MP Willie, and Joe Devlin, are being driven to the meeting, under voluntary escort by a small group of cheering female mill workers, many carrying green flags. Passionate renditions of 'God Save Ireland' can be heard all around.

When the speakers finally convene inside the marquee, they are greeted by a banner facing the platform: 'Ulster Welcomes Churchill'. Those present have paid between a half crown and a shilling – almost a day's pay for the mill girls, but more affordable for working men – for their tickets, the cheapest of which are for the standing-only areas to the right and left of the stage. Tickets have been available for anybody to buy, so while the audience is predominantly nationalist, an unknown – but likely substantial – number of unionists and people of no political persuasion are also present.

Despite the cold and the incessant patter of rain on the canvas, some of which drips through the cover on to the crowd, the atmosphere is one of great cheer as a brass and string band goes through its repertoire of Irish tunes in the hour before the event proper begins.

Taking the stage, Churchill is greeted by a standing ovation and wild cheering that lasts for several minutes. He stands before the crowd, beaming with pleasure, as the roars are accompanied by the waving of white handkerchiefs, hats and walking sticks. Beginning his speech minutes later, he must wait first for his audience to finish a rendition of

'For He's a Jolly Good Fellow', before he provokes loud and prolonged cheers by announcing that he comes before this audience 'on the eve of a Home Rule Bill'.

Suddenly, he is interrupted, when a woman from the grandstand shouts, in a clear northern Irish accent: 'Will you give self-government to the women of Ireland?' Churchill's reply hits the right note: 'I think we had better leave that question for the Irish parliament to decide.' Whether the interrupter hears the reply is not clear – she is the first of at least four women to be ejected for heckling Churchill about the denial to women of the right to vote.

Churchill detests these interruptions, which have become a constant at every political meeting. 'We all hate the suffragettes for spoiling our speeches, but they make Winston very bitter because they ruin his perorations,' Lloyd George will tell Liberal peer Lord Riddell; 'His perorations, prepared with the utmost care, are completely wrecked and spoiled by little voices calling out "Mr Churchill! What about votes for women?"'

Ignoring the steady flow of such calls, Churchill sets out one of the government's key arguments for the introduction of Home Rule: its failure to resolve the Irish question is damaging Britain's standing abroad, and in particular its relationship with the United States. This problem has become more acute as Irish influence overseas has grown.

> In their own island the Irish race have dwindled. While the population of Europe has overflowed that of Ireland has ebbed away; but elsewhere all over the world they have held their own, and in every country where the English language is spoken the Irish are a power – a power for good or a power for ill, a power to harm or a power to help us – a power to unite us, a power to keep us asunder. What can we say of these Irishmen who, we are assured, are in their own island incapable of managing their own affairs, but who in every other part of the English-speaking world have won their way out of all proportion to their numbers to positions of trust, affluence and authority, particularly political authority?
>
> Speaking as an English minister I must say that, on the whole, in varying degrees, no doubt with notable exceptions, they have been

our enemies. They have been filled with feelings of resentment and anger against the British power and name [a voice: 'But no longer!'], and they have counterworked our interests. ... They have been an adverse force in our colonies. They have on more than one occasion unfavourably deflected the policy of the United States. They are now the most serious obstacle to Anglo-American friendship we have got.

Imagine how much brighter the future would be for all if Britain had Ireland's aid instead of its enmity, he adds, before proceeding to give details of the Home Rule legislation planned by the government. It will seek to assure Protestants, he says, that they will not suffer discrimination under the new regime. To safeguard against this, the Irish parliament 'will be so constituted, both in its house of commons and in its senate, as to be fully and fairly representative of the Irish nation of Protestants as well as of Catholics, of urban as well as of agricultural interests, of minorities even more than majorities'.

But other 'ramparts' will be erected against oppression, including provisions safeguarding religious freedom for Protestants and Catholics and powers vested in the Westminster parliament, 'backed by all the forces of the Crown', to block any bill brought forward by the Irish parliament that goes beyond the scope of its powers.

But what will those powers be? The Home Rule Bill, he says, will give the Irish parliament 'real responsibility' in financial affairs. While Ireland's financial system will need to fit into 'the framework' of the United Kingdom, its parliament 'will be able to grip and to control large areas of taxation, and it will have the power, within reasonable and wise limits, to supplement its income by new taxation'. This is immediately interpreted by some as meaning that the Irish parliament will have control over excise, i.e. internal taxes, but not over border taxes (customs).

The British exchequer, he adds, will continue to underwrite the land purchase scheme for tenant farmers that has been successfully in place for some years now, and it will continue to pay old age pensions in Ireland.

The financial provisions of the new bill, then, can be summarised in four parts, he says: the Irish financial system must be consistent with that of the United Kingdom; the obligations of the imperial parliament at Westminster will be discharged; the Irish parliament will have 'the real financial responsibility'; and there will be no setback to Irish economic and social progress.

British statesmen, Churchill adds, have never dealt fairly with the Irish claim for self-governance.

> And yet, why should not Ireland have her chance? Why should not her venerable nationhood enjoy a recognised and respected existence? Why should not her own distinctive point of view obtain a complete expression? Why should the empire, why should the world at large, be deprived of a new contribution to the sum of human effort? History and polity, justice and good sense alike demand for this race, gifted, virtuous and brave, which has lived so long and has endured so much, that it should not, in view of its passionate desire, be left out of the family of nations, and should not be lost forever among indiscriminated multitudes of men.

In spite of his high-flown words about Irish nationhood, Churchill makes it clear that what is being contemplated for Ireland is not complete independence, but an enhanced role within the British Empire. Talk of separation of Ireland from England is 'idle chatter', he says; the two are bound together until the end of time by natural forces and circumstances. But he sounds a warning about the consequences of failing to meet nationalist aspirations: 'The faith of Irish nationality is inextinguishable. The quarrel would go on here and all over the world.'

Churchill will prove to be the most unreliable supporter of Home Rule in the Cabinet, but his affection for Ireland is probably genuine, given that his earliest memories are of growing up in the Phoenix Park in Dublin in the late 1870s, where he was first 'menaced with education', when his grandfather was lord lieutenant and living in the Viceregal Lodge.

'My nurse, Mrs. Everest, was nervous about the Fenians,' he will recall in his autobiography. 'I gathered these were wicked people and there was no end to what they would do if they had their way. On one occasion when I was out riding on my donkey, we thought we saw a long dark procession of Fenians approaching. I am sure now it must have been the Rifle Brigade out for a route march. But we were all very much alarmed, particularly the donkey, who expressed his anxiety by kicking. I was thrown off and had concussion of the brain. This was my first introduction to Irish politics!'

Now, standing on a Belfast stage more than three decades later, Churchill finishes his speech by picking up and wielding the stick with which unionists have been beating him since his visit to Belfast was announced last month, and answering the charge of filial impiety. In the past few weeks he has been reminded 'often and again of the words Lord Randolph Churchill used a quarter of a century ago'.

> The reverence I feel for his memory and the care with which I have studied his public life make me quite content to leave to others to judge how far there is continuity between his work and any I have tried to do. I am sure the Liberal Party will never become an instrument of injustice and oppression to the Protestants of Ulster. I know this is a duty in which the people of Ulster must not fail; it is a task and a trust placed on them in the name of Ireland, in the name of the British empire, in the name of justice and goodwill – to help us to settle the Irish question wisely and forever now. There is the task which history has assigned to them, and it is in a different sense that I adapt and repeat Lord Randolph Churchill's words, 'Ulster will fight, and Ulster will be right'.
>
> Let Ulster fight for the dignity and honour of Ireland, for the reconciliation of races and the forgiveness of ancient wrongs, for the unity and consolidation of the British empire, for the spread of charity and enlightenment among men. Then indeed, Ulster will fight, and Ulster will be right.

After the cheers have subsided, John Redmond – speaking in the name of 'the overwhelming majority of the people of Ireland' – thanks Churchill for his 'magnificent advocacy' of the nationalists' cause. He accepts 'every word' of the speech just given; there are no limits to which the Irish Party will not go to provide safeguards to the Protestant population. Nevertheless, the 'arrogant and intolerable claim of a minority in Ulster must not be allowed to override Ireland, Great Britain and the empire.'

> With Mr Churchill's imperial argument I absolutely agree. We want to make a settlement with our Protestant fellow countrymen, and one of our chief reasons for wanting it is that we may come, at last, into our rightful place in the empire, which we have built as well as they [loud cheers].

After a resolution of thanks to Churchill is passed, the visitor declares – to more cheers – that 'we have done a good day's work and I do not think any of us will ever have any cause to regret it.' The audience then rises and sings 'God Save the King', an uncharacteristic act at a Belfast nationalist gathering, explained most likely by the mixed nature of the audience and the goodwill generated by Churchill's visit and the government's Home Rule policy.

On his return journey down the Falls Road, Churchill is again enthusiastically hailed by large numbers of nationalists, including several youths who clamber on to the steps of his car and succeed in shaking his hand. A decidedly more unreceptive crowd is waiting for him on a densely packed Royal Avenue, but his convoy takes a sudden turn on to a different route from the one by which it came, and soon the Churchill party is on a special train out of Belfast and back to Larne – where a lone protester shakes his fist at Churchill and cries 'Traitor! Traitor! Traitor!' – before the seething masses gathered outside the Grand Central Hotel have any inkling that their quarry has escaped.

For some time they stand, squeezed one against the other, once again repeatedly singing 'Rule, Britannia!' and 'God Save the King'. Then word spreads that the First Lord of the Admiralty is well on his way back to London, and the crowd quietly disperses. John Redmond, too, is on his way home to Aughavanagh, satisfied in the knowledge that another staging post has been passed on the road to Irish freedom.

Chapter 5 ～

WHERE GLADSTONE STOOD

I personally thank God that I have lived to see this day.

Two irreconcilable forces have been unleashed, and the momentum behind the Home Rule campaign on one side and opposition to it on the other looks unstoppable. Nevertheless, John Redmond is unperturbed. The re-establishment of a parliament in Ireland, after an absence of more than a century, is now inevitable, and practical details are being worked out.

Since the unveiling of the Parnell monument in October 1911, he has addressed a series of public meetings in Britain to explain the case for Home Rule. He then suffered a severe physical setback on 29 December when the horse-drawn carriage in which he was travelling in County Wicklow with his wife and daughter and fellow MP J.J. Clancy collapsed, throwing the entire party on to the road, although only Redmond was injured.

After several weeks convalescing at Aughavanagh, Redmond returned to the public stage in time for the Churchill meeting in Belfast in February. In the meantime he and John Dillon have been pushing senior Cabinet ministers for as far-reaching a measure of Home Rule as possible. A committee of experts established by the government to examine the financial relations between Ireland and Britain, chaired by retired Inland Revenue Chairman Sir Henry Primrose, has already recommended full fiscal autonomy for the new Irish administration. This, however, is rejected by a Cabinet sub-committee on Home Rule, which includes David Lloyd George, Winston Churchill and Irish Secretary Augustine Birrell. It asks another of its members, Postmaster General Herbert Samuel, to draw up an alternative scheme.

As Redmond prepares for the mass rally on O'Connell Street in Dublin on 31 March, which fills the capital's main thoroughfare from end to end and at which Patrick Pearse makes his 'red war in Ireland' speech, Birrell keeps him posted on the details of the imminent Government of Ireland Bill – or Home Rule Bill, as it is generally known.

In the days following the O'Connell Street demonstration, Redmond receives the final draft. The fiscal scheme drawn up by Samuel is a disappointment. Instead of full fiscal autonomy, the bill sets out a complicated arrangement under which all Irish tax revenues would be paid into the imperial exchequer, and in return London would provide the Irish government with a block grant for the administration of exclusively Irish affairs. London would continue to administer certain 'reserved services', as hinted at by Churchill in his Belfast speech, including old age pensions, land purchase and general tax collection. In summary, parliament will later be told, the financial arrangements in the first year would result in about £10.8 million in Irish tax revenue being collected by the British exchequer; it would then hand this money – plus an additional £2 million – back to the Irish executive, giving it some £12.8 million to run the country.

The details are not a surprise to Redmond and Dillon, who were shown a first draft of the Samuel proposals as early as 12 January. The Irish leaders immediately objected to the scheme and sought the complete fiscal autonomy recommended by the Primrose committee. Despite the government's refusal to concede to this demand, Redmond remains in good heart as the government prepares to introduce the bill in the House of Commons. He believes the most important thing is to secure Home Rule in the first place and that there is still room for negotiation on the details.

Such is the sense of anticipation at the proximity of Home Rule that Dillon feels the need to warn Redmond, in advance of a trip he is planning to Dublin, to avoid his usual headquarters, the Gresham Hotel. 'It is at present uninhabitable,' Dillon writes. 'It is beset with a swarm of office-seekers from morning til night.'

∿

On 11 April 1912, the long-awaited day arrives. Just before 3 p.m., loud cheers ring out in the House of Commons at the sight of the white-haired prime minister, Herbert Asquith, entering the chamber from behind the Speaker's chair. Moments later, the Liberal and nationalist MPs are cheering again as John Redmond moves slowly and quietly to his seat below the gangway, an aisle stairs that divides the chamber in two. Then, at the stroke of three o'clock, it is the turn of the unionist MPs to stand and voice loud approval as a smiling Edward Carson takes his seat on the front opposition bench. Conservative and Unionist Party leader Bonar Law receives a similarly rapturous welcome when he takes his seat a few minutes after the proceedings have begun.

There is a palpable sense of history being made, and Irish supporters of Redmond and his party make up a significant proportion of those in the packed public gallery. Many other Irish people, who filled the lobby of the House of Commons earlier in the day, have left disappointed, having been unable to secure entry tickets.

A solemn Asquith stands at 3.05 p.m. to ask for leave to introduce a bill to amend the provisions for the government of Ireland. He begins by reminding the house that it is 19 years since William Gladstone stood at the same table at which he is now standing, to begin his second attempt to bring in a measure providing 'for the better government of Ireland'. Asquith says he will now 'take up the narrative where Mr Gladstone was obliged to leave it'.

> While the fortunes of political parties in the house have ebbed and flowed over the years, one thing has remained consistent: the demand for home rule by a large majority in Ireland.
>
> We have had as a nation peace and war, adversity and prosperity, shifting issues, changing policies; but throughout the welter and confusion, amid all the varying phases and fields of our electoral and parliamentary campaigns, one thing has remained constant, subject neither to eclipse nor wane, the insistence and persistence of the Irish demand [cheers]. It remains today, in April 1912, what it was in January 1886, and what in the interval it has never ceased to be: a demand preferred by four-fifths of the elected representatives of the Irish people.

Ulster is the only province where there is a genuine division of opinion, he points out, and even there the picture is not as uniform as presented.

Taking Ulster as a whole, the province of Ulster is represented at this moment, how? By 17 unionists and 16 home rulers [cheers]. These figures in themselves are quite sufficient to show the misleading character of the pretence that Ulster would die rather than accept home rule.

That is not to underestimate the hostility to Home Rule of the majority of those in north-east Ulster, he says. He hopes to demonstrate that their concerns have not been ignored in the bill now being presented, but a minority cannot be allowed to veto the demands of 'the vast majority of the nation, repeated and ratified ...' Here Asquith is interrupted by a Conservative MP, Sir Clement Kinloch-Cooke, who shouts: 'What nation?!' To further cheers from the Liberal and nationalist MPs, Asquith responds: 'What nation? The Irish nation – repeated and ratified time after time during the best part of the life of a generation.'

Step by step, Asquith builds the case for Home Rule, not just for Ireland, but as a principle in itself. Indicating that similar schemes will later be brought forward for England, Scotland and Wales – a concept commonly referred to as 'Home Rule all round' – the prime minister argues that the imperial parliament in London is overburdened and, consequently, inefficient.

Look at the question paper of this house on a Monday or Thursday in any week you like to select. What does it include, or, rather, what does it not include? Delay in the postal service of some hamlet in Connemara, a dispute about trawling in the Moray Firth, a decision perhaps in a poaching case by some rural bench in Wales ... and, perhaps, the international relations between Great Britain and Germany.

Home Rule for Ireland is just the first step in a larger policy to address this problem, he says. Much of Asquith's speech, however, is taken up in setting out the detailed measures of the bill. It proposes a bicameral parliament, made up of a house of commons of 164 elected members, and a 40-seat senate. The London government will appoint the members of the first senate, but as they complete their eight-year terms and vacancies arise, replacements will be made by the Irish government. The idea of making the senate a nominated rather than elected body, Asquith explains, is to ensure that minority interests are represented.

The Dublin parliament is to have power to 'make laws for the peace, order, and good government of Ireland', but a number of areas – including the army and navy, matters affecting the crown and treaties with foreign countries – are to remain under Westminster control. The Royal Irish Constabulary (RIC) is also to stay under London's jurisdiction, but only for six years, after which it will come under the authority of the administration in Dublin. The Lord Lieutenant in Ireland will have power to veto any legislation considered to exceed the Dublin parliament's powers. Westminster will remain in control of taxation, delegating only limited powers in this area to the Irish parliament.

Ireland will retain 42 seats in the House of Commons in London – about half the current number – and Irish MPs there will continue to have a vote on all matters. There are also measures to protect religious freedom, aimed at negating the Ulster unionists' claim that Home Rule will mean 'Rome rule'.

Asquith's two-hour address concludes in fiery exchanges with Bonar Law and other unionist leaders, whom he accuses of introducing 'a new style' of politics in their opposition to Home Rule. He expresses particular anger at a speech made by Law in Belfast in recent days in which the opposition leader said: 'In order to remain for a few months longer in office, his majesty's government have sold the Constitution.'

Uproar ensues when Law interjects to say that he stands over the accusation, and Asquith is forced to deliver the concluding passages of his speech in the face of a cacophony of shouted interjections from all sides of the chamber.

We put this bill forward as the responsible advisers of the crown as the embodiment of our own honest and deliberate judgment. [Cheers and opposition laughter and shouts of 'Toe the line!'] What is your alternative? [MPs: 'Tariff reform!'] Are you satisfied with the present system? [MPs: 'Quite!'] Were you satisfied with it two years ago? What do you propose to put in its place? Have you any answer to the demand of Ireland [MPs: 'Yes!'] beyond the naked veto of an irreconcilable minority, and the promise of a freer and more copious outflow to Ireland of imperial doles? [MPs: 'Hear, hear!']

There are at this moment between 20 and 30 self-governing legislatures under the allegiance of the crown. They have solved, under every diversity of conditions, economic, racial, and religious, the problem of reconciling local autonomy with imperial unity. Are we going to break up the empire by adding one more? The claim comes this time, not from remote outlying quarters, but from a people close to our own doors, associated with us by every tie of kindred, of interest, of social and industrial intercourse, who have borne and are bearing their share, and a noble share it has been, in the building up and the holding together of the greatest empire in history. [Cheers, then an MP: 'Cheering our defeats in South Africa!' and another MP: 'Did Lynch do that?'] That claim no longer falls on deaf ears. There has been reserved for this parliament, this House of Commons, the double honour of reconciling Ireland and emancipating herself.

When Asquith sits down, the cheers from the government and nationalist benches soon give way to equally loud bellows for the first speaker from the opposition. Edward Carson's hawk-like features and self-possession, combined with a precision in his speech, finely tuned over many years in the law courts, make him one of the most imposing figures in the house. He begins with a gleeful assertion: he does not mind in the least being accused of what the prime minister calls 'the new style of politics' when he states that 'more ridiculous or fantastic proposals' than those just outlined by Asquith have never been put before this or any other parliament.

In a lengthy and scornful address laden with sarcasm, Carson rejects the government's bill measure by measure.

The new senate, the great safeguard of that contemptible minority which I attempt to represent in this house, is to be a nominated body. That is a radical proposition. Any such proposal as that is a deliberate insult to this House of Commons. What is the use of it? Nominated by whom? Nominated, I suppose, by the imperial government. Will it be nominated, or could it be nominated, against the wish of the honourable members who will be retained in this house, and supported by a parliament in Dublin which you yourselves created? The thing is fantastic. It is worth nothing, like all the other safeguards that you have put forward.

Carson's central argument is that once an Irish parliament is established, no safeguards or checks and balances will prevent it pursuing separation from the British Empire and complete independence, notwithstanding the protestations from nationalist MPs that this is not their aim. Even John Redmond, he points out, said during the debate in 1893 on Gladstone's second Home Rule Bill: 'As the bill now stands no man in his senses can regard it as a full, final, and satisfactory settlement of the Irish question. Sir, the word "provisional", so to speak, has been stamped in red ink across every page of this bill.'

'Will the Irish members tell us that this [latest bill] is going to be accepted as a final settlement? I venture to think that not one of them will,' says Carson. Irish unionists, he concludes, will oppose the bill with all their energy, at every stage and every moment it is before the house.

That is our duty. We believe it to be an unnecessary bill. We believe it to be a fatal bill for our country, and an equally fatal bill for yours, and, above all things, we believe it to be involved in the greatest series of dishonourable transactions that have ever disgraced any country.

The cheers are still resounding in Carson's ears when Redmond rises to speak. If Carson's visage is akin to a hawk's, Redmond's features are owl-like, his transparent, wide eyes contrasting with his opponent's impenetrable stare, and carrying a permanent hint of hurt or anticipated disappointment. But when Redmond speaks, he comes into his own, deploying to great effect the skills first learned at elocution classes in Clongowes Wood College in Kildare and developed in the school's debating competitions. His melodic timbre and eloquence make him one of the most popular speakers in the British parliament.

He begins by welcoming the bill with – as the *Times* of London will mockingly observe the next day – 'a detachment and admiration which to the uninitiated might suggest that he did not recognise the work of his own hands'. The truth is that while Redmond has been consulted on all stages of the preparation of the bill, it falls considerably short of what he had hoped for, especially in the area of fiscal independence. But, recognising that a great breakthrough has been achieved and that his life's work is coming to fruition, he welcomes the bill in effusive terms:

> It is a great measure and we welcome it [cheers]. This bill will be submitted to the Irish national convention [cheers], and I shall without hesitation recommend to that convention the acceptance of the bill [cheers].

He also rejects Carson's claim that for nationalists the bill is merely a first step towards the separation of Ireland from the British Empire.

> We on these benches stand precisely where Parnell stood. We want peace with this country. We deny that we are separatists, and we say we are willing, as Parnell was willing, to accept a subordinate parliament created by statute of this imperial legislature, as a final settlement of Ireland's claims.

'If I may say so reverently,' he adds, 'I personally thank God that I have lived to see this day.'

> I believe this bill will pass into law. I believe it will result in the greater unity and strength of the empire; I believe it will put an end once and for all to [An MP: 'Cattle driving!'] the wretched ill-will, suspicion, and disaffection that have existed in Ireland, and to the suspicion and misunderstanding that have existed between this country and Ireland; I believe it will have the effect of turning Ireland in time – of course, it will take time – into a happy and prosperous country, with a united, loyal, and contented people.

Twelve days later, at the Mansion House in Dublin, Redmond is given an ecstatic welcome by five thousand delegates at a nationalist convention called to consider the bill. Delegates representing a broad range of nationalist opinion, including county and district councils, the Ancient Order of Hibernians and the United Irish League – the Irish Party's grassroots organisation – attend the event. In truth, there is no real discussion on the merits of the bill, and the only note of discord is struck by the one hundred or so members of the Irish Women's Franchise League, who are refused permission to send a delegation to the meeting and are held outside by a large force of policemen.

Inside, there is not a single note of dissent in what *The Times* of London will next day describe, not unfairly, as 'an excellently stage managed event'. But there is nothing fake about the euphoric reception given to Redmond when, led by the Irish National Foresters in their picturesque regalia, he mounts the stage shortly after 11 a.m. He begins on a sombre note, moving a resolution of sympathy with the relatives of all who died on-board the Belfast-built ocean liner the *Titanic*, which sank on its maiden voyage eight days previously, before going on to tell his audience that the Home Rule Bill is the greatest and most satisfactory measure offered to Ireland, and is a justification and vindication of the Irish Party's policy.

The convention unanimously passes a motion accepting the bill as 'an honest and generous attempt to settle the long quarrel between the British and Irish nations'. The Irish Party is also given a mandate to negotiate amendments to the bill as it sees fit.

Not all of nationalist Ireland is convinced that the bill is the 'greatest measure'. In a statement issued in the days preceding the nationalist convention, the General Council of County Councils – representing local authorities throughout the country – criticises the financial provisions of the bill, describing them as 'unsatisfactory' and 'in need of drastic amendment'. Among the 'minimum terms' it says the Irish people should accept are the retention by Ireland of the taxes collected within its borders, the control of Irish revenue by an Irish staff, and for the Irish treasury to be responsible for all Irish services.

The failure of the Irish Party to secure full fiscal independence will continue to be a source of controversy as debate over the bill continues.

Nevertheless, for John Redmond this is a moment of triumph, one he has been working towards for more than 30 years. Although a Member of Parliament since he was 24, his involvement in parliamentary life goes back even further than that. Born into one of Wexford's leading merchant families in 1856, Redmond has politics in his blood. He was three when his grand-uncle, John Edward Redmond, entered the House of Commons as MP for Wexford. The Redmonds had been Catholic landed gentry until their estates were confiscated following the Cromwellian conquest of Ireland in the seventeenth century. After that, some members of the family went into military service abroad, while others pursued commercial interests at home.

John Redmond's great-grandfather, who had the same name, was one of the founders of Redmond's Bank in Wexford, which merged with the Bank of Ireland in 1834. The banker's son, John Edward, the MP, was also responsible for major commercial and public projects in Wexford, including the building of a local railway line.

John Edward died in 1865. Seven years later his nephew, William Archer Redmond – John Redmond's father – was elected to the Wexford seat in the House of Commons, where he immediately threw in his lot with the new Home Rule party being established by Isaac Butt. Within four years of his election, however, his health had begun to fail and in 1876, aged 19, John Redmond went to London to assist his father in his parliamentary work, while also studying for the bar.

His life had been immersed in the affairs of the House of Commons for several years before his election as a youthful MP. He is now 55 and the party he leads has grown old with him. Its usefulness has been questioned by many among the younger generation, who have increasingly come to view the Irish MPs as ineffectual and detached from their constituents. For the first time since before the Parnell split of 1890, the party is seen as relevant and dynamic. Redmond has proved the doubters wrong, and the wholehearted endorsement of his policy at the Mansion House meeting confirms his status as the undisputed leader of the Irish nation.

But he has not yet conquered Ulster, and the resistance there to his campaign for Home Rule has just taken a new, and sinister, twist.

Chapter 6 ∿

WHAT ANSWER FROM THE NORTH?

We are not out for holiday-making.

John Redmond has his Home Rule Bill, and almost all of nationalist Ireland is behind him, but the pace of events is quickening on both sides. Two days before the introduction of the bill in the House of Commons, the Ulster unionists stage their biggest demonstration yet to step up their confrontation with the British government.

The Balmoral agricultural showgrounds in south Belfast is the setting for what Edward Carson will describe as 'the greatest assembly that has ever met in any country'. It is certainly one the biggest ever seen in Ireland or Britain, and surpasses in numbers the turnout for the mass Home Rule rally addressed by Redmond on O'Connell Street in Dublin just over a week earlier.

The protest, on 9 April 1912, carries the explicit message that the Ulster loyalists are now on a war footing, beginning as it does with a military-style procession by up to a hundred thousand members of unionist clubs, Orange lodges and the Apprentice Boys of Derry, many of them in the regalia of their organisations. After parading through streets bedecked in blue, white and red and lined with supporters, to the ubiquitous sound of flutes and drumbeats, they split into two columns on arrival at Balmoral, one passing each side of a small pavilion where the unionist leaders Bonar Law, Edward Carson, Lord Londonderry and Walter Long stand to take a salute.

As was the case for the Home Rule rally in Dublin, four speakers' platforms have been erected. From one of these, perhaps seduced by the impressive display of militarism, Lord Charles Beresford – a Conservative MP who once represented the County Waterford constituency and whose family own the hundred thousand-acre

Curraghmore estate in Portlaw – warns of the inevitability of 'civil war' if Home Rule is forced through.

The marchers make up only half the estimated attendance of two hundred thousand, some of whom will have been stirred by 'Ulster 1912', a poem by Rudyard Kipling published in that day's *Morning Post* newspaper:

> The dark eleventh hour
> Draws on and sees us sold
> To every evil power
> We fought against of old
> Rebellion, rapine hate
> Oppression, wrong and greed
> Are loosed to rule our fate,
> By England's act and deed ...
>
> Believe, we dare not boast,
> Believe, we do not fear –
> We stand to pay the cost
> In all that men hold dear.
> What answer from the North?
> One Law, one Land, one Throne.
> If England drive us forth
> We shall not fall alone!

Kipling's 'answer from the North' is bolstered by the presence of several thousand southern unionists, many of whom have travelled by rail from Amiens Street station in Dublin.

Acknowledging this, Carson, in an introductory speech from the central platform reported in the following day's *Irish Times*, says 'it is mainly an Ulster assemblage, but we welcome here my own fellow citizens from Dublin [cheers], from Wicklow [cheers], from Clare [cheers], yes, from Cork, rebel Cork [cheers], who are now holding the hand of Ulster'.

And what have we met for? To pronounce in the most solemn and deliberate way that we are determined to maintain our privileges as citizens of a United Kingdom. We are not out for holiday-making. We are here to meet a revolution in the only way that a revolution can be met – by realising our responsibilities and not caring about the consequences, determined that we shall defeat it [cheers].

Many are here at great sacrifice, many are here from long distances, but they care nothing about that. We have one object in view, that is the object of victory – and we are going to win [cheers].

The Liberal government, Carson tells the crowd, has removed the constitutional protections that enabled them to defeat the Home Rule Bills of 1886 and 1893.

I tell you that when they are trying to force this Home Rule policy upon us by methods of this kind, it gives us the right to say: 'Your bill has no moral force. We will not accept it, and as you have treated us with fraud, if necessary we will treat you with force' [loud cheers].

The government, he declares, is unable to deal with the Home Rule question judicially or fairly, 'because if they dared to say one word John Redmond says "Come, Mr Asquith, toe the line" [laughter]. Yes, you are dealing with a toe-the-line government [laughter] and that is the one form of exercise with which they are acquainted and at which they are prepared to take the first prize [laughter].'

Twenty years previously, Carson reminds his audience, many of them gathered at a great meeting at which the Duke of Abercorn gave them a simple phrase that embodied their whole political faith: 'We will not have Home Rule.' With that simple faith they beat Mr Gladstone and his allies, he says, and with that same simple faith they will beat the policy of Home Rule again. He concludes his short address by asking the enormous crowd to raise their hands and repeat after him: 'Never, in any circumstances, will we submit to Home Rule.'

The more the Ulster unionists get to know Edward Carson, the more they like him. But the man standing before them is not easy to get to know. Steadfast and purposeful in public, he conveys an air of invincibility; far less self-assured in private, he obsesses about his health and is frequently confined to bed with one ailment or another.

One thing on which his admirers and detractors agree is that he does not lack courage, moral or physical. As a boarding school pupil in Portarlington, where he was given the nickname 'Rawbones' – abbreviated by himself to 'Bones' when signing his letters – because he was tall and ungainly and of delicate physique, he was known for standing up to bullies, even when that meant fighting bigger boys himself.

Signs of his unflinching courage are still clear to all, including his supporters at the Balmoral rally. The star turn at the event, however, is not Carson, but Bonar Law, the Canadian-born leader of the Conservative Party, who is here with some seventy of his party's MPs. As he mounts the platform, Law – who is of Ulster Scots descent – is received with prolonged cheers before Carson hands him an address of welcome, on paper, stating as he does so: 'Mr Bonar Law, I present you with this address on behalf of this great assemblage. All I ask in return – as I am the Leader of the Irish Unionist Party – is that you and I in the presence of this, our nation, should shake hands over this question.'

The two men then grasp each other's hands amid loud cheering. In this symbolic act, soon to be backed with explicit commitments, Law ties the Conservative Party to the Ulster Unionists' extra-constitutional campaign to defeat Home Rule. For John Redmond, a constitutional politician to his core, the rules of the game have suddenly changed.

Within weeks, Law will leave no room for doubt about how far beyond constitutional boundaries his party is prepared to go in support of their Ulster unionist brethren. For today, he is content to tell his audience that he comes to them 'as the leader of the Unionist Party in the House of Commons, with two objects':

> I come to give you the assurance which I give you now – that we who represent that party regard your cause, not as yours alone, nor ours alone, but as the cause of the empire; and that we shall do all that man can do to defeat a conspiracy as treacherous as has ever been formed against the life of a great nation [cheers].

Home Rule, he adds, would bring no benefits to nationalist, never mind unionist, Ireland.

> On what ground either of reason or of justice is Home Rule defended? It is defended on this ground only: that the Irish people demand it. The Irish people demand it. Then who and what are you?! [cheers]

There is not a single grievance that nationalists can point to which the British parliament and people have not been ready to redress, he says. 'They are in the main a Catholic population in a Protestant country, but they enjoy, and will always enjoy, religious liberty in a measure as great, probably greater, than in any Catholic country.'

Commenting on the event the following day, the nationalist *Freeman's Journal* will describe this remark by Law as an 'instructive glimpse' into the unionist mind and how it perceives the Catholic majority. 'They are a "Catholic minority in a Protestant country". They ought to be thankful they are not persecuted. Their natural destiny is to be subject to a Protestant ascendancy with Mr Bonar Law as the Protestant head-piece.'

Law, in his address, has much more to say that will not be well received by the nationalist press. Men do not constitute a nation because they happen to live on the same island, he asserts, and Ireland 'is not, and never has been' a nation.

> There are two peoples in Ireland, separated from each other by a gulf of religion, or race, and, above all, of prejudice, far deeper than that which separates Ireland as a whole from the rest of the United Kingdom ['hear, hear!']. I do not suggest, and you do not ask, that the minority should exercise any ascendancy over the majority. But you do ask, and you have the right to ask, that a majority, because it is in Ireland, should not dominate a minority because it is also in Ireland.

The Protestant minority, he continues, makes up a quarter of the population of Ireland, but in 'influence, in character, in everything which goes to make the strength of nations', it is far more important than that. It pays half the taxation of Ireland and 'probably does half the trade', and in Belfast alone it contributes two-thirds of the customs dues.

'I say to you with all solemnity,' he concludes, 'you must trust to yourselves.'

> Once again you hold the pass for the empire. You are a besieged city. Does not the picture of the past, the glorious past, with which you are so familiar, rise again before your eyes? The timid have left you [laughter]. Your Lundys have betrayed you, but you have closed your gates [cheers]. The government by their Parliament Act have erected a boom against you, a boom to cut you off from the help of the British people ['Never! Never!']. You will burst that boom! [Loud cheers.] The help will come, and when the crisis is over men will say of you in words not unlike those once used of Pitt, 'you have saved yourselves by your exertions, and you will save the empire by your example' [loud cheers].

The event concludes with the passing of a resolution assuring the Conservative leader that the opposition of the Irish unionists to Home Rule is unaltered and unalterable, and expressing the conviction that a Home Rule parliament would lead to racial and sectarian strife and to lasting injury to commerce, and would be the first step towards the disintegration of the empire.

At the moment of the resolution's adoption, a union flag measuring 48 feet by 25, said to be the largest ever woven, is unfurled, to loud roars of approval, from a signalling tower in the middle of the grounds. Carson, standing beside Law, leads the gathering in prolonged cheering before quietness descends and 'God Save the King' is sung. On their way back to the Northern Counties Railway Station en route to London, the two leaders are briefly carried shoulder high by some in the departing crowds. For a further two hours the bands parade through the city as everybody who was there basks in the glory of the greatest show of unionist strength ever displayed.

The 'one gap in our ranks' identified by John Redmond nine days earlier at the Home Rule rally in Dublin looks like a very large gap indeed.

Chapter 7 ~

'CHEERS FOR THE LIBERATOR!'

Give them the hatchet! Set fire to them!

Ireland is now the dominant issue in British politics. On 9 May 1912, the Home Rule Bill is read in the Commons a second time and passes by 372 votes to 271, but the 'Ulster question' is no closer to being resolved. Then the debate takes a turn. On the evening of 11 June, Thomas Agar-Robartes, a young Liberal MP of aristocratic stock who will lose his life in the Great War that is soon to come, rises in the House of Commons to move an amendment.

Why not, he suggests, remove counties Antrim, Armagh, Down and Londonderry from the provisions of the bill? 'If this amendment is carried,' he says, 'the Home Rule majority of the people in Ireland will have Home Rule, and, on the other hand, the unionist majority in north-east Ulster will be excluded from the provisions of the bill, and will be enabled to retain their liberties and their political allegiance with this country. The chief danger of disturbance and civil war will thus be removed.'

Although MPs have had the customary advance notice of the amendment, Agar-Robartes' proposal is greeted with silence. It is as if nobody dare express a view on this radical idea. Explaining his delay in rising to respond, Irish Chief Secretary Augustine Birrell says he thought some of the members from Ulster might have wished to speak first. He has 'no hesitation' in saying, however, that the government does not intend to accept this 'somewhat fantastic proposal'.

The reality, however, is that what the MPs have just heard on the floor of the Commons is less a 'fantastic' new proposal than the sound of a cat escaping from a bag. The possibility of separate treatment for Ulster as a way out of the Home Rule impasse has, in fact, been a topic of discussion among Cabinet members for some time.

As early as ten months previously, in August 1911, Birrell himself wrote to Winston Churchill, a fellow member of the Cabinet's Home Rule sub-committee, suggesting that each county in Ulster be allowed to decide by referendum whether or not they wished to be part of the new Home Rule regime. Those that opted out could be asked to vote again after a transitional period of perhaps five years. Birrell's rather optimistic view – from the Irish nationalist perspective – was that only Antrim and Down would choose to remain outside the Home Rule fold.

Churchill saw merit in the idea and six months later, on 6 February, two days before he addressed an enthusiastic nationalist audience in Belfast, he and David Lloyd George proposed to the Cabinet that the Ulster counties be given the option of voting to exclude themselves temporarily from Home Rule. After a lengthy discussion the idea was rejected, but Prime Minister Herbert Asquith, in his report of the Cabinet meeting to King George, said that 'special treatment' for Ulster might have to be considered at a later stage, depending on the strength and character of the province's resistance to the bill.

Asquith's position on the matter, then, appears to be one of pragmatism rather than principle. The government will face down the Ulster loyalists unless they protest too strongly. It's a policy that will become known, disparagingly, as one of 'wait and see'. This may not be the man John Redmond needs at his back when the going gets really tough, as it soon will.

Agar-Robartes' intervention, bringing into the open the suggestion that Ulster – or some of its counties – might be excluded from the bill presents a challenge, not only for John Redmond but also for Edward Carson. He has fought Home Rule to date on the basis that it would be bad for Ireland as a whole, and not only the Ulster loyalists whom he represents. If he now accepts the idea that Home Rule is fine as long as Protestant Ulster is not forced to submit to it, won't his 'principled opposition' to the measure be exposed as a sham? Worse, won't he be open to the accusation that he has abandoned his fellow southern Protestants to their fate in a jurisdiction to be run by the disreputable leaders – the cattle mutilators and boycotters, as he has called them – of nationalist Ireland?

There is intense interest, then, in what the next speaker has to say when Birrell sits down after declaring the government's opposition to the Agar-Robartes amendment.

Carson's close confidant Bonar Law, leader of the Conservative and Unionist Party – now formally established as such following a merger between the Conservatives and Liberal Unionists, and commonly referred to simply as the Unionist Party – rises to his feet. His short but rambling speech initially skirts around the issue and keeps MPs in suspense. Finally, however, he affirms that his party will support Agar-Robartes' proposal. 'While we oppose this bill root and branch,' he explains, 'yet we are discussing it in [the] committee [stage], and the ground on which we are discussing it is that we will support any amendment which, bad as the bill seems to us to be, would make it less bad than it was before the amendment was introduced.'

Two days later, Carson confirms to the house that he is prepared to accept the 'basic principle' of Agar-Robartes' amendment, but says that the detail will require further consideration. For example, he says, Tyrone and Fermanagh have a claim to exclusion from the bill that is equal to the four counties mentioned in the amendment, and he could 'never agree' to leave them out of a scheme for separate treatment.

In a sombre address free from rhetoric, he reiterates his view that Home Rule would be 'disastrous' for Ireland, and he remains opposed to the bill in its entirety. He does not want to see Ireland truncated, but if Home Rule is to come, the best way for Ulster to help the people in the south and west of the country is for its representatives to remain in the Westminster parliament.

He is followed immediately by Redmond, who begins by acknowledging the 'moderation and calmness' of Carson's speech and promising to try to imitate it, but he doesn't hold back in his criticism of the Agar-Robartes proposal, describing it as 'absurd'.

> We say it is illogical and unworkable, that it is not asked for by any section of unionists in Ireland ... Above all, we oppose it because it would destroy for ever our most cherished ambition, namely, to see the Irish nation in the near future made up of every race and every creed and every class working unitedly for the well-being and

freedom of the Irish race and doing so through the instrumentality of a native government which, in the words of Thomas Davis, 'shall rule by the right and might of all, yet yield to the arrogance of none'.

Redmond also makes an appeal to members of the Liberal Party who, although friendly to the Home Rule movement, might be tempted to support the amendment as a potential settlement of the Irish question. Edward Carson and his colleagues, he argues, have made it clear that while they support the Agar-Robartes proposal, they do not see it as a potential compromise, but rather as an opportunity to 'wreck' the bill in its entirety.

His analysis is immediately confirmed by Ulster Unionist MP Charles Craig – brother of Sir James, on whose estate Carson made his first speech to a mass unionist audience the previous September. 'I think it is a wrecking amendment,' he says, 'and so much the better. I would use any means to wreck the bill. That is one reason why I will vote for the amendment.'

Speaking in the same debate, Lloyd George confirms that the government did consider the exclusion of Ulster or some of its counties from the Home Rule Bill, though he neglects to mention that he himself advocated such a measure four months earlier. Ireland, he points out, has always been treated by the Westminster parliament as a separate and single entity, and until now there has never been a demand for special treatment for Ulster on any matter.

'If there were a demand from Ulster that Ulster should be treated separately,' he says, 'then, of course, the government should give it serious consideration. When has it ever been made? It has not been made, not even in this debate.' The only reason the Protestants of Ulster would support the amendment, he also argues, is if they saw it as a means of wrecking the entire bill.

The 'real claim' of Ulster, Lloyd George adds, is 'not that she should be protected herself, not that she should have autonomy herself, but the right to veto autonomy to the rest of Ireland. That is an intolerable demand.'

The amendment is defeated, but as the debate continues inside and outside parliament, Carson and Law become increasingly inflammatory in their language. At a boisterous protest meeting in the Albert Hall in London on 14 June, Carson – after several swipes at Redmond, the 'dictator of the government' – denounces the Liberals' policy as 'a declaration of war' against Ulster. 'We will accept the declaration of war. We are not altogether unprepared. I think it is time that we should take a step forward in our campaign, and I will recommend that to be done.'

Four days later, in the Commons, Law makes the extraordinary claim – for the leader of a conservative party in a constitutional democracy – that the government knows 'there are stronger influences than parliamentary majorities'. No government, he adds, would dare to use its troops to drive the people of Ulster out of the United Kingdom. 'They know, as a matter of fact, that the government which gave the order to employ troops for that purpose would run a greater risk of being lynched in London than the loyalists of Ulster would run of being shot in Belfast.'

Despite the wild talk of shootings and lynchings if Home Rule is passed, it is a sanguine Asquith who visits Dublin on the evening of Thursday, 18 July to make a speech in defence of the Government's Home Rule policy. Remarkably, it is the first visit to Ireland by a serving prime minister of Britain, and he is greeted with what one Liberal-supporting newspaper – the *Daily Chronicle* – describes as 'almost feverish joy'.

On arrival by ferry at Kingstown harbour at 8.30 p.m., Asquith, accompanied by his wife Margot and daughters Violet and Lizzie, is greeted by a cheering crowd of ten thousand, many of them waving green flags bearing the words 'We Want Home Rule'. Local bands create a festive air with a selection of Irish harmonies, and a priest in the crowd, one of the many clergymen present, is so carried away by the moment that he is heard by an *Irish Independent* reporter to call for 'cheers for the liberator!'

In the city centre, vast but orderly crowds line the streets as the prime minister, accompanied by Redmond and the other Irish Party leaders, make their way in carriages in a torchlight procession – though darkness has not yet descended – from Westland Row train station to the Gresham Hotel on O'Connell Street, where a reception is to be held.

Hats, handkerchiefs and walking sticks are waved enthusiastically in the Asquiths' direction, and Margot, clutching a 'We Want Home Rule' flag in one hand, waves back with a handkerchief in the other. The cavalcade is accompanied by the Ireland's Own band and a guard of honour of the Irish National Foresters. At its head, incongruously, is a sixty-strong delegation on horseback from the Anti-Taxi Association, made up of jarveys opposed to the issuing of taxi licences for motor cars.

When the procession turns the corner into College Green shortly after 9.30 p.m., loud cheers go up and several rockets are fired into the evening sky. A band at the gates of Trinity College strikes up a rendition of 'The Memory of the Dead', prompting the multitude to break into song: 'Who fears to speak of Ninety-Eight?/Who blushes at the name?...'

As the crowds surge towards Asquith's open carriage, the police lines are broken. Amid scenes of 'unbounded enthusiasm' – as the *Independent* will describe it – 'deafening' cheers ring out again and again, while handkerchiefs are waved from nearby windows. Asquith, visibly taken aback by the exuberance of his reception, rises to his feet and bows towards Trinity College. His attention is drawn away, however, by a touch on his shoulder from his wife, who points him towards the Bank of Ireland building opposite Trinity, which was once the home of an Irish parliament and is soon to be so again. As the prime minister turns to face the building and wave his hand, shouts go up from the crowd: 'The Old House!'; 'We will be there very soon!'

It is a dramatic moment, but a very different kind of excitement is about to unfold.

While the convoy slowly makes its way through the heaving masses and up O'Connell Street, a young woman forces her way towards the carriage carrying Asquith and Redmond, produces a small hatchet from her handbag, and flings it at the prime minister. The axe misses Asquith, who is standing in acknowledgment of the cheering crowds, but catches the seated Redmond on the right ear. Word of the attack by Mary Leigh, a member of the suffragette movement in England, quickly reaches a contingent of Redmond supporters waiting in the Gresham to greet the Irish leader and his guests. The news could not be more distressing: Redmond, those present are told, has been killed in an assault.

For a few minutes there is panic, until the cavalcade arrives at its destination and Redmond emerges displaying nothing more than a superficial cut. Leigh, it turns out, was not acting alone. While she was waiting outside the General Post Office for her chance to attack the prime minister, two of her fellow English suffragettes – with whom she had travelled to Dublin for the occasion – were attempting to set fire to the Theatre Royal on Hawkins Street, where Asquith is to speak the following night.

The scenes outside the Gresham after the arrival of the procession at 10.15 p.m. surpass, in excitement and intensity, those of the great Home Rule rally of the previous March, according to the *Independent*. Thousands of men, women and children have filled the street and they are joined in song when the Ireland's Own band strikes up the ubiquitous air 'A Nation Once Again'. Inside the hotel, Asquith proudly shows off the axe with which his would-be assailant has apparently just tried to assassinate him.

Further loud and prolonged cheers greet Asquith and Redmond, sporting a sticking plaster on his ear, as they make short speeches from a balcony of the hotel, but the main event takes place the following night at a crammed Theatre Royal, where Asquith receives a welcome so vigorous it seems to shake the building. Standing to speak, he has to wait for six minutes for the cheering – followed by a lengthy rendition of 'For He's a Jolly Good Fellow' – to subside before he can begin. Watching the handkerchief- and hat-waving crowd from a box above them, Violet and Lizzie appear thrilled by the spectacle.

The news Asquith brings is that the Home Rule Bill will go to the House of Lords before Christmas. And, he reminds his audience, the upper house no longer has the power to reject the measure, only to delay it. When a man interrupts with a shout of 'What about votes for women?', he is – as the London *Times* will put it the next day – 'picked out of the crowd and hurled into the street with admirable precision and terrifying velocity'. Two or three further interruptions – also by men – on the same theme are the only other notes of discord, as Asquith tells his audience what they have come to hear: Ireland is a nation and the views of a minority in one section of it must not be allowed to frustrate the wishes of the majority.

In the streets outside, however, the atmosphere turns ugly and violent when the Irish Women's Franchise League attempts to hold a public meeting on Beresford Place at the same time as Asquith is delivering his address. Speakers including Margaret Cousins, a founder of the league, are heckled by a hostile crowd of some two hundred and the shouts heard include 'Have you got any hatchets or explosives in your pockets?' and 'Burn them! They are unfit to live!' A woman in the crowd yells 'We don't want votes!' and the crowd then drowns out the speakers with a loud rendition of 'A Nation Once Again'.

Police, fearing a riot, force the women off the platform and march them, under the protection of some forty officers, up Lower Abbey Street. They are followed by an expanding and increasingly aggressive crowd, and by the time they reach O'Connell Street, the throng has grown to a thousand. The women are placed on the Rathmines tram, which leaves under police protection to a chorus of boos and under a hail of missiles. But the episode does not end there. The now out-of-control mob sets about attacking women – some of them suffragettes, others just passers-by – on and around O'Connell Bridge. Amid cries of 'Throw them into the river!', 'Give them the hatchet!' and 'Set fire to them!', some women are physically attacked and have their clothing torn.

Among those 'roughly handled' by the crowd, reports the *Independent*, is the social activist Countess Markievicz, who declines a police request that she get on board a tram and heads instead for Liberty Hall, proclaiming that she is 'going back to Jim Larkin', referring to the militant trade unionist.

Distressing as these scenes are, they will not have perturbed John Redmond, who has taken no interest in the suffragettes' campaign and is unlikely to have been won over by the hatchet-wielding Mary Leigh. For him, Asquith's visit has been a success beyond all expectation and there is no reason to doubt that the government remains fully committed to the delivery of Home Rule.

Just eight days later, however, on 27 July, there is a reminder that the issue is far from settled. At a rally of more than ten thousand gathered in warm sunshine at Blenheim Palace in Oxfordshire – home of the Duke of Marlborough and birthplace of Winston Churchill – Bonar

Law removes any doubt about how far the Conservative and Unionist Party is prepared to go in support of the Ulster campaign.

Accusing the government of attempting to force through Home Rule 'at the bidding of Mr Redmond' – the mention of whose name draws groans from the crowd – against the will of the British people, Law, quoted at length in the following day's London *Times*, says his party does not acknowledge the Liberals' right 'to carry a revolution by such means'.

> We regard [the government] as a revolutionary committee which has seized by fraud upon despotic power [cheers]. In our opposition to them we shall not be guided by the considerations, we shall not be restrained by the bonds, which would influence us in an ordinary political struggle. We shall use any means [loud cheers], whatever means seem to us likely to be effective. That is all we shall think about. We shall use any means to deprive them of the power which they have usurped and to compel them to face the people whom they have deceived. Even if the Home Rule Bill passes through the House of Commons, what then? I said in the House of Commons, and I repeat here, that there are things stronger than parliamentary majorities.

Law's logic is clear: it is not the Unionist Party that is departing from the constitutional path in its determination to resist an Act of parliament that brings in Home Rule. Rather, it is the 'revolutionary' government that has torn up the normal rules of politics. And his concluding comments raise the temperature even more. After expressing doubt that the government would ever attempt to impose its will on the people of Ulster by force of arms, he continues:

> But I am sure of this: that if the attempt were made, the government would not succeed in carrying Home Rule. They would succeed only in lighting fires of civil war which would shatter the empire to its foundations.

He reminds his listeners that in the past, before he was leader of the Unionists, he said that Ulster would be justified in resisting Home Rule by force.

> I said so then, and I say now, with a full sense of the responsibility which attaches to my position, that if the attempt be made under present conditions, I can imagine no length of resistance to which Ulster will go in which I shall not be ready to support them and in which they will not be supported by the overwhelming majority of the British people.

The audience rises as one and applauds this declaration for several minutes.

Speaking next, Carson devotes much of his address to an attack on John Redmond, drawing cries of 'Shame!' when he reminds the crowd that the Irish leader expressed support for the Boers in their war with Britain just over a decade earlier and then questioning, by way of an anecdote, Redmond's professed loyalty to the crown.

> When Queen Victoria, just before her death, went over to Dublin, and the corporation [city council], in a fit of generosity, came forward to honour the sovereign, what did Mr Redmond do? He made a speech in which he said the corporation had degraded the capital of Ireland by debasing itself at the feet of the sovereign.

He concludes with typically stark words for Prime Minister Asquith and his Cabinet:

> We will shortly challenge the government to interfere with us if they dare, and we will with equanimity await the result. We will do this regardless of all consequences, of all personal loss, or of all inconvenience. They may tell us if they like that that is treason; it is not for men who have such stakes as we have at issue to trouble about the cost. We are prepared to take the consequences.

Law's and Carson's comments are unlikely to calm an increasingly tense situation in Ulster. Sporadic rioting and acts of intimidation against supporters of Home Rule have been taking place throughout the province since early July. The worst cases have been in Belfast, where loyalist lynch mobs have attacked opponents in the streets and two thousand Catholic workers, as well as five hundred Protestants who refused to join the newly formed unionist clubs, have been violently forced out of their jobs in the shipyards.

On 31 July, in a House of Commons debate on the crisis, Irish nationalist and Labour MPs blame Carson and Law for inciting the disturbances, several pointing in particular to a speech by Carson on 24 June in which he said he intended to go to Ulster and 'break every law that is possible'. The two men and other Unionist MPs deny the charge, arguing that the situation is not as bad as it has been portrayed and that loyalists have been acting in response to nationalist provocations. Law then takes the opportunity to emphasise that he stands over his comments in Blenheim the previous weekend: 'Whatever else may be said of the remarks I made on Saturday, this at least cannot be said, that they were made thoughtlessly. I have been carefully considering them for a long time, and I did what I rarely do – I actually wrote down the words I used.'

Law's statement prompts a prescient question from Asquith. If the leader of the opposition is really saying that the minority in Ireland has the right to use force to resist a Home Rule act – at this point Law nods to indicate that this is indeed his position – then what, asks Asquith, if the shoe was on the other foot? If the Conservatives were back in power and refusing to grant Home Rule to Ireland, wouldn't the nationalist majority be entitled to appeal to Law's own logic and resist the government's position by force?

The moment you lay down, as the leaders of the constitutional party lay down, the doctrine that a minority – I do not care what minority, if you like a majority – are entitled, because a particular act of legislation is distasteful to their views, and, as they think, oppressive to their interests, to resist it by force, there is an absolute end to parliamentary government. That, sir, is the real significance of the right honourable gentleman's statement. It is a declaration of war against constitutional government.

Asquith's warning is followed by an even more damning condemnation of Law's and Carson's methods by Winston Churchill. In a letter to his constituency chairman in Dundee, published in *The Times* on 12 August, he accuses the two men of using 'foolish and wicked words' to incite civil war in Ireland. But he suggests, in typically scornful language, that the two unionist leaders have no intention of delivering on their threats. 'They would be unspeakably shocked and frightened if all this melodramatic stuff in which they are indulging were suddenly to explode into real bombs and cannon.'

It is true, says Churchill, that 'men have been found and will be found again in the world to dare and suffer all things in resistance to tyranny or to a foreign conqueror. But these are not the circumstances; and – with all respect – these are not the men.'

Such strident talk on the government side, however, serves only to camouflage its weakening resolve in the face of the unionists' campaign, and the first evidence of this comes from Churchill himself. In a letter to Redmond on 31 August, he makes a 'personal' suggestion. The opposition of 'three or four Ulster counties' is now the only obstacle standing in the way of Home Rule, he says, and in his view 'something should be done to afford the characteristically Protestant and Orange counties the option of a moratorium of several years before acceding to the Irish Parliament'. Churchill adds that in his belief the time is approaching when such an offer should be made, 'and it would come much better from the Irish leaders than from the Government'.

A fortnight later, on a visit to Dundee, he floats another idea: why not set up a federal system of government for the entire United Kingdom, with populous areas such as greater London, the Midlands, Yorkshire and Lancashire all having their own parliaments? Confirming that it is the government's intention to bring in self-government for Scotland and Wales after it is established in Ireland – the scheme known as 'Home Rule all round' – he says that a parliament for England would be too powerful and might end up quarrelling with the imperial parliament at Westminster – hence his idea, which he again stresses is personal and has not been discussed with the government, to break England into several self-governing areas.

There may be little chance of any of this happening, but the subtext of Churchill's proposal is clear: if parliaments for Yorkshire and Lancashire can be contemplated, then separate treatment for Ulster in the case of Home Rule for Ireland is surely also a possibility.

Redmond has no intention of making any such proposal, but Churchill's letter and subsequent musings in Dundee are evidence that the Ulster unionists are gaining ground and that government ministers are starting to think about a compromise. And the unionists' campaign, in fact, is only beginning.

Plans to make 28 September 'Ulster Day' have just been announced by the Ulster Unionist Council. Carson and his followers are about to deliver their biggest statement yet.

Chapter 8 ~

ULSTER DAY

If there is a row, I'd like to be in it with the Belfast men.

In the autumn of 1912 Protestant Ulster is mobilising like never before. After the success of the monster rallies at Craigavon a year earlier and at Balmoral at Easter, the loyalist men of the north are about to deliver a novel show of unity and strength: by signing in their tens of thousands an oath of fidelity to the anti-Home Rule cause.

As the day for the signing of the Ulster Solemn League and Covenant – Ulster Day, 28 September – approaches, the province is abuzz with activity. The build-up begins on 18 September in Enniskillen, where nearly thirty thousand people – many of them farmers and their families who have travelled by horse-drawn carriage from the surrounding area – gather on the town's Portora Hill to hear Edward Carson describe himself as a soldier in the firing line, sworn to resist 'the most nefarious, the most unprovoked attack upon our liberties that has ever confronted a God-fearing people'.

The following day the Ulster Unionist Council meets at Craigavon to sign off on the wording of the covenant. At 4 p.m. Carson emerges on to the steps in front of the building, bareheaded and smoking a cigarette, and – flanked by fellow council members – reads the proposed pledge to waiting journalists. Loosely based on the seventeenth-century Scottish Solemn League and Covenant, drawn up to defend the independence of the Presbyterian Church of Scotland, the Ulster version declares:

> Being convinced in our consciences that Home Rule would be disastrous to the material well-being of Ulster as well as of the whole of Ireland, subversive of our civil and religious freedom, destructive of our citizenship, and perilous to the unity of the Empire, we, whose names are underwritten, men of Ulster, loyal

subjects of His Gracious Majesty King George v, humbly relying on the God whom our fathers in days of stress and trial confidently trusted, do hereby pledge ourselves in solemn Covenant throughout this our time of threatened calamity to stand by one another in defending for ourselves and our children our cherished position of equal citizenship in the United Kingdom, and in using all means which may be found necessary to defeat the present conspiracy to set up a Home Rule Parliament in Ireland. And in the event of such a Parliament being forced upon us we further solemnly and mutually pledge ourselves to refuse to recognise its authority. In sure confidence that God will defend the right we hereto subscribe our names. And further, we individually declare that we have not already signed this Covenant. God save the King.

That evening, Carson is led into Lisburn town centre by a large procession of men, some carrying torches and others the ubiquitous dummy rifles with which thousands have been drilling in preparation for armed conflict. Fife and drum bands play 'The Boyne Water' and 'Protestant Boys' before Carson tells an audience of ten thousand in the town's marketplace that there is no sacrifice he is not prepared to make in the fight to prevent the government separating Ulster from Great Britain. The following night it's the turn of Derry, where Carson arrives – again under escort of unionist club representatives practised in military drilling – to speak to a capacity crowd in the Guildhall.

Next stop is Coleraine, as rallies continue throughout the province for several more days, culminating in a great demonstration in Belfast on the night before Ulster Day. Carson, standing on a platform in front of the Ulster Hall – and against a backdrop of electric lights spelling out the declarations 'We will not have Home Rule' and 'Ulster will fight' – concludes his speech to an audience of twenty-five thousand with the shouted words: 'We tell the enemy that if they wish to fight – then by heaven we will fight!'

Ulster Day, a Saturday, has been designated a public holiday by Belfast Corporation and a day of religious observance by Protestant churches. Carson begins proceedings by attending a religious service at the Ulster Hall before making a ceremonial walk to the nearby Belfast

City Hall in the company of other unionist leaders, escorted by 200 members of the city's Orange lodges and unionist clubs, all wearing bowler hats and carrying walking sticks. At the head of the procession is the banner that was – it is claimed – carried before King William III at the Battle of the Boyne.

In the city hall's grand entrance room, a circular hall with a marble staircase, Carson is greeted by Belfast Lord Mayor Robert McMordie and members of the corporation in their robes of office, and other dignitaries. A copy of the covenant sits on a round table draped in the union flag. The recent spell of good weather has held up for the day and sunlight streams through the stained glass windows. Silence descends as Carson picks up a silver pen and becomes the first to sign the document. He hands the pen to the second signatory, Lord Londonderry, who in turn is followed by the leaders of the Protestant churches.

For the remainder of the day and well into the night, until the hall is closed at 11 p.m., a continuous flow of men come in to sign the covenant. Rows of desks have been placed on two floors of the building, so that as many as 540 can sign at the same time. Back at the Ulster Hall, women are queuing in equally large numbers to sign a separate declaration in support of the covenant. Similar scenes are replicated all over Ulster, with men and women going to sign the covenant or declaration at local centres after attending religious ceremonies in the morning. In Dublin some two thousand Ulster-born unionists sign the covenant at the offices of the Irish Unionist Alliance in Grafton Street.

The documents remain open for signing for a few more days, after which it is established that the covenant has been signed by 237,368 men and the declaration by 234,046 women.

Nationalist newspapers view the proceedings with derision. In an article headlined 'The Belfast Farce', the *Freeman's Journal* says of Ulster Day: 'As a political portent it has no reality. The desperate efforts to invest it with importance only emphasise the mock heroics and the bluff. The wooden cannon painted to look like the real thing is symbolical of the theatrical posturings and rantings constituting the so-called Ulster menace.'

The unionist *Irish Times* takes a sharply different view. Reflecting in an editorial on the 'wonderful scenes in Belfast', it states: 'The Northern demonstrations began ten days ago amid the jeers and laughter of English Radicals and Irish Nationalists. These noises are silenced now. Ulster has convinced the whole United Kingdom of the utter sincerity of her hostility to the Home Rule Bill.'

~

John Redmond refrains for a time from making any public statement on the covenant, but his brother Willie, the MP for East Tyrone, in a speech to constituents, dismisses it as 'a joke'.

Willie has just returned from an 18-month fundraising tour of Australia and New Zealand, where the uniformly warm welcome he received contrasted with the reception he and John faced on a similar mission to the same countries in 1883, undertaken at the behest of Charles Stewart Parnell. The 27-year-old John was then the newly elected MP for New Ross; Willie, five years his junior, would soon follow him into the House of Commons.

Their visit coincided with the opening of the trial of the killers of Lord Frederick Cavendish and Thomas Burke in the Phoenix Park a year earlier, and the negative headlines this generated for Irish nationalists led to much hostility towards the Redmonds as they traversed Australia and then New Zealand, addressing political meetings. Some newspapers called for their public appearances to be boycotted, and there were even demands for them to be deported.

They overcame the opposition, though, and over the following ten months raised £15,000 for the nationalist movement. The success of their joint enterprise did not stop there. While in Australia John had met and married Johanna Dalton, a member of a wealthy and influential Irish-Australian family, while Willie was later to marry her niece, Eleanor. Not everybody connected with the Daltons approved. A fracas broke out at John and Johanna's wedding in Sydney after the owner of the hotel where the brothers had been staying described the Redmonds, within earshot of Willie, as a 'pack of scrubbers' and suggested that John was an adventurer who had come to Australia to look for a wife and a fortune.

John's marriage to Johanna was a happy one, resulting in the births of Esther ('Essie') , William ('Billie'), and Johanna ('Joey'). It was cut short by tragedy, however. On 12 December 1889, Redmond returned to his home in Dublin from a day at his legal practice in Tipperary to be told that Johanna had died giving birth to a stillborn child. She was 28. Their eldest child at the time was five. For the rest of his life, Redmond will keep a memento of her with the note: 'My darling wife's hair and the flower she gave me the first time I met her in Sydney'.

∼

After the celebrations in Belfast around the signing of the Ulster Covenant, the next stop for Edward Carson is Liverpool. He departs Belfast in the evening by ferry, in the company of other unionist leaders including Lord Londonderry and the Liverpool Tory MP F.E. Smith, to the sound of revolver shots fired in salute by members of the Queen's Island Unionist Club and to the sight of bonfires on each side of Belfast Lough. His ship, named *Patriotic*, sails off to the sound of tens of thousands of supporters singing 'Rule, Britannia!', 'Auld Lang Syne' and 'God Save the King'. On arrival at Liverpool the following morning the travelling party is cheered off the boat by a gathering of thousands of dock workers. Bands play, banners are held aloft and the crowd sings a hymn frequently heard at Ulster loyalist rallies:

> O God, our help in ages past,
> Our hope for years to come,
> Our shelter from the stormy blast,
> And our eternal home.

At a rally in the city that night, Carson tells a crowd numbering more than a hundred thousand: 'If there is a row, I'd like to be in it with the Belfast men, and I'd like to have you with them, and I will!' There is even greater fighting talk from Smith, whose inflammatory speeches both inside and outside the House of Commons are becoming a feature of the Ulster campaign. Smith, the future Lord Birkenhead, tells the crowd that just this afternoon he has been talking at the Conservative Club in Liverpool with three large shipowners, who told him: 'If and when it comes to a fight between Ulster and the Irish nationalists, we will undertake to give you three ships that will take over to help Ulster in her hour of need 10,000 young men of Liverpool [cheers].'

Not content with visions of Ulster unionists and Irish nationalists engaging in war, Smith draws further roars of approval when he adds: 'In the words of a great leader, if the government dares to order the army to march upon Ulster, they will be lynched upon the lamp-posts of London.'

The more reflective Carson, however, realises that something more than incendiary speeches will be required if the unionists' campaign is to succeed. He is conscious that the Home Rule Bill is soon set to pass all stages in the House of Commons, and once it goes to the Lords there will be no prospect of its being amended. The upper house will have no power to vary the bill, but only to delay it by two years. If he has any alternative card to play, he knows it must be played now.

While Carson is considering this, an unexpected development comes close to derailing the bill and putting the Liberals out of office. On 11 November, the government – carelessly failing to ensure it has a majority of MPs present – suffers a sensational defeat in the Commons on a financial amendment to the bill, provoking loud and sustained cheers from the opposition benches and shouts of 'Resign!', 'What about Home Rule now?', 'Goodbye!' and 'Take your pension!' as ministers scurry from the chamber to hold an emergency meeting of the Cabinet.

Rather than resign from office, Asquith and his ministers opt to do something that the opposition claim is unprecedented; they decide to go back to the Commons and seek to rescind the amendment, which was tabled by Conservative MP Sir Frederick Banbury and would have the effect of making the bill unworkable. Asquith's attempt two days later to give effect to this decision leads to scenes of great disorder in the chamber, which carry on after the Speaker adjourns the sitting, saying that it is 'useless to continue'. For a moment, it looks as if MPs on the two sides will come to blows, but in the event the only one to suffer a physical assault is Winston Churchill.

Leaving the chamber with Cabinet colleagues amid cries of 'Rats!' from Tory MPs, the First Lord of the Admiralty takes out his handkerchief and waves it to encourage cheers for Asquith, who is also departing. Before putting the handkerchief back in his pocket, Churchill waves it towards the opposition. This prompts Unionist

MP Ronald McNeill – the future Lord Cushendun – to pick up the Speaker's copy of the standing orders and fling them at Churchill, striking him on the side of the face and causing a bruise. Churchill makes to retaliate but is held back by two Liberal colleagues. The angry scenes suddenly dissolve into laughter when Labour MP Will Crooks shouts, 'Should auld acquaintance be forgot!'

McNeill apologises in the Commons at the next sitting, and the crisis blows over almost as suddenly as it erupted when Asquith and Bonar Law find an agreed way out of the mess created by Banbury's amendment. The Home Rule Bill is back on track.

A month later, on 13 December, Carson recommends a change in policy to the standing committee of the Ulster Unionist Council: the time has come, he argues, to actively seek the exclusion of Ulster from the bill. The committee accepts his recommendation, adopting a motion saying that in taking this course it 'firmly believes the interests of Unionists in the three other provinces of Ireland will be best conserved.'

This is a radical change in stance by the Ulster Unionists that has the potential to transform the campaign against Home Rule. They did, of course, support Thomas Agar-Robartes' amendment seeking to exclude four Ulster counties from the bill, but that was a tactical stance and part of their overall campaign to wreck the measure in its entirety. Now, for the first time in all of the anti-Home Rule campaigns, including those of the Gladstone era, Ulster is demanding to be treated as a separate entity from the rest of Ireland.

On 30 December, an open letter from the Irish Unionist MPs to Prime Minister Asquith, giving notice of the change of policy, is published in the newspapers. In essence, it says that the MPs see the exclusion of Ulster from the bill as the only means of avoiding an armed conflict.

'To drive out a loyal, industrious, thriving, and contented population from under the authority of the Imperial Parliament and Executive to which they cleave and to place them under a Government which they abhor, is an act of gross tyranny unparalleled in the history of our country,' the letter states.

'Such tyranny it is right to resist; but, while we approve, we cannot be blind to the grave mischiefs which are involved even in righteous resistance. It is therefore plainly our duty as members of Parliament representing those whose fate is involved to do whatever we can to avert the evils we foresee. We ask you, therefore, to accept our amendment as the only way to preserve the threatened peace of the realm.'

Asquith will deliver his response to this appeal in the new year. Whatever the prime minister's answer, John Redmond faces a new set of challenges in his fight to secure a Home Rule parliament for all of Ireland. The decision of the unionists to, in effect, concede the measure for the rest of Ireland as long as Ulster is left alone has suddenly changed the rules of the game.

Chapter 9 ~

CARSON'S ARMY

We will go on, and eventually we will defeat you.

On 1 January 1913, Edward Carson stands up in the House of Commons to move an amendment excluding 'the province of Ulster' from the Home Rule Bill. In a speech earnest in tone and devoid of rhetoric, he emphasises that the Ulster Unionists' new stance is not an attempt at compromise. They remain against the bill 'root and branch' and besides, he says, compromise would be impossible because John Redmond has made it clear that removing Ulster from the bill would not be acceptable to nationalists.

Carson says that nobody who was in Ulster in the period leading up to the signing of the Ulster Covenant could have failed to conclude that the signatories were 'grimly in earnest' in their opposition to Home Rule, 'and grimly determined at whatever hazard and cost to themselves, never to submit to the degradation of a parliament set up in Dublin to rule them'. He repeats the view expressed in the letter to prime minister Herbert Asquith, published in December, that removing Ulster from the bill may be the only way to avoid bloodshed.

I do not set myself up, as honourable members of this house so often do, as a sort of infallible pope, but I say from the bottom of my heart and with all the sincerity that is possible that I am as firmly convinced as I stand here that never without the use of force, which everybody would deprecate, can you compel these men to break their covenant and submit to Home Rule.

The house must now make up its mind as regards the truth of that situation. We who believe it, at all events, have a very plain duty. We have the plain duty of trying to avert what we believe would be the greatest disaster to the United Kingdom that has occurred for some hundreds of years. We have the perfectly plain duty of trying if we can by every constitutional means in our power to obtain for these men what they, whether rightly or wrongly, think they can obtain for themselves by force if you pass the Act of parliament. I do not think anybody will deny that that is our duty.

He defends the decision to propose the removal from the bill of the entire nine counties of Ulster, including those with strong nationalist majorities where support for Home Rule is strong, on the basis that this is fairer than having the province spoken for at Westminster by MPs 'representing practically one religion'.

Asquith, who begins by complimenting Carson on his 'very powerful and moving speech', says that his proposed amendment – as the Ulster Unionist leader 'knows perfectly well' – would mean 'the wrecking of the whole bill'. He also argues that, whatever about the merits of Thomas Agar-Robartes' proposal to remove four Ulster counties from the Home Rule Bill, there is no basis for Carson's view that the entire province ought to be taken out.

If this amendment were carried, the whole of Ulster would be excluded. What is Ulster? I have here a very useful map in which Ulster is coloured. By looking at that map I see that, dividing Ulster according to its representation – leaving population for the moment – between those who are in favour and those who are against Home Rule, the whole of the north-west, the whole of the south, the larger part of the middle – by the middle, I mean the county of Tyrone – are almost unanimously in favour of Home Rule. That is a geographical fact, there can be no dispute about it whatever.

Carson's amendment, he adds, is 'totally unsupported by logic or reason', and amounts to a claim 'on the part of a relatively small minority in Ireland to frustrate the aspirations and defeat the wishes of the Irish people as a whole'.

John Redmond, next to speak, also begins by acknowledging the sincerity of Carson's 'serious and solemn speech'. But he dismisses the prospect of an armed insurrection in Ulster if the bill goes through unaltered. As grounds for this stance, he cites the similar warnings that

were issued when northern Protestants opposed the disestablishment
of the Church of Ireland in 1869, when the language used was 'equally
... strong' and the threats 'quite as unveiled' as is the case today.

> We know what happened. As soon as the quite honestly alarmed
> Protestant opinion of Ireland found that they were not injured
> either in their civil or religious lives by the legislation that had been
> passed, that all their fears had been groundless, all talk of civil war
> disappeared.

His belief, 'fortified by the experience of history', is that when
Protestants find that Home Rule involves no attack on their rights,
property, liberties or religion, they will 'as good citizens' fall in line
with the legislation 'and bring to the service of what, after all, is their
country as well as ours, all those great qualities which, for my part, I
believe will be perhaps the most valuable in the government of Ireland
in the future'.

The effect of Carson's position, Redmond argues, is that Home
Rulers – 'men who believe in the principle of this great measure, men
who believe in the right of the majority of the people of Ireland to
govern themselves in their own affairs' – are being asked to sacrifice
their principles and convictions 'for nothing'. Given that Carson
has made it clear that his amendment is not being put forward as a
compromise, and that the unionists' opposition to Home Rule is to
continue unaltered in all circumstances, the nationalists are being
asked to support a measure that would not even give them 'a mutilated
bill' in return.

The Irish Party leader concludes with atypical flourish:

> Ireland for us is one entity. It is one land. Tyrone and Tyrconnell are
> as much a part of Ireland as Munster or Connaught. Some of the
> most glorious chapters connected with our national struggle have
> been associated with Ulster – aye, and with the Protestants of Ulster
> – and I declare here today, as a Catholic Irishman, notwithstanding
> all the bitterness of the past, that I am as proud of the heroism of
> Derry as of Limerick.

Our ideal in this movement is a self-governing Ireland in the future, when all her sons of all races and creeds within her shores will bring their tribute, great or small, to the great total of national enterprise and national statesmanship and national happiness. Men may deride that ideal; they may say it is a futile and an unrealisable ideal, but they cannot call it an ignoble one. It is an ideal that we, at any rate, will cling to, and because we cling to it, and because it is there embedded in our hearts and natures, that it is an absolute bar to such a proposal as this amendment makes, a proposal which would create for all times a sharp and eternal dividing line between Irish Catholics and Irish Protestants, and a measure which would for all time mean the partition and disintegration of our nation. To that we as Irish nationalists can never submit.

The debate continues without rancour before a row flares between Conservative leader Bonar Law and the ever-pugnacious Winston Churchill, after Law says that the loyalists of Ulster would prefer 'to accept the government of a foreign country rather than submit to be governed' by Irish nationalists. Churchill describes this comment as extraordinary and unprecedented for 'any responsible member of parliament', never mind the leader of the Conservative and Unionist Party. 'This then is the latest Tory threat, that Ulster will secede to Germany,' he says, drawing angry shouts from the opposition benches of 'Scandalous!' and 'Who said Germany? Why Germany?'

Overcoming further heated interruptions throughout, Churchill concludes his speech – the last in the debate – with a declaration that the government will not be found wanting if an opportunity arises to reach a settlement of the Home Rule issue by consent. 'We can find no such opportunity in an amendment which is in itself unworkable and impracticable, and which is accompanied by assertions of inveterate and implacable hostility towards the Irish policy which we have carried so long through so many struggles to the threshold of success.'

Carson's amendment is duly defeated, and 15 days later the bill passes its third reading in the House of Commons and is referred to the House of Lords, where at the end of January it is rejected, as expected, after a four-day debate. But the government quickly revives the bill in the Commons, and there will be nothing the upper house can do to prevent it becoming law before the end of 1914.

While the bill is being debated in the House of Lords, the Ulster Unionists suffer an embarrassing setback when they lose the Derry seat in the House of Commons in a by-election. The result leaves the nationalists holding the majority of Ulster's seats in the Commons – 17 as opposed to the unionists' 16.

This awkward fact does nothing to slow the momentum of the loyalists' campaign to keep the province out of a Home Rule administration, and early in the year a decision is taken by the Ulster Unionist Council's standing committee to take the next inevitable step in its programme to set up a provisional government for Ulster in the event of a parliament being established in Dublin. A government must have an army, and so the UVF is born.

With the help of senior figures in the British military establishment, a commander-in-chief is secured: Lieutenant General Sir George Richardson, a retired officer of the British Indian Army who now lives in Ireland.

In July, the 65-year-old Richardson takes up his new post as general officer commanding of the UVF, which is now nearly sixty thousand strong and is gaining new recruits every day. Only men who have signed the Ulster Covenant are allowed to join. On an inspection tour of the UVF's 'battalions' around the province, Richardson is accompanied by Carson, who tells the men that they are no longer a collection of unrelated units – now they are an army, under single command.

As the military preparations in Ulster have intensified, so have the accompanying fiery speeches. In March, Charles Craig MP tells his constituents in Antrim that £10,000 spent on rifles would be 'a thousand times stronger' than the same spent 'on meetings, speeches and pamphlets'.

Opening a new drill hall in Belfast on 16 May, Carson – who has resumed political activities following the death of his wife, Annette, on 6 April – tells an audience of some three thousand working-class loyalists that they have no quarrel with their fellow Irishmen in the south; their quarrel is with the government. But they will use force if driven to do so.

I have only this to say to you: 'go on, be ready!' [Voices: 'We will!'] You are our great army, it is on you we rely. Under what circumstances you will have to come into action, you must leave to us. These are matters which give us grave consideration, which we cannot and ought not to talk about in public. You must trust us that we will select the most opportune moment or, if necessary, taking on ourselves the whole government of the community in which we live. I know a great deal of that will involve statutory illegality, but it will also involve much righteousness.

On 10 June, in the House of Commons, Carson delivers what Redmond, rising to speak immediately after him, describes as his 'most violent speech' yet in the chamber. 'You may laugh at us, you may jeer at us,' says Carson, 'but we will go on, and eventually we will defeat you. For my own part, with all my heart, I will continue to support these men in the north of Ireland, and I will take full responsibility for every resistance that they are able to organise.'

Redmond responds with a prophetic warning about the danger of a violent revolt in the south of Ireland if talk of an insurgence in the north is allowed to gain hold.

Rebellion is threatened. Rebellion is justified in high quarters. The rebellion of a portion of the population of four counties, because they disapprove of the [Home Rule Bill] before any wrong has been done, and before any oppression has been attempted, would be a crime and a calamity. Rebellion by over three-fourths of the people of a country distracted, tortured, and betrayed, deprived of the rights of freemen, and condemned to a barren policy of coercion, would be too horrible a thing to contemplate; and it is because this is so that I rejoice with all my heart to believe and to know that this bill is safe, and that the future of Ireland is assured.

In the same debate, Lord Charles Beresford, one of the first to speak of civil war, when he addressed the unionist demonstration at Balmoral in April 1912, raises the stakes by talking of a potential 'religious war' in Ireland if Home Rule goes through. Furthermore, says the 67-year-old

Beresford, while he is too old to be of anything other than poor service, he is prepared to go to Ulster and 'be one of the first to be shot down if troops are sent to Ireland'.

By now, the importation of arms into Ireland by agents acting for the loyalists has begun, though their campaign suffers a setback when between six thousand and seven thousand Ulster-bound rifles sourced in Italy are seized by police from a stable yard in Hammersmith, London.

Undaunted by the negative publicity arising from the seizure, Carson and the other Irish unionist leaders begin a tour of Scotland and England to drum up support for the Ulster cause, and are greeted by enthusiastic crowds in Glasgow, Edinburgh, Leeds, Norwich and other cities. Redmond and Joe Devlin, accompanied by senior colleagues in the Irish Party, follow with a tour of their own to the same locations. Departing on a train from St Pancras station in London, Redmond tells a crowd that has gathered on the platform to cheer him off: 'You know the mission on which I am embarking. I am going to defend my country against misrepresentation and calumny ... I am going wherever the foes of my land go to blacken her!'

Carson recovers from a bout of neuritis in time to engage in renewed fighting talk and threats of law-breaking at a 12 July celebration in Craigavon. Speaking to a crowd estimated at between a hundred thousand and a hundred and fifty thousand, he calls on the people of Ulster to refuse to pay taxes if a Home Rule parliament is put on the statute book, and warns the government that if it attempts to impose Home Rule on Ulster, it will have to fight not only the loyalists of the province, but those in Scotland and England who are on their side. He also claims that he is getting at least six letters a day from army officers asking to enrol in the Ulster campaign. The government knows perfectly well, he says, that it cannot rely on the army 'to shoot down the loyalists of Ulster' – a statement that John Redmond will learn to his cost is entirely justified.

Carson also reads a message to his audience from Bonar Law, on behalf of the Conservative and Unionist Party, reiterating its support for any action the Ulster loyalists feel compelled to take, whether constitutional or not.

The Ulster Unionist leader's incitements to law-breaking are becoming so blatant that speculation arises that he could face prosecution. Government ministers and nationalist leaders are against the idea, however, knowing that such a move would merely enhance Carson's standing among his followers.

Confirmation that unionists would like nothing more than to see Carson locked up comes in the House of Commons on 7 August, when the prospect of his arrest is raised – by the unionists themselves – and treated with much levity. Ronald McNeill – whose accuracy of aim with the Speaker's standing orders on a previous occasion left Winston Churchill with a bruised face – asks Irish Chief Secretary Augustine Birrell if the government intends to arrest Carson, and if so, on what charge? After Birrell answers that the government has no such intention, another Ulster Unionist MP, Andrew Horner, suggests that it is the clear duty of the government to arrest Carson 'if it is true, as the government and their supporters here assert, that his speeches are treasonable and that he has incited to rebellion, or are the government convinced that the Ulster resistance to Home Rule is too strong to cope with?'

Amid laughter on both sides of the house, the nationalists' deputy leader John Dillon interjects to ask if there is not now 'abundant evidence that the right honourable gentleman is exceedingly anxious to be arrested?' Birrell maintains the humorous tone in concluding the short exchange: 'Everyone knows perfectly well that criminal proceedings based on speeches must be always a matter of somewhat delicate discretion. I do not know whether the honourable gentleman [McNeill] acts on behalf of the right honourable gentleman [Carson] in requesting me to proceed with his arrest, but I shall still continue to regard it as a matter for my own discretion.'

Back home at Aughavanagh after his successful tour of Scotland and England, John Redmond might well reflect that, while the prospect of arresting Carson is regarded by all sides as a joke, nationalists in Ireland have always been far more likely than unionists to be imprisoned for their politics. Even Redmond, the arch constitutionalist and respected parliamentarian, has served time for his involvement in campaigning for the rights of tenant farmers.

In 1888 he was jailed for five weeks for using 'language of intimidation' against a Wexford landlord, Captain Thomas Walker, who had evicted a farmer named John Clinch. In a speech in support of Clinch, Redmond had declared:

> If Captain Walker is determined on fighting this man he will very soon find out that in fighting him he is fighting the people of this county ... The injustice done to this man will confront him wherever he goes and wherever he puts his feet. Until the injustice is remedied he will find nothing in the county, either in the hunting-field or anywhere else, except the hostility of men who resent injustice.

At his court hearing in Wexford, where he was met on arrival in the town by a large crowd of supporters and a brass band, Redmond represented himself and made no attempt to challenge the facts of the case. His response to being sentenced, as reported in the *Freeman's Journal*, drew applause from the public gallery: 'That finishes the business, I presume. I do not intend to delay, and can only say that I have the greatest possible satisfaction in going to jail.'

Redmond was jailed in Wexford and served some of his sentence in the company of his brother Willie, already imprisoned for inciting tenants to resist the sheriff amid violent scenes at another eviction in the county. They had to sleep on planks and endure a diet of bread and water, the latter a punishment for refusing to exercise in the yard with prisoners convicted of ordinary criminal offences.

More than two decades later, Redmond has reason to feel satisfied that his long campaign to secure an independent Irish parliament is at last bearing fruit. The government has held firm in the face of everything the Unionist Party has thrown at it, and the Home Rule Bill is on course to become law next year. But his peace of mind is abruptly destroyed by an unexpected intervention in the debate that has the potential to destroy much of the progress he has made over the previous three years.

In early September *The Times* publishes a letter from Lord Loreburn suggesting a conference of all the parties to try to resolve the Irish question by consent. A member of the Liberal Cabinet until his retirement in 1912, Loreburn was one of the government's strongest advocates of Home Rule and an opponent of the suggestion that Ulster or part of it might be excluded from the scheme. His sudden reappearance to appeal for compromise is a devastating blow to Redmond and his fellow nationalist MPs.

Compromise in the case of Irish Home Rule can mean only one thing – separate treatment for Ulster. John Redmond is now in a fully fledged fight to prevent the partition of Ireland.

Chapter 10 ∾

LET'S PRETEND

Irish nationalists can never be assenting parties to the partition and mutilation of their nation.

Lord Loreburn's letter to *The Times*, published on 11 September 1913, throws the Irish Party into a state of confusion and panic. John Redmond and his colleagues realise that the former lord chancellor's intervention could have catastrophic consequences. It has the potential to dent the government's resolve not to countenance the partition of Ireland as a solution to the current crisis, and will be seen by the Ulster unionists as evidence that their campaign is having an impact – senior Liberals are clearly scared of what will happen if Home Rule goes through unaltered. The nationalist MPs immediately set about trying to limit its impact.

In the letter, which takes up half a page of the newspaper, Loreburn says that either the passing of the Home Rule Bill (which he supports) or its defeat will most likely spark a violent reaction in Ireland. 'No good purpose can be served ... by ignoring the certainty that the passage of this Bill will be followed by serious rioting in the North of Ireland,' he writes. And if the bill is 'by some accident' rejected and not replaced by an acceptable alternative, even greater disorder can be anticipated as nationalists find their aspirations for self-government dashed because of civil strife in the north.

It would be 'a delusion', he concludes, to think that the choice is between two paths, one leading to fury and bloodshed, and the other to tranquillity. 'Both of the paths which are open at this moment, unless some common agreement can be reached, must certainly take us into serious trouble. Is there, then, really nothing that can be done except to watch the play of irreconcilable forces in a spirit of indolent resignation?'

He proposes a conference between the leaders of all the parties concerned – the nationalists, unionists, government and opposition.

Proceedings would be confidential, 'so that everyone should enjoy unrestrained freedom in pointing out difficulties, or in advancing or withdrawing suggestions'. However, if the conference broke up without agreement, the final position of all parties should be published. 'The country will suffer if things go wrong,' he says, 'and the country is entitled to know what stands in the way of things going right.'

A few days later, a copy of Loreburn's secret memorandum to the Cabinet setting out his proposal in more detail is sent to Redmond in Aughavanagh. Its contents are even worse than Redmond anticipated. Loreburn suggests 'concessions' – Redmond underlines the word as he goes through the document – that the government might make, not as part of a final settlement, but merely to get the Ulster Unionists into preliminary talks.

The Liberal peer proposes a Home Rule scheme involving distinctive treatment for the four Ulster counties with the largest unionist populations. They would be treated as an 'enclave' to be administered by their own 'Ulster Minister'. No law affecting the four counties could be passed by the Irish legislative assembly without the consent of a majority of the MPs from the four counties themselves.

Loreburn says that such a scheme could be a first step towards a wider system of federation or devolution for the entire United Kingdom, which, he points out, Lord Lansdowne, the Conservative leader in the House of Lords, has indicated he supports. 'If the case of Ireland were treated as a beginning, there would be an irresistible argument that Ulster could not object to Ireland being treated first, with the rest to follow, upon strict condition that the fullest regard were had to the peculiar apprehensions of Ulster.'

With the prospect in mind of future devolved parliaments for England, Scotland and Wales, he also proposes that the imperial parliament at Westminster should maintain total control over tax collection in these countries and in Ireland. He goes further: given likely Ulster fears that the Dublin parliament might not distribute revenues fairly, the Westminster parliament could have the power to step in to ensure a fair allocation. This idea is unlikely to correspond with John Redmond's idea of Home Rule.

Loreburn believes, however, that these proposals, or something on similar lines, should be enough to enable Lansdowne to persuade Edward Carson to enter talks. If the parties involved are unwilling to enter such a conference, 'then I think it would be right that the Government should announce their readiness to make concessions for the sake of peace, and specify how far they are ready to go and state their willingness to meet and discuss with a view to a settlement'.

The unionist press makes hay with this development. In an editorial on the day Loreburn's letter is published, *The Times* triumphantly declares: 'Here, for the first time, on the eve of a great political crisis, and, it may be, of national disaster, a distinguished Liberal statesman makes public confession of his belief that, as a permanent solution, the Irish policy of the government is indefensible.' An equally exultant *Irish Times* describes the letter as an acknowledgement that the government's Home Rule Bill is 'profoundly unsatisfactory' and if enforced must have 'disastrous results, not only for Ireland, but for the whole Kingdom'.

Nationalist papers attempt to minimise the significance of the intervention, and in an interview at his home in Killiney, County Dublin, the Irish Party's deputy leader John Dillon says he 'cannot see any useful purpose' in entering a conference of the type proposed by Loreburn unless it is based on acceptance of 'the principle of Irish Home Rule'.

Carson is even more dismissive, telling his audience at a political meeting in Durham that while he recognises Loreburn's good intentions, the former Liberal minister does not see the gulf that exists between himself (Carson) and John Redmond on the matter of how Ireland should be governed, and any conference on the issue 'must prove abortive'. Referring to Loreburn's forebodings about the threat of civil strife, Carson adds: 'Is it not strange that all this has never occurred before to the Liberal Party when they took up this bill, and when Mr Asquith and Mr Redmond, meeting together day after day without any concern for us, framed this measure? They thought it was all plain sailing. Apparently, they had never heard of a place called Ulster.'

Despite the negative reaction from both sides, it will soon become clear that Loreburn has dropped a hand grenade into the Home Rule controversy that will change the terms of the debate.

Its immediate impact is to place unionists on the front foot as they celebrate the first anniversary of the signing of the Ulster Covenant. Carson undertakes an inspection tour of UVF contingents throughout the province, accompanied for much of it by the ever-provocative F.E. Smith.

At an inspection on 20 September at Ballyclare, County Antrim of 2,500 volunteers and an ambulance section comprising 30 nurses in uniform, Smith declares that he cannot believe that even a government 'as corrupt and guilty' as the present one would mobilise the English army to march on Ulster. But if that 'unhappy moment' arises, the Conservative and Unionist Party will regard itself as absolved from allegiance to the government. 'From that moment we will say to our followers in England, "to your tents, O Israel!", from that moment we will stand by the side of Ulster, refusing to recognise any law and prepared with you to risk the collapse of the whole body politic to prevent this monstrous crime.'

It is not Smith's comments, however, but something Carson says on the same day that makes the newspaper headlines. Addressing volunteers following a later inspection at Antrim Castle, he makes an astonishing claim: 'I tell the government that we have promises and pledges from some of the greatest generals in the army; they have given their word that when the time comes, if it is necessary, they will come over and help us to keep the old flag flying and defy those who would dare to invade our liberties [cheers].'

On the same day, something very significant happens behind the scenes. Carson – most likely influenced by Lord Loreburn's intervention and the increased prospect it has brought of a negotiated settlement – writes to Bonar Law to suggest that the exclusion of Ulster from the Home Rule Bill might actually be an acceptable compromise.

This is a marked change in policy because Carson's earlier proposal to take Ulster out of the bill was made in the context of the unionists' continued opposition to the measure as a whole. Furthermore, he is now preparing to drop his insistence that the entire nine counties of Ulster be excluded from Home Rule. 'I am of opinion that on the whole things are shaping towards a desire to settle on the terms of leaving "Ulster" out,' he writes to Law. A difficulty arises as to defining

Ulster and my own view is that the whole of Ulster should be excluded but the minimum would be the 6 Plantation counties and for that a good case could be made.'

Carson appears to be referring to the six counties with the largest Protestant populations – Antrim, Down, Derry, Armagh, Tyrone and Fermanagh – rather than the actual counties of the Ulster Plantation. He acknowledges that unionists in the south and west of Ireland would object to a deal that leaves them under the jurisdiction of a Home Rule parliament. But he feels 'certain' that excluding Ulster, or at least six counties of it, 'would be the best settlement if Home Rule is inevitable'.

This is a change in position, which will in time increase John Redmond's difficulties immeasurably. It is much easier keeping the government onside as long as the Ulster Unionists remain truculently opposed to any settlement that involves granting self-rule to Ireland; if they show a willingness to meet the Liberals half way, the nationalist party will be in a much more awkward position.

For the moment, though, the battle lines remain drawn as they were from the start of the contest and Carson, in public at least, maintains his stance of implacable opposition to Home Rule. His pronouncement at Antrim Castle that the army, or at least some of its most senior officers, is ready to defy the orders of the government is followed by a meeting of the Ulster Unionist Council which confirms the arrangements for establishing a provisional government for the province in the event of Home Rule coming to pass. An executive committee is formed, with Carson as its chairman. A military council and committees dealing with finance, education, the law, customs and excise, and the Post Office are among those appointed. There is also a transport board and a railway board. And plans to create an indemnity fund of £1 million to compensate UVF members for any loss or injury suffered, and to support the widows and dependants of those killed, are also announced.

In a speech to council delegates, Carson says there is no alternative to the stance which the unionists are taking. 'Surrender is out of the question. I do not believe the prime minister himself, if I spoke to him in confidence, or he to me, would say "go and announce your surrender in Belfast". Impossible!'

Three days later, Redmond dismisses the provisional government as a joke. Speaking in Cahersiveen, County Kerry, at the start of an autumn campaign in support of Home Rule, he says amid much laughter: 'For my part, I have always all my life endeavoured to take such solemn, weighty, and respectable persons [as Carson, Lord Londonderry and James Craig] seriously, but upon my word the provisional government is too much for me.'

'I remember,' he tells his audience in the town's Carnegie Hall, 'when we were children we used to play a game called 'let's pretend'. We used to sit in a circle. Some of us pretended we were kings or queens or princes; some of us pretended we were giants, some that we were wild beasts, and ogres. It seems to me that this is a game Sir Edward Carson and his friends are engaged in at the present moment [loud laughter].'

An open-air public meeting later in the day threatens to go badly wrong when the speakers' stage partially collapses and throws about a hundred people to the ground, including Redmond's wife, Amy. Nobody suffers anything worse than bruising, however, and the Irish Party leader goes on to comment publicly for the first time on Lord Loreburn's intervention.

He says, in essence, that Loreburn's proposal is dead in the water because it has been dismissed – 'with brutal insolence' – by the Ulster Unionists. But he does not hide the truth that, in any case, the nationalists have no interest in facilitating the Liberal peer's scheme. The Irish Party 'stands for the whole bill, and nothing but the bill', he insists, and there can be no question of it going into a conference that is not based on the principle that Ireland is to have its own parliament and government.

I am told that we ought to agree to any conference without any condition whatever. That is to say, that having succeeded after 30 years of unparalleled sacrifice and labour in convincing the electorate of Great Britain and a large majority in the House of Commons of the justice and necessity of an Irish parliament and executive, and having seen a bill to carry that principle passed twice by a majority of over 100, and on the eve today of its final passage, we should now, in the face of Sir Edward Carson's arrogant and irreconcilable declarations, go into a conference, where the whole question of the principle of Home Rule would be put back once again into the melting pot – that we cannot and will not do [loud cheers].

The Ulster Unionists' 'attitude of truculence, of bluster, of lawlessness and of recklessness' is born of despair, he says, adding: 'We know that we have won our fight. They know that they have lost it [cheers].'

∾

In the north-east of Ireland, however, the fight continues. On the same day that Redmond is speaking in Cahersiveen, the parades of volunteers in the run-up to the first anniversary of Ulster Day reach a climax with an inspection of twelve thousand members of the Belfast UVF by Carson and Sir George Richardson, the retired general recruited in the summer to command the new force. The following day, 28 September, the first anniversary of the signing of the covenant is marked throughout Ulster at services of Protestant churches, including the Church of Ireland, which has designated it 'a special day of intercession and prayer on behalf of our native land'.

An official commemoration service at the Ulster Hall, attended by Carson and Smith and jointly celebrated by clergy of the Presbyterian, Church of Ireland and Methodist churches, concludes with all present raising their right hand and swearing a declaration to stand by the Ulster Covenant and 'follow wherever Sir Edward Carson might lead'.

Where that might be becomes clearer within days with confirmation that Lord Loreburn's intervention has had exactly the impact the nationalist party feared. Parliament is in recess and Redmond is at home in Aughavanagh when T.P. O'Connor is invited to a meeting with Chancellor of the Exchequer David Lloyd George.

Lloyd George tells O'Connor that Winston Churchill has had a discussion with Bonar Law, who said that the Conservatives were willing to go into a conference on Home Rule, but only if the Liberals consented to the right of Ulster to decide by plebiscite whether it should come under an Irish parliament. In a letter to the party leaders back in Ireland on the following day, 1 October, O'Connor says Lloyd George showed no desire to push the nationalists into accepting this plan. 'He recalled that he had proposed at the beginning of the struggle that Ulster should get this option, feeling confident then that it would be refused, and that he still thought this would have been wise tactics. But he accepted that this plan was now out of date (by the way, Loreburn was its most vigorous opponent); and he discussed quite calmly and amicably our difficulty in agreeing to a proposal which would look like a betrayal of our fellow-Nationalists in Ulster,' O'Connor writes.

Lloyd George also tells O'Connor that the Cabinet is almost unanimous on the matter, the only possible exception being Churchill, who feels he cannot support coercive action against the Ulster Unionists if they are prepared to accept Home Rule for the rest of Ireland, while remaining within the Westminster fold themselves.

A week later, on his annual visit to his constituency in Dundee, Churchill adds to Redmond's difficulties in a speech – reported verbatim in *The Times* – in which he offers a forthright defence of the government's 'clear and unswerving policy' on Home Rule, only to immediately suggest that it is time to compromise with the unionists.

It is obvious that the claim of north-east Ulster for special consideration for itself is a very different claim from the claim to bar and defeat Home Rule and to block the path of the whole of the rest of Ireland, and it is a claim which, if put forward with sincerity, not as a mere wrecking manoeuvre, cannot be ignored or pushed aside.

Churchill emphasises the need for agreement before any change will be made to the government's bill, but Redmond recognises that the speech amounts to a potential capitulation to the unionists' demands.

At around the same time he receives a letter from the Bishop of Raphoe, Patrick O'Donnell, warning him of 'growing apprehension' on the part of Catholics in the north of Ireland about the talk of a conference such as that proposed by Lord Loreburn.

O'Donnell, a future cardinal and Catholic primate of Ireland, is an active and influential supporter of the Irish Party and his views carry weight. He tells Redmond: 'If anything special is attempted for Ulster by the Government you will have a most troublesome business on hand. I have been saying to people that nothing special should be entertained by the Government that would not be satisfactory to the Nationalist majority in the [north-east].'

Redmond knows that he needs to retake control of the increasingly perilous situation and several days later, on 12 October, he has an opportunity to reaffirm the nationalists' position at a great rally of supporters in Limerick. Before an audience of fifty thousand drawn from all parts of Munster, he hints that a degree of autonomy for Ulster – a concept commonly described as 'Home Rule within Home Rule' – might be acceptable, but the partition of Ireland is out of the question.

> Irish nationalists can never be assenting parties to the partition and mutilation of their nation. Ireland is a unit from north to south and from east to west [cheers]. It is true that within the bosom of a nation there is room for many local diversities of treatment of government, but a unit Ireland is and Ireland must remain, and we can never assent to any proposal which would create a sharp and eternal dividing line between Irish Catholics and Irish Protestants [cheers].

The Ulster loyalists' campaign, he tells his appreciative audience, is nothing more than 'the manoeuvres of defeated men seeking to cover their retreat'.

Redmond knows he needs to say more, however. He must try to undo the damage caused by Churchill's speech in Dundee, but without opening a rift between himself and a senior member of the government. He takes time to endorse much of what Churchill said before coming to the point:

> Mr Churchill, in his speech in Scotland, alluded to the possible exclusion of a portion of Ireland and a portion of Ulster on condition that both parties in England agree to pass a bill to make it a real settlement. Now I have to say here today that that suggestion is a totally impracticable and unworkable one. Let me point out that it has no friends in Ireland. No section of nationalist opinion has ever suggested or tolerated the idea. No responsible leader of the Unionist Party in Ireland has ever put forward that idea as a

means of settlement of the Irish question, and when it was put forward in the House of Commons the men who proposed it in so many words said they put it forward simply as a means of wrecking and killing the Home Rule Bill.

Redmond's words, reported in full in the *Freeman's Journal*, are well received by his Munster audience but in one respect at least Churchill is right and Redmond is wrong: as Churchill pointed out in his speech, Edward Carson's disposition has changed. Unionists are no longer seeking to exclude Ulster from the Home Rule Bill as a means of wrecking the entire scheme; rather, they are now prepared to drop their opposition to a Dublin parliament as long as the loyalist counties of Ulster are left alone to remain under Westminster jurisdiction.

And Redmond's problems don't end there. Herbert Asquith is now actively seeking a compromise with the unionists, and two days after Redmond's speech to the cheering masses of Munster, the prime minister holds the first of a series of confidential talks with Bonar Law on the possibility of finding an agreed resolution. The meeting takes place at the Cherkley Court mansion in Surrey of Sir Max Aitken, the future press baron Lord Beaverbrook. The atmosphere is frosty and Asquith's attempt to break the ice by remarking on the beauty of the surrounding countryside is met with silence by Law, the Conservative leader, who is not – as Aitken puts it – 'a scenery man'.

No progress is made, but at a second secret meeting at the same venue on 6 November, the two have a hypothetical discussion about how Ulster might be excluded from the Home Rule Bill and under what conditions. Asquith asks Law if Edward Carson would be satisfied with taking out the four counties with Protestant majorities, but is told that in Law's opinion the minimum Carson would settle for is six counties. Whether the prime minister is really negotiating at this point, however, or merely trying to discover the opposition's bottom line will be a matter for debate.

Between his two meetings with Law, on 25 October Asquith delivers a keenly anticipated speech to his constituents in a packed village hall in Ladybank, in south-east Scotland. His 40-minute address, devoted almost entirely to Home Rule, mirrors that of Churchill in Dundee a fortnight earlier. It includes a stout defence of the government's position and a warning that the threats of violence from Ulster will be met 'by every appropriate and adequate measure'. He also rules out Lord Loreburn's proposal of a conference of the parties, on the basis that it would serve no practical purpose.

Unionists express dismay at the hardline tone of the speech. Captain James Craig MP tells the Belfast correspondent of *The Times* that Ireland is 'apparently doomed' and the 'forces of Hibernianism and disorder' have prevailed, adding: 'Mr Asquith's message is one of war upon a loyal Protestant and Imperial province, but there is not an Ulster covenanter who will flinch from the conflict.'

The Belfast-based *Northern Whig* is even more scathing: 'Mr Asquith's truculent speech at Ladybank should give entire satisfaction to his master, Mr Redmond, and to the Ancient Order of Hibernians. It is just the sort of speech that might have been expected from Mr Asquith, who, since he entered into the foul conspiracy with the Nationalists, has been their most subservient tool.' Asquith's 'master', however, will not have missed the fact that amidst all the hard talk the prime minister has sent an unmistakeable message to the Ulster unionists that a compromise may be on the table.

The line in Asquith's speech that Craig *et al.* have conveniently ignored is that there is no scheme dealing with the concerns of the Ulster unionists that the prime minister is not prepared to consider, provided certain conditions are met. The first of these is that nothing can be allowed to interfere with the establishment of an Irish parliament and executive in Dublin. And nothing is to be done 'which will erect a permanent, or an insuperable, bar in the way of Irish unity'.

The message to the Ulster unionists is plain. The government is not for turning on Home Rule for Ireland. Neither will it sanction a scheme that condemns Ireland to permanent partition. But that clearly leaves room for at least a temporary exclusion of Ulster, or a portion of it, from the Home Rule Bill.

John Redmond's negotiating skills are about to be tested to the limit.

Chapter 11 ∿

THE GOVERNMENT WAVERS

There was no civil war. There was a revolution and the king disappeared.

The handwritten letter from the prime minister is marked 'secret'. Opening it on Thursday, 13 November 1913, John Redmond reads Herbert Asquith's message: 'I am anxious to have a talk with you, but owing to your engagements and mine I understand that this cannot be until Monday.' Redmond is due to make a speech in Newcastle on the Friday evening, and Asquith expresses confidence that the Irish leader 'will be careful not to close the door on the *possibility* of an agreed settlement'.

'I will only add, for the moment, that I am by no means sanguine that anything of the kind can happen,' the prime minister continues. 'Indeed I assure you of the firm and unshaken determination of my colleagues and myself to attain with your help our common object.'

Redmond's train journey to Newcastle, in the company of Amy, is one he is unlikely to forget. The pair are attacked in their compartment by a suffragette who declares herself to be Irish. After striking Redmond in the face with her fist and attempting to throw the astonished couple's umbrellas out of the train window, she empties two bags of flour over her victims, telling Redmond as she does so: 'You're a nice man being leader of the Irish Party!' She is detained by police on arrival at Newcastle, but – the *Irish Independent* reports – Redmond declines to press charges. The nationalist leader has greater worries on his mind.

Redmond is deeply frustrated by the indications that the Ulster unionists' campaign is slowing the momentum behind Home Rule and his exasperation is clear in his speech before a large crowd of Liberal Party supporters at Newcastle Town Hall. The crowd responds with cheers at his impassioned recounting of the history of the Home Rule movement and its origins.

Ireland is asking for nothing new. Ireland had a parliament of her own, going back in history almost as far as the parliament of England. During the last 18 years of that parliament Ireland showed an increase in prosperity and in commerce and in industrial effort not paralleled in any other country in Europe at the time [cheers]. In 1800 that parliament was destroyed ...

During that dreadful period [since then], now more than a century, there were three unsuccessful insurrections in Ireland put down ruthlessly, put down in the blood of the people. There were famines every ten years. In one great famine, as you know, Ireland lost two millions of her people. ['Shame! Shame!'] During that dreadful period, when England's population increased and multiplied, the population of Ireland fell one-half. Her industries were destroyed. Ireland, which in the 18 years before the Union was the most prosperous country in Europe; in the 18 years after the Union she sank to the lowest state of industrial stagnation and decay. And, mark you, during this period the Irish nationalists, who went to your parliament at Westminster, against their will and to protest against the destruction of the parliamentary liberties of their country, in spite of all provocation, rendered all through that century good for evil and by their votes supported, aye and often by their votes carried, every popular reform that the century has seen passed for the British people [cheers]. And all this time, during this terrible period of famine, discontent, industrial stagnation, insurrection, suffering, and bloodshed, Irish soldiers fought the battles of the empire throughout the world [cheers].

The opponents of Home Rule are engaged in 'a gigantic game of bluff', he declares, and the Ulster unionists' position 'so ridiculous and audacious' that one can find no parallel for it in the history of constitutional government in any land upon earth.

One small handful of men in one small corner of one province in Ireland declare they will not allow this bill to pass [laughter] – this bill, mark you which has a majority of Ireland at its back, a majority of Great Britain at its back, and the whole empire practically unanimous [cheers]. They will not allow it to pass, and, if it is passed in spite of them, then they swear by high heaven they will declare war [laughter] upon their fellow countrymen in Ireland, upon the empire, and upon the throne itself ['Shame! Shame!']. Now, let me say to you English people this one serious word. If such an obstacle as that were allowed to prevail, if such a threat as that were allowed to become effectual, there is an end of all constitutional government [cheers], an end to all liberty, an end to all law-and-order, aye, an end to all civilised society.

Opponents of Home Rule speak of Ulster, Redmond adds, but what is Ulster?

It is a province that consists of nine counties, which returns to parliament 17 Home Rulers and 16 anti-Home Rulers [cheers]. It is a province where the population is very nearly evenly divided between Catholics and Protestants, and, allowing for a margin, which I believe to be a large one, of Protestant Home Rulers, Ulster today consists of a population the majority of which is in favour of Home Rule [cheers].

The idea of excluding Ulster from the Home Rule Bill is, therefore, so 'patently absurd' that opponents of the measure have been forced to fall back upon the 'four counties'. But the truth, he insists, is that Belfast and the four counties are more dependent on the rest of Ireland for their prosperity than the rest of Ireland is on them.

I say that the exclusion of Ulster or any part of Ulster [from Home Rule] would mean the ruin of its prosperity. But to us, exclusion would mean something more. It would mean the nullification of our hopes and aspirations for the future Irish nation. It would mean the erection of sharp, permanent, eternal dividing lines between Catholics and Protestants, whereas our ideal has been an Irish nation in the future made up of a blend of all races, of all classes, and of all creeds [prolonged cheers].

Those holding out against Home Rule for Ireland, Redmond asserts, are the members of 'that cursed ascendancy whose spirit has been the cause of all the miseries and misfortunes of our country'.

> No, it is not fear of religious persecution, it is not fear of unjust taxation which animates our opponents, it is fear of the loss of the old ascendancy. And today, in defence of that unholy monopoly and ascendancy, these men threaten civil war on the empire and the throne. Their threats are idle [cheers]. In Ireland we will never submit to them [loud cheers].

Nevertheless, Redmond adheres to Asquith's request not to close the door on the possibility of an agreement with his opponents. He believes it would be worth paying 'a large price' to secure a settlement by consent and he does not want Home Rule to come 'in the garb of a humiliating defeat for any section of my countrymen'.

> All I say tonight is this: let these men say what they want [cheers], and I repeat what I have so often declared, that there is no demand, no matter how extravagant or unreasonable it may appear to us, that we are not ready to consider carefully so long as it is consistent with the principle for which generations of our race have battled – namely the principle of a settlement based upon the national self-government of Ireland. (loud and prolonged cheers) … But I say here – and let it be clearly understood I mean what I say [cheers] – we will not be intimidated or bullied into the betrayal of Ireland [cheers].

On the following Monday morning, Redmond arrives at the home of Liberal MP Edwin Montagu, 24 Queen Anne's Gate – a tranquil street of elegant town houses close to the Palace of Westminster – for an hour-long meeting with the prime minister, who tells him of the discussions he has held with Bonar Law. Asquith reports that the Conservative leader told him that both he and Edward Carson were anxious to find a settlement of the Home Rule question. Law thought the matter could be settled by the total and permanent exclusion of Ulster from the bill – Ulster to mean an area to be settled by agreement.

'[Asquith] gave no countenance whatever to his idea,' Redmond writes later in his notes of the meeting, 'and asked whether there was any other direction in which [Law] saw hope of a settlement. [Law] answered, he thought not, and said that the suggestion of what is called "Home Rule within Home Rule", or administrative autonomy, was impossible. They separated without anything more definite having taken place, and without any arrangement for another meeting.'

Asquith also tells Redmond that, after he apprised the Cabinet of his conversations with Law, a wide-ranging discussion ensued on whether a settlement might be found that would prevent bloodshed in Ulster. Herbert Samuel, the postmaster general, suggested giving Ulster members in the Irish parliament a power of veto over legislation affecting Ulster, but this was rejected after a few moments' consideration. One suggestion, however, did engage the Cabinet for some time. This was a proposal by David Lloyd George to the effect that a certain area to be agreed on should be excluded from the Home Rule Bill for five years, but after that time would automatically come under the Irish parliament's jurisdiction.

Lloyd George acknowledged that this idea could not be the basis of an agreed settlement, as Edward Carson and his friends would never support it. But it would, he argued, prevent an immediate outburst in Ulster, as men could not possibly go to war to prevent something that wasn't going to happen for five years. The prime minister assures Redmond that he does not support this suggestion. He told the Cabinet, indeed, that it would probably result in the government's defeat in the House of Commons, as 20 to 30 Liberal members would probably vote against it, as possibly would the Irish Party.

A week later, in response to a request from Asquith, Redmond sets out his party's position in a memorandum for the prime minister. He makes three fundamental points: under no circumstances must the government offer to compromise on the Home Rule Bill – the onus to make any such offer should be placed on Bonar Law and the Conservatives; the partition of Ireland would be a disaster and must be avoided; and fears of an armed rebellion by the Orangemen of the north are exaggerated.

Any offer by the government, he argues, would be seen as evidence that the 'Orange threats' are working and would be used by the Tory party as a basis for further demands. Nationalists in Ulster would be 'shocked' by any suggestion that Ulster might be excluded from the bill. 'Such exclusion, apart from its mutilation of Ireland, would expose our people in North-East Ulster to intolerable oppression,' he adds, prophetically.

Taking Ulster out of Home Rule would also create administrative confusion and have serious political consequences, Redmond contends. 'It would tend to perpetuate the sectarian differences we seek to extirpate. It might even accentuate these differences.'

If Bonar Law is made to take the initiative and propose the exclusion of Ulster from the bill, he suggests, the unionists' opposition to Home Rule will be seriously undermined. Their argument that they are standing up for Protestant liberties would be exposed as a sham if it was shown that they were prepared to abandon the Protestant minority in the south to their fate under an Irish parliament. 'It seems to me thus incontestable that an offer from the Liberal Ministry has all the disadvantages in tactics, whereas, leaving the offer to come from Mr Bonar Law, presents him with all the difficulties, party and otherwise.'

On 25 November, a meeting with Lloyd George confirms Redmond's fear that the government is becoming increasingly jittery over the Ulster unionists' campaign. The chancellor tells Redmond that his memo to the prime minster has been read to the Cabinet, and there was unanimous agreement with his argument that it would be a fatal mistake for the government to make an offer of compromise at this time.

He insists, however, that an offer will have to be made at some stage, and sooner than they might think. The government has discovered 95,000 rounds of ammunition in Belfast and has decided to issue a proclamation to seize the entire cache. It also has reason to believe that Edward Carson's next move will be to hold a review of armed men, and it is determined to suppress this.

Lloyd George says it is the Cabinet's view that it will be necessary to accompany such coercive measures with 'some offer to Ulster', and he believes his own proposal – the exclusion of a certain portion of Ulster from the Home Rule Bill for five years – is the best option. Redmond declines to argue other than to say he stands 'absolutely' over his memorandum.

But Lloyd George concludes with a threat: if no offer is made to Ulster, then under certain circumstances Edward Grey, Lord Haldane, Winston Churchill and, he implies, himself might all resign from the Cabinet. That, says the chancellor, would be 'a very serious thing' for Home Rule and for Redmond personally. Redmond records his response in his note of the meeting: 'I pointed out to him that, so far as I personally was concerned, the consequences would not be nearly so serious as they would for him personally, that the debacle would mean the end of his career and the end of the Liberal Party for a generation – perhaps, indeed, for ever. He admitted this.'

Most disquieting for Redmond is his impression that Lloyd George believes the Irish Party would agree to anything rather than face the break-up of the government. 'In view of this I spoke to him more strongly and more frankly than, perhaps, was absolutely necessary,' he notes.

~

The pace of events has quickened noticeably, and on 26 November, the day after his meeting with Lloyd George, Redmond receives another handwritten note from the prime minister, marked 'confidential':

Dear Mr Redmond,
I am greatly obliged to you for your letter of the 24th. I read it to my colleagues in the Cabinet, and I need not say that they gave, and will continue to give, the most careful consideration to your statement of your views.
For the moment, I will, on their behalf and my own, only say this:
(1) There is no question at this stage of our making any 'offer' or 'proposal' to Mr Bonar Law, though I may think it expedient to finish the conversation with him which was broken off at our last interview.
(2) We must, of course, keep our hands free, when the critical stage of the Bill is ultimately reached, to take such a course as then in all

the circumstances seems best calculated to safeguard the fortunes
of Home Rule.
Very truly yours
H.H. Asquith

The following day, Redmond meets Irish Chief Secretary Augustine
Birrell, who gives him a much more upbeat assessment than Lloyd
George's. Birrell dismisses as 'ridiculous' the idea that the chancellor's
proposal to exclude Ulster from the bill could lead to any kind of
settlement, and tells Redmond that members of the Cabinet are bitterly
opposed to it. Birrell also says nothing definite has been decided about
seizing arms from the Ulster unionists; he thinks that something will
be done, but he does not agree with Lloyd George that taking such
action would necessitate an offer being made to Ulster. 'He was in the
best of spirits,' Redmond writes in a memo of the meeting, 'and quite
confident about everything.'

On the same day, 27 November, Asquith makes an uncompromising
speech to supporters in Leeds which indicates a hardening of the
government's resolve and infuriates unionists. Although he makes
no reference to his private meeting with Bonar Law in October, he
dismisses the call made by the Tory leader at that meeting for a general
election to take place before the Home Rule Bill goes through. Two
general elections took place in 1910 and the Liberal Party made it clear
before each of them that, if elected, it intended to bring in Home Rule
for Ireland, he says. 'This demand for a general election ... is one of
the idlest demands that was ever put forward [cheers]. No. There is no
ground for demanding a general election.'

In the only note of conciliation, the prime minister says that he has
not closed the door to the possibility of a deal that could bring peace,
but his conclusion could hardly sound better to John Redmond's ears
if the Irish leader had scripted it himself.

We are not going to make, either upon our own initiative or at
the suggestion of others, any surrender of principle [cheers]. We
mean to see this thing through [loud cheers]. We took up the Irish
cause from a conviction that time has strengthened and deepened

that, as a matter of right, Home Rule was due to Ireland, and that, as a matter of policy, it was sanctioned by the highest interests of our parliament and our imperial development [cheers]. The Irish members, representing the vast majority of the Irish people, have trusted us with a loyalty that has never wavered. For that loyalty we hope to show a worthy counterpart and that trust we most certainly shall not betray [cheers].

But not all of Asquith's Cabinet are singing from the same hymn sheet on the Ulster question. On the same day as the prime minister's address in Leeds, Winston Churchill has a long conversation with the Conservative MP Austen Chamberlain on board the Admiralty yacht *Enchantress*, during which Churchill says that the Cabinet has never excluded separate treatment for Ulster and that it is not bound to the Irish nationalists. These remarks, disclosed by Chamberlain in a political memoir, are not publicised at the time, of course, and for the moment all the focus is on the government's apparent unwillingness to make any concessions that might upset John Redmond.

On 28 November, Law and Carson take their anti-Home Rule campaign to Dublin, beginning their day with a visit to Lord Iveagh at his residence on St Stephen's Green – the future home of the Irish Department of Foreign Affairs.

As the two men pose for press photographs outside the building, they are accosted by two suffragettes – Hanna Sheehy Skeffington and Meg Connery – who attempt to force them to take handbills containing 'Questions for Mr Bonar Law'. A mixed crowd of nationalist and unionist supporters has gathered to watch proceedings and – in a scene reported in the following day's *Irish Independent* – some cheer on the women, while others groan. There are shouts of 'Home Rule!', 'No Home Rule!', 'Parnell!', 'Redmond!' and 'Keep your powder dry!' An indignant Sheehy Skeffington is dragged away by a police sergeant who, with support from a constable, frogmarches her to the nearby Lad Lane police station, followed by a crowd. She is subsequently charged with assaulting the sergeant and jailed for a week.

In the meantime, Law and Carson have been guests for lunch at the City and County Conservative Club on Dawson Street, where Law makes his most inflammatory speech yet about the prospect of an army revolt in response to any attempt to coerce Ulster into Home Rule. Suggesting that Asquith should turn his mind 'to the history of the great revolution' of 1688, when the Catholic King James II was overthrown, Law continues:

> Then the country rose against a tyranny. It was the tyranny of a king, but other people besides kings can exercise tyranny, and other people besides kings can be treated in the same way. I remember this, that King James had behind him the letter of the law just as Mr Asquith has now. He made sure of it. He got the judges on his side by methods not dissimilar from those by which Mr Asquith has a majority of the House of Commons on his side. There is another point to which I would especially refer. In order to carry out his despotic intention the king had the largest paid army which had ever been seen in England. What happened? There was no civil war. There was a revolution and the king disappeared. Why? Because his own army refused to fight for him [cheers].

The main event of the pair's visit, however, is a speech by Law that night in the Theatre Royal – the venue where the prime minister made his famous rallying call in favour of Home Rule 16 months previously. Once again, the theatre is packed with an enthusiastic, flag-waving, cheering crowd. This time it is the union flag on display, and 'the effect of 4,000 of these fluttering from floor to ceiling of the great building was highly impressive', reports *The Times*.

Responding to Asquith's hard-hitting speech in Leeds the previous night, Law tells his audience that the prime minister's remarks show that either the government has decided to obey John Redmond's orders or it plans to bluff its way through the crisis before climbing down at the last moment. 'If that is their idea, they will be playing with fire.' Each mention of Redmond's name draws boos and groans from the crowd, until Law asks them to desist from doing so: 'I shall never get on if you show your feelings every time I mention the name.'

Law's earlier wild words about army insurrection and his clear exasperation with the government are most likely a source of comfort to Redmond. They suggest that, in spite of Lord Loreburn's untimely intervention and the signs of a weakening of resolve by Churchill and perhaps some of his Cabinet colleagues, the unionists remain frustrated at their failure to bully the prime minister and his government into submission. And if Law and Carson are losing, then Redmond must be winning.

Everything points to his having negotiated well and succeeded over the past few weeks in calming ministers' nerves over the threatened Ulster rebellion. No sooner has one challenge been successfully met, however, than another presents itself. This one emanates from much closer quarters, and it has the potential to fatally undermine Redmond's authority in Ireland.

Chapter 12 ～

THE SOUTH BEGINS

*You have never tried to win over Ulster. You have never
tried to understand her position.*

As darkness falls on Dublin city centre, a tall, broad-shouldered
man standing on a platform steps forward into the light and
delivers a speech that fills his audience in Beresford Square with
renewed enthusiasm for the increasingly bitter struggle in which they
are occupied. 'Are you going to continue the fight?', he asks, drawing
cries of 'Yes! Yes!'

> This fight means emancipation for you and yours. ... We must
> triumph, we cannot fail. We don't preach bigotry or hatred, but
> brotherhood and good fellowship. Our gospel means success ...
> make up your minds, that this fight is going to be a fight without
> any conference or any compromise – a fight to a finish.

Cheers go up as Jim Larkin, watched by a reporter from the *Freeman's
Journal*, continues: 'When this struggle is over great things will be
spoken of you and great songs sung of you. The greatest thing that
will be told of our race in history will be the story of how the hungry
men and women and children of Dublin stood together and came
successfully out of the fight! [Loud cheers].'

For two months now, Dublin has been convulsed by the industrial
dispute in which Larkin and his followers are engaged against the
city's employers, led by the *Irish Independent*'s owner, William Martin
Murphy. The Dublin lockout, as it will come to be known, could not
have come at a worse moment for John Redmond and his nationalist
party colleagues. After a decades-long fight by the Irish MPs, Home
Rule is within touching distance and the last thing they need is to get
dragged into an extremely bitter fight between the capital city's workers
and employers.

The party's position is summed up in a forthright letter from John Dillon to T.P. O'Connor on 1 October 1913: 'Dublin is Hell! And I don't see the way out. Murphy is a desperate character, Larkin as bad. It would be a blessing to Ireland if they exterminated each other.'

Apparently unwilling to take sides, Redmond's response to the crisis was not to respond at all. He is mocked for this by Bonar Law in his speech at the Theatre Royal in Dublin, in which Law says that it is 'amazing' that no attempt to end the labour dispute has been made by the nationalist leaders. '[Redmond] has left it severely alone, and it surely is a curious omen for the success of the Home Rule Bill, if it were ever to become law, that the Irish leader is not in a position, or, at all events, does not care, to show his face in the three largest cities in Ireland.' Law's exaggerated claim is that Redmond is unwelcome in Dublin, Belfast and even Cork – where William O'Brien's All-for-Ireland League holds sway over the Irish Party.

Larkin, the leader of the workers on strike or locked out, is also scornful of Redmond, describing him and Carson, in a speech in London on 10 October, as 'both the mouthpieces of the capitalist class'.

In a letter to the *Freeman's Journal* published on 5 November, the Irish Party's Galway City MP Stephen Gwynn attempts to explain the 'extraordinary difficulty' in which he and his colleagues find themselves as a result of the labour dispute, 'when such a matter, so intimately Irish, has to be dealt with by an alien Government, which we cannot afford to weaken. Heaven knows how one has wished for the open arena of an Irish assembly, in which this matter could be thrashed out, and in which people might assume their natural groupings without fear of consequence.'

Gwynn allows no doubt about his own admiration for Larkin: 'The Irish working classes have shown in this strike that they can produce a leader and can follow a leader. He will not always break their ranks on a false issue. It is this combination of qualities which makes Syndicalism [a revolutionary doctrine involving workers seizing control of industry and government] a practicable policy.'

Some other party MPs take a different view. In a letter to the newspapers published on 24 September, the Leix (Queen's County) MP P.J. Meehan declares himself a 'convinced believer in the principles of trade unionism' and says that any movement that would bring about an improvement in conditions for unskilled workers is deserving of support. However, he adds, 'public opinion is against Larkin, his methods and doctrines ... because the Irish people cannot tolerate a man who blasphemously arrogates to himself a Divine mission, avows his predilections for hell under certain conditions, and publicly gives utterance to doctrines at variance with the Divine law, and denounces the clergy as paid hirelings in the pulpit, and accuses them of preventing their flocks from improving their worldly conditions.'

Meehan's opinion of Larkin is more typical than Gwynn's among the few party MPs who have anything at all to say about the dispute; most choose – like their leader – to keep well out of it, seeing only potential damage to the Home Rule cause from any decision to take sides.

While Jim Larkin poses no threat to Redmond's position as undisputed leader of nationalist Ireland, the same spirit of rebellion animating the trade union leader and his followers raises a potential challenge to Redmond's long-held status from another quarter.

On 1 November 1913, *An Claidheamh Soluis* ('The Sword of Light'), the official organ of the Gaelic League, an organisation dedicated to the promotion of Irish language and culture, publishes an article by the Professor of Early Irish History at University College Dublin (UCD), Eoin MacNeill. 'The North Began' praises the Ulster volunteers led by Edward Carson for seizing their own destiny from the control of the British Empire, and suggests that nationalists in the south of Ireland should arm themselves in similar fashion.

MacNeill's article is seized upon by a small group of Irish Republican Brotherhood (IRB) members who have been considering the establishment of an armed volunteer organisation in the south to counter the threat to Home Rule posed by Carson's putative army in the north. The IRB is a secret revolutionary organisation dedicated to the overthrow of British rule in Ireland. It lacks popular support, but in MacNeill it sees a respected potential figurehead for a new volunteer body.

An approach is made to MacNeill, who agrees to be involved in the initiative, and on 25 November 1913, the Irish Volunteers are inaugurated at a public meeting in the Rotunda Rink in Parnell Square, Dublin. Many of the estimated seven thousand in attendance – most of them young men, including a large contingent of students from MacNeill's university – are confined to overflow halls as the main auditorium is full.

The proceedings descend into chaos when the new movement's provisional secretary, Laurence Kettle, attempts to read its manifesto but is shouted down by members of the recently formed Irish Citizen Army, trade unionists who accuse Kettle – a farmer and engineer with Dublin Corporation – of being a strike-breaker.

Those given a hearing, however, include MacNeill and a young barrister and schoolteacher, Patrick (P.H.) Pearse, who tells the crowd that the significance of the evening is that several thousand Dublin people have 'resolved at last to become Irish citizens'. The bearing of arms is not only the proudest right of citizenship, he adds, but its most essential duty. 'Irishmen cease to be citizens and become a mob when they throw away the arms with which they have achieved a measure of freedom.'

Pearse will go on to describe the Volunteers as 'a weapon' to be used by John Redmond in the fight to secure Home Rule, but the Irish Party leader is not grateful for this unwanted gift. He has brought Ireland to the brink of his goal through strictly constitutional means, and the last thing he wants now is an armed body of men, over whom he has no control, lining up behind him.

Within a week of the Rotunda meeting, a panicked Liberal government makes matters worse for Redmond by banning the importation of arms into Ireland. The move enrages supporters of the already five thousand-strong Irish Volunteers, who know that their Ulster counterparts have been importing arms and openly drilling for the past 18 months without government interference.

A report in the unionist *Irish Times* on 8 December by the paper's Belfast correspondent underlines the extent of he problem: 'The Royal proclamation prohibiting the importation of military arms and ammunition into Ireland was the principal topic of conversation in Belfast to-day, and the more the document is discussed the more amusement does it create among Ulster unionists. The idea of prohibiting arms into Ulster when it is notorious that modern rifles with suitable ammunitions have already arrived in thousands during the past eighteen months is a proceeding which can only cover the Government with ridicule.'

A short report in the *Irish Independent* of 10 December provides further evidence that the arms ban has come too late to prevent an insurrection in Ulster. It quotes an unnamed rifle manufacturer from Birmingham as saying that between 35,000 and 40,000 firearms have been sent from that city to Belfast. 'You may take it from me', he says, 'that Ulster is armed to the teeth.'

In a speech in Plymouth, Edward Carson mocks the government's 'great proclamation' prohibiting the importation of arms and makes it clear that he will be telling his followers to ignore it. In the face of such provocations, the Irish Volunteers begin an impressive recruitment drive, putting John Redmond under increasing pressure to deliver a final agreement with the Liberal government before matters spin out of control. But Redmond's worst fears about weakening government resolve in the face of the Ulster unionists' threats are about to be confirmed.

Asquith, meanwhile, having left Bonar Law puzzled by his silence since their last meeting on 6 November, confounds the opposition leader further by inviting him to another meeting on 3 December, and still making no serious proposal as to a settlement. He then switches his attention to Carson, holding two equally unfruitful meetings with the Ulster Unionist leader, leaving his opponents with the clear impression that he is trying to draw them into making the first move while also playing for time.

∾

As the new year of 1914 arrives, John Redmond receives a letter at his home in Aughavanagh from a frequent correspondent, Bishop O'Donnell of Raphoe. 'Though you have no need of them,' begins the bishop, 'it will do no harm for me to send you some thoughts on politics that have been passing through my mind.' He tells Redmond that the Ulster unionists are not really minded to fight, but even if they do he can be assured that the nationalists of the north will offer no resistance. Redmond can therefore assure the government that there will be 'no huge trouble' in Ulster, and on that basis he can insist that 'the little Bill ... go through as it now is, or no worse than it now is'.

Redmond has every reason to worry, however, that the little bill is about to cause him big problems. January brings respite on one front at least when the Dublin labour dispute ends. Larkin's followers must return to work defeated, but the stand they have taken will inspire future generations. Redmond's eye, though, remains focused on one prize only, and on 2 February he sits down with Herbert Asquith and Augustine Birrell to find out what the government plans to do next on the Home Rule Bill.

Asquith begins by briefing him on the series of meetings he has held since December with Law and, separately, Carson. He assures Redmond that no offer was made by him to the unionist leaders. He did make some 'tentative suggestions', but none was seriously discussed. Both men, the prime minister adds, held obstinately to their position that nothing short of the total exclusion of Ulster from the Home Rule Bill would lead to an agreed settlement. But it is the government's view that taking Ulster, or any part of it, out of the bill – even temporarily – would lead to 'the most disastrous' results for Ireland. He and his Cabinet colleagues remain firmly opposed to such a measure.

The prime minister goes on to explain, however, that the situation is complicated by domestic political issues. Among these is the Army Annual Bill, which must be passed into law by a certain date in March or April, otherwise the army must be disbanded. He expects that the opposition in the House of Commons will threaten not to sanction the bill until they know how the army is going to be used in Ulster, possibly provoking such extreme disorder that the whole business of parliament will be held up.

Asquith's conclusion is that to ensure the Home Rule Bill is safeguarded, it is necessary to make Ulster an offer. He doesn't believe that any offer – barring the exclusion of Ulster from the bill – will be accepted. But if a sufficiently good offer is made and rejected, the Ulster unionists' opposition to Home Rule will lose all moral force, he believes.

Redmond, having barely had a moment to digest the convoluted logic of Asquith's thinking, then listens as the prime minister outlines an astonishing series of concessions that he plans to offer the unionists, all of them recorded in Redmond's memo of the meeting. The first is to take the Irish Post Office out of the Home Rule Bill, leaving it under the control of the Westminster parliament. Redmond immediately protests that this would not appease a single individual in Ulster and would be a gratuitous giving away of something regarded as most valuable to the Irish nationalists.

Asquith's second idea is to place a number of areas, including education, under local administrative control in Ulster. And he also proposes to grant Ulster members of the Irish parliament the power to appeal to Westminster against the application to Ulster of certain legislation passed by the parliament in Dublin.

The prime minister points out that at this stage these are merely personal proposals and he has not yet brought them to Cabinet, though he expects that his colleagues will be guided by his views on the matter. He neglects to mention that he has already made proposals on these lines to Edward Carson, in their recent talks, and that they were flatly turned down.

A fuming Redmond sets out his objections at once. To their opponents, such concessions would amount to an abandonment of the bill, he argues. The Ulster unionists would not accept these concessions anyway, and it would be 'quite impossible' for the Irish Party to support proposals of such a character.

Asquith protests that he did not expect the nationalists to support his plan. All he asks of them is that they be prepared to make large concessions in the interest of securing an agreed bill, as long as they meet the minimum conditions Redmond and his colleagues have themselves laid down: namely the creation of an Irish parliament and executive and the maintenance of a united Ireland.

The prime minister adds that he is to meet the king on Thursday and he is happy to meet Redmond again at any time of his choosing, or to consider any document the Irish leader wishes to send him. Redmond notes that Birrell, usually a strong advocate of the nationalist cause, takes practically no part in the 90-minute meeting.

Asquith's reference to his planned meeting with King George is an indication of the pressure the prime minister has come under to find an agreed settlement to the crisis. The king has become increasingly jittery over the issue and has been on the prime minister's case for several months, telling Asquith in a memorandum in August 1913: 'I cannot help feeling that the Government is drifting and taking me with it.'

The following month he wrote to Asquith to ask if he intended to use the army to suppress disorder in Ulster and whether it would be wise, or fair to the army or the king himself as its head, to do so. 'You will, I am sure, bear in mind that ours is a voluntary Army,' he continued. 'Our soldiers are none the less citizens; by birth, religion and environment they may have strong feelings on the Irish question; outside influence may be brought to bear on them; they see distinguished retired officers already organising local forces in Ulster; they hear rumours of officers on the active list throwing up their commissions to join this force.' He went on, not for the first time, to press the prime minister to hold a conference to try to resolve the impasse.

Several months on, rumours persist that the king may intervene to force a dissolution of parliament and bring about a general election, or insist upon a referendum on Home Rule before agreeing to sign it into law. There is even talk of him dismissing the Cabinet, the first time since 1834 that a monarch would have exercised their power to do so.

In any event, Asquith's proposed climbdown has created a crisis for the nationalist party. After consulting senior colleagues, Redmond writes a long letter to Asquith on 3 February urging him to change his mind. A compromise offer to the unionists on the lines he has proposed would be rejected by them out of hand, he argues, and it would allow the opposition to claim that the government had finally admitted that its Home Rule Bill could not be carried.

With the matter due to come before the Commons again in the coming days, Redmond beseeches Asquith to confine his comments in the house to an offer to consider any proposals made to him, as long as they are consistent with the establishment of an Irish parliament and executive and do not pose a threat to 'the integrity of Ireland'. Should he do so, he will have the Irish nationalist MPs' wholehearted support.

A day later Birrell tells Redmond that his letter has been read to the Cabinet and will be acted upon. The Irish question now has the undivided attention of the government and on 9 February the Cabinet meets again, devoting its entire discussion to Home Rule. Birrell writes to Redmond immediately and discloses that 'a great difference of opinion' has arisen. Asquith proposed offering non-specific concessions to the unionists in the areas of administrative autonomy and legislative vetoes, 'but eventually it seemed to be the view of the majority that it was better he should say nothing', writes Birrell, underlining certain words himself.

The prime minster, he adds, is not prepared to reiterate his general offer to consider any proposals put forward, as Redmond has urged, as he is 'very sick' of making such declarations. But while he knows what Asquith won't say, he is still unsure what the prime minister will say in the Commons on the following day. 'I feel sure the Cabinet won't be willing to wait very long before making up their minds as to what ought to be offered publicly to Ulster,' he writes.

Replying at once, Redmond again insists that it would be a 'fatal mistake in tactics' to offer any specific changes to the bill at this stage. Such a move, he says, would kill any chance of a compromise being reached, as the nationalists would have no option but to reject any proposals designed to weaken the bill.

Parliament is due to resume 10 February, the next day, following the Christmas recess, but before MPs gather in the Commons an interesting new proposal to resolve the crisis is made in that day's edition of the *Times*. In a letter to the paper Sir Horace Plunkett, a former unionist MP for South Dublin, says the two ideas floated to date – administrative autonomy for Ulster within an Irish parliament, or the province's exclusion from the Home Rule – are objectionable, because both would isolate Ulster and thereby impair Irish unity.

He suggests that Ulster should enter a Home Rule parliament on the basis that it may leave after a certain period if it so wishes. 'The only chance of success for the experiment of Irish national unity is that all parties should enter the scheme freely,' he writes. 'The only way to induce the Ulster unionists to enter it freely is to give them the power of leaving it if, after a fair trial, they find it impracticable.'

Plunkett's suggestion catches the eye of the prime minister, who tells the House of Commons immediately that he finds it a remarkable

proposal that 'deserves a good deal of study'. Should all the parties find
Plunkett's idea acceptable, he would welcome it 'without a moment's
hesitation'.

But observers who have been keenly awaiting Asquith's own
suggestions to deal with the crisis are left disappointed. The government
recognises 'to the full' the situation that has developed and knows that
it must take the initiative in putting forward a potential resolution,
he says. But he makes no specific proposals, promising instead that
the government will bring forward its ideas for a settlement without
'undue delay'.

The following day, 11 February, the House of Commons spends
more than seven hours debating a resolution by the Conservative MP
Walter Long stating that it would be 'disastrous' to proceed with the
Home Rule Bill 'until it has been submitted to the judgment of the
people' – in other words, at a general election.

In a stirring speech, Edward Carson castigates Asquith for his failure
to bring forward specific proposals the previous day.

> I say that the position, at all events to us Irish unionists in this
> house, is an intolerable one. We are asked to sit here quietly and
> patiently, to vote for estimates, to vote, I suppose, for the pay of the
> army, which you are so ready to say that you will send, but which
> you never will send, over to Ulster.

Carson says he will not be led into making proposals of his own until
he has heard what the government has to say, but he emphasises
that the delay in resolving the crisis has caused attitudes in Ulster to
harden.

> They are always talking of concessions to Ulster. Ulster is not
> asking for concessions. Ulster is asking to be let alone. When you
> talk of concessions, what you really mean is, 'We want to lay down
> what is the minimum of wrong we can do to Ulster.' Let me tell
> you that the results of two years' delay and the treatment we have
> received during these two years have made your task and made our
> task far more difficult. You have driven these men to enter into a

covenant for their mutual protection. No doubt you have laughed at their covenant. Have a good laugh at it now. Well, so far as I am concerned, I am not the kind of man who will go over to Ulster one day and say, 'Enter into a covenant', and go over next day and say, 'Break it'. But there is something more. You have insulted them. I do not say the prime minister has done so. I would be wrong if I were to say that he has done so. He has treated them seriously, but the large body of his colleagues in the rank-and-file of his party have taken every opportunity of jeering at these men, of branding them as braggarts and bluffers and cowards, and all the rest of it. Well, do not you see that having done that, these men can never go back, and never will go back, and allow these gibes and insults and sneers to prove true.

Despite having said that he will not put forward any proposals at this stage, the Ulster Unionist leader does, in effect, make one. Should the prime minister move to exclude Ulster from the bill, Carson says, it would be his 'duty to go to Ulster at once and take counsel with the people there'. He makes clear that in such a scenario he would recommend acceptance of the government's offer.

He then chides John Redmond and the government for trying to compel Ulster to come under a Dublin parliament rather than seeking to win their argument by example and persuasion.

Believe me, whatever way you settle the Irish question, there are only two ways to deal with Ulster. It is for statesmen to say which is the best and right one. She is not a part of the community which can be bought. She will not allow herself to be sold. You must therefore either coerce her if you go on, or you must, in the long run, by showing that good government can come under the Home Rule Bill, try and win her over to the case of the rest of Ireland. You probably can coerce her – though I doubt it. If you do, what will be the disastrous consequences not only to Ulster, but to this country and the empire? Will my fellow countryman, the leader of the nationalist party, have gained anything? I will agree with him – I do not believe he wants to triumph any more than I do. But will he have gained anything if he takes over these people and then applies for what he used to call – at all events his party used to call – the enemies of the people to come in and coerce them into obedience? No, sir, one false step taken in relation to Ulster will, in my opinion, render for ever impossible a solution of the Irish question, I say this to my nationalist fellow countrymen, and, indeed, also to the government: you have never tried to win over Ulster. You have never tried to understand her position. You have never alleged, and can never allege, that this bill gives her one atom of advantage ... I say to the leader of the nationalist party, if you want Ulster, go and take her, or go and win her. You have never wanted her affections; you have wanted her taxes.

Asquith is so impressed by Carson's speech that he is moved to write him a letter of congratulations afterwards. But it draws an angry riposte from Redmond. While acknowledging that Carson's 'powerful' speech 'deeply moved' him, he denies the suggestion that the prize he is seeking is control of Ulster's taxes: 'Sir, I repudiate that statement. No such desire animates either my colleagues or myself.' This draws loud cries of dissent from Conservative MPs, but Redmond scornfully dismisses them: 'I care not about the assent of Englishmen,' he says. 'I am fighting this matter out between a fellow countryman and myself, and I say it was an unworthy thing for him to say that I am animated by these base motives.'

And so the English, Scottish and Welsh MPs sit and watch as two southern Irishmen, one-time colleagues on the legal circuit, fight out their private duel on the floor of the House of Commons.

When Redmond goes on to say that Ulster is a province in which Catholics are 'not very far short' of being half the population, Carson interrupts: 'Two hundred thousand short.' Redmond counters: 'That is so, and allowing for a margin, as you must fairly do, of Protestant Home Rulers, it is a province where the majority against Home Rule is not really overwhelming, but there is a majority against it. It is a province in which, if you take out the one city of Belfast from your calculation, there is then a Catholic majority, and a large nationalist majority, over the whole province. In view of these facts, it is absurd to contend that honourable gentlemen, when they speak of Ulster, mean the whole province of Ulster.'

But Redmond knows that he and Carson are merely sparring. The government's promise of new proposals has ensured that the real fight is about to begin.

Chapter 13

ULSTER SAYS NO

We don't want sentence of death with a stay of execution of six years.

T he Liberal government wastes no further time in trying to find a compromise to end the impasse. On 16 February 1914, Chancellor of the Exchequer David Lloyd George presents a paper to the Cabinet – a copy of which is furnished to John Redmond – containing an imaginative proposal.

To have any hope of succeeding, Lloyd George writes, any plan from the government to end the stalemate must have two 'essential characteristics':

> (1) It must be an offer the rejection of which would put the other side entirely in the wrong, as far as the British public is concerned; and
>
> (2) It must not involve any alteration in the scheme of the [Home Rule] Bill; so that if it is rejected the Unionists cannot say, 'Why, you yourselves admitted that your Bill needed amendment'.

Lloyd George says he can think of only one suggestion that would meet both of these conditions. He proposes giving each county in Ireland the right to hold a referendum to 'contract out' of the bill for a period of time, to run at least until after the next general election.

There is more to Lloyd George's proposal than meets the eye; it is not just a manoeuvre to defuse the immediate crisis by allowing the Ulster counties to vote themselves out of Home Rule for a limited time. The key element of his plan is that an election must take place before the specified period of exclusion is up. This is an attempt to address a fundamental objection to the Home Rule Bill by the Conservatives and their Ulster Unionist allies, who argue that the British electorate was never consulted about the major change to the country's constitutional arrangements that Home Rule would entail.

This perceived objection is disputed by government ministers and John Redmond, who argue that the Liberals' commitment to introduce a Home Rule Bill was clear to everybody during the two election campaigns of 1910. For the past three years the argument has been carried on incessantly: did the electorate know that a vote for the Liberal Party was a vote for Home Rule?

Neither side is going to concede the point, but the critical thing for Lloyd George is that Bonar Law has accepted that if the Liberals are returned to power following another general election at which it is clear that Home Rule is part of the governing party's platform, the Conservatives will have no further grounds for supporting armed resistance in Ulster.

Lloyd George's scheme would allow the four most unionist counties in Ulster – he doesn't anticipate any others voting to exclude themselves – to remain outside a Home Rule parliament until after their case has gone before the British electorate. If the Liberals win the next election, they will have the mandate to implement Home Rule which the Conservatives currently claim they lack, and the Conservatives in turn will have to accept the verdict of the British people and withdraw their opposition. If the Tories win the election, they can do as they see fit; a Home Rule parliament for the remaining 28 counties in Ireland will be already up and running, and it will up to the government of the day to decide what to do with the other four.

'The great advantage of this scheme lies in the fact that it is in no sense an admission that any part of the present Bill is defective,' Lloyd George writes. 'It is merely an offer, limited to the affected counties, of an opportunity for that corner of Ireland to put its own case before the British electorate. With the exception of these four counties, the whole of Ireland would come immediately under the operation of the Home Rule Bill.'

Lloyd George's proposal presents the Irish Party with a dilemma. It is clear now that the government has shifted its position under the threat of an uprising in Ulster, and some concessions are going to be made. If Redmond and his colleagues are to remain in a position of influence, they will have to engage with the government on its terms. A simple rejection of the Lloyd George plan will not suffice. But the partition of Ireland is not something the nationalists can countenance.

Joe Devlin, the Belfast MP and de facto leader of the Ulster nationalists, is given the task of formulating a response to the chancellor. In a confidential memo for the government, Devlin reiterates the nationalists' argument that the danger posed by the UVF is 'grotesquely exaggerated'. Home Rule supporters in Belfast, who would be among the first victims of any outbreak of loyalist violence, 'regard the whole thing with absolute contempt, and are astonished that anybody outside Belfast should take it seriously', he writes.

He acknowledges the reality, however, that the government is poised to offer concessions to the Ulster Unionists. It is the Irish Party's position that in this event, the unity of Ireland in the Home Rule Bill must be preserved, and there should be no barrier put in the way of having all Irish people placed under the jurisdiction of an Irish parliament 'at the earliest possible moment'.

'We believe the case would be met by permitting 'Ulster' to claim exclusion after, say, ten years if her representatives were not satisfied with their treatment in the Irish Parliament,' he writes. In other words, the nationalists are now adopting the proposal made by Sir Horace Plunkett in his letter to *The Times* of 10 February.

Devlin suggests two additional concessions that could be offered to the loyalists: extra representation in the Irish parliament, and a different arrangement of the senate – the upper house to be established under Home Rule – to provide the unionists with additional safeguards against unfair treatment. 'This method of meeting the demand for concession to "Ulster" would preserve the main principles of the Bill intact, whilst offering terms to "Ulster" which all reasonable men must consider generous,' he concludes.

Lloyd George, however, is not convinced, and writes back to the nationalist leaders within a few days to argue the merits of his own plan over Devlin's. The government's information, he says, is that Devlin underestimates the threat of civil disturbance in Ulster. Granted, talk of 'civil war' is overstating things, but 'riots on a large and menacing scale' are in prospect.

The government, he adds, is aware of the difficulties confronting the Irish leaders and 'the impossibility of their assenting to any proposal which would involve the division of Ireland'. The Plunkett proposal favoured by Devlin would be an 'admirable way out of the difficulty' but for one problem: it most likely would not have the unionists' support. And without that, he argues, the threatened riots would still take place and the new Irish parliament would be established in the midst of a 'blood feud' between it and the Ulster Protestants. 'Ten years count as nothing in a bloodstained quarrel of this kind, and at the end of that experimental period the defeated Protestants and their sympathisers would certainly, under such circumstances, vote the exclusion of Ulster.'

A further advantage of his plan, he argues, is that if the Ulster unionists have to submit to Home Rule after the exclusion period has elapsed, it 'will be very difficult for them to get up another movement such as they have organised at great expense during the past couple of years'. If Edward Carson is forced to lead his troops down from the hill on which they currently stand, it will be very hard to march them back up again in a few years' time.

Lloyd George, then, is not for budging, but there is still much negotiating to do before the government's position is settled. At around the same time as the chancellor responds to Devlin's memo, Redmond receives a typically upbeat note from Birrell, the Irish chief secretary, assuring him that the prime minister has no intention of offering immediate concessions and will maintain the line that the government will not be bullied or intimidated by threats of bloodshed.

As word begins to filter out that the government is poised to concede to the Ulster unionists' demands and take at least part of the province out of the Home Rule scheme, northern nationalists become increasingly concerned. The newly formed Irish Volunteers organisation has been steadily building support and in February it announces plans for a major rally in Derry on 14 March. It urges every Home Rule supporter to attend 'and thus strengthen the hands of Mr Redmond and the Irish Party in any action they may take in the House of Commons'.

Redmond, fearful that the rally could provoke clashes between nationalists and loyalists, writes at once to the Bishop of Derry, Charles

McHugh, urging him to use his influence to have the demonstration called off. A disappointed McHugh accedes to the request but makes it clear, in his letter of reply, that he disagrees with Redmond's stance: 'The great object of the meeting was to give the Liberal Party to understand that the Nationalists of the North have their rights as well as the Orangemen, and that, while agreeable to make concessions, they were not prepared to accept a state of things that would be worse than if they had never stood up for Home Rule.'

Against this increasingly tense background in the north and throughout nationalist Ireland, negotiations on a revised Home Rule Bill intensify. On Friday, 17 February, Redmond, John Dillon and Joe Devlin meet Lloyd George and Birrell at the headquarters of the Treasury in London. The discussion goes well for the Irish Party leaders, with Lloyd George telling them that the prime minister agrees with their view that the nationalists should not be asked to support any changes to the bill unless they have already been accepted by the unionist opposition. Redmond also seeks an assurance, and receives it from Lloyd George, that any compromise put forward by the government will be its 'last word' on the matter, and no further concessions will be offered.

The following Monday, Redmond, Dillon and Devlin, this time accompanied by T.P. O'Connor, are in 10 Downing Street for a meeting with Asquith, Lloyd George and Birrell. Asquith repeats the assurance that whatever concession is offered by the government will be its last word. The Ulster Unionists are, in effect, to be given one final 'take it or leave it' offer.

On the same evening Redmond submits a detailed memorandum to the government outlining how far the Irish Party is prepared to go in the interests of securing a deal. He again expresses a preference for the 'Plunkett plan', giving Ulster the option of seceding from Home Rule after ten years. But, while not explicitly consenting to the Lloyd George county-exclusion plan, the memo acknowledges that this is the one the government favours as 'offering the best tactical advantages'.

Redmond says that he understands the latest proposal to encompass several things: the right of Ulster counties to remain outside an Irish parliament would be limited to three years, covering the period in which an election must take place; it must be implemented by a suspensory clause to the Home Rule Bill, meaning that after three years the counties concerned would automatically come under Home Rule without the need for further legislation; no other change of any kind would be made to the bill; and the Irish Party reserves its right to be consulted about how the excluded counties would be governed.

He specifies one further, fundamental consideration from the Irish Party's perspective: it can consider submitting this proposal to its people for consideration only on the basis that it is 'the price of peace', an expression Redmond uses repeatedly throughout the memorandum. If peace is not to be guaranteed in return for such a major concession, the government should proceed with the all-Ireland bill as it stands and face the consequences.

Redmond and his party have made a concession that only weeks earlier they could not have imagined themselves contemplating: they are prepared to accept an Irish parliament that does not have jurisdiction over all the counties of Ulster, albeit for a temporary period only and provided certain conditions are met.

But the concession has not been granted lightly. A few days later, Lloyd George tells his friend Sir George Riddell, the proprietor of the *News of the World*, that he has had a tough job. 'The Irish are rare negotiators. They bluff so well that you really cannot tell whether they are bluffing or not.' Coming from Lloyd George, an ace negotiator and a first-class bluffer when the occasion demands, this is high praise indeed.

Asquith replies to Redmond two days later, on 4 March, accepting the nationalist leader's terms. The outlines of an agreement are now in place, and the first task facing the Irish Party is to secure the support of those who will be most affected by it – the northern nationalists. To this end, Joe Devlin and South Down MP Jeremiah MacVeagh are dispatched to Ulster to sell the deal. Most crucial will be the backing of the Catholic hierarchy, and Devlin soon reports back to Redmond that bishops McHugh of Derry and O'Donnell of Raphoe are on board.

There is much concern about the potential reaction of Cardinal Michael Logue, a supporter of the cultural revival movement who has distrusted the leadership of the Irish Party in all its guises as far back as the time of the Parnell divorce case and earlier. But after meeting the Catholic primate on 5 March, MacVeagh writes to Redmond with good news: 'We were at Armagh to-day for two hours, and with splendid results. He was most gracious, and said he thought you had done the best possible under the circumstances. He prefers the Plunkett scheme, but would not let the other scheme stand in the way of peace. "The Bill must be saved," was the last thing he said to us. It was well we went, for he was restive until everything was explained to him. Of course he doesn't love the concessions, but will not object. We then motored to Newry and saw Dr [Henry] O'Neill [the Bishop of Dromore], who is also in agreement. We go to-morrow to Monaghan and Cavan.'

Devlin subsequently writes with confirmation of the positive outcome to their mission: northern nationalists will accept the terms of the deal, although 'not with the best grace ... they regard the compromise as extremely disappointing, but they feel we have done our best under all the circumstances.'

On 6 March, the proposals setting out the full scheme for the plebiscites in Ulster are circulated to members of the Cabinet. Voters are to be asked a question 'in something like the following form':

Are you in favour of the exclusion of the county from the Government of Ireland Act, 1914, for a period of _____ years?
Are you against the exclusion of the county from the Government of Ireland Act, 1914, for a period of _____ years?

Belfast is to be treated as a county for the purpose of the plebiscites, prompting Redmond to win a big concession from Asquith: if Belfast is to have a separate vote, Derry must be given that option too. This opens the way for Derry City, with its nationalist majority, to vote its way into a Home Rule parliament. But Redmond, in turn, makes a major concession of his own: Birrell tells him that Asquith, on reflection, has concluded that to be certain that an election must take place in the intervening period, it will be necessary to exclude the Ulster counties from Home Rule for five years rather than three. Redmond writes to the prime minister to tell him that an extension of the three-year period will increase the Irish Party's difficulties and cause 'the deepest disappointment', but he is prepared to accept it if Asquith considers it 'absolutely essential'.

Asquith does consider it essential. In fact, when he writes back to Redmond to express gratitude, five years has suddenly become six. Only a six-year exclusion can provide a guarantee that an election will take place during the period concerned, he says. From this moment on, however, Asquith and his colleagues speak of the necessity of having not just one but two general elections after the Irish parliament is established before the Ulster counties are required to come under its jurisdiction.

With Redmond having made this additional concession, then, the scene is finally set for the prime minister to tell the nation how the government plans to bring about an end to the crisis over Home Rule. On 9 March, the House of Commons is packed 'from wall to wall' – as the next day's London *Times* will describe it – as MPs and visitors gather in hushed anticipation of what Asquith will say when he moves the second reading of the Government of Ireland Bill. Members sit tightly wedged together and many have to squeeze themselves into standing positions at the perimeters of the chamber.

As Asquith arrives to take his place, he is cheered by his Liberal Party colleagues, but the Irish nationalist MPs uncharacteristically remain silent. The prime minister appears relaxed and confident, laughing at something Birrell whispers in his ear just before he begins his address at 3.45 p.m.

Speaking in a firm and deliberate tone, Asquith says that the government remains as convinced as ever of the merits of the Home Rule Bill as it stands. But if the bill is passed unchanged, there is a prospect of 'acute dissension and even civil strife' in Ulster. 'On the other hand, if at this stage Home Rule were to be shipwrecked, or permanently mutilated, or indefinitely postponed, there is in Ireland as a whole at least an equally formidable outlook.'

> The hazards in either event are such as to warrant in all quarters, I think, not, indeed, a surrender of principle, but any practical form of accommodation and approach which could lead to an agreed settlement. And it is obvious – it is no use blinking the fact – that such a settlement must involve, in the first place, on the side of our

opponents the acceptance of a Home Rule legislature and executive in Dublin, and, on the other hand, on the side of our supporters some form of special treatment for Ulster – for the Ulster minority – over and above any of the safeguards contained in this bill.

Before outlining the government's proposal, Asquith tells the house he prefers either of two alternative schemes. One of these is the Plunkett plan, allowing the Ulster counties to remove themselves from Home Rule for a period of time; the other, 'Home Rule within Home Rule', was put forward by Foreign Secretary Edward Grey, he says. Under this scheme Ulster would be included in an all-Ireland parliament, but if a majority of the province's representatives opposed any measure brought forward there, it could not be implemented in Ulster without the approval of the parliament at Westminster.

This is a scheme which Asquith likes very much, but it has 'one very serious drawback', he admits, to laughter from all sides of the house: 'It does not commend itself to any of the parties concerned.'

That leaves the government with a proposal it regards as 'an expedient' rather than a final settlement. Immediately after the passing of the Home Rule Bill into law, Asquith tells the house, any of the Ulster counties that so wishes may hold a plebiscite on remaining outside the scheme for six years. At the end of the exclusion period – which would begin from the date of the first meeting of the new Irish parliament – the counties concerned would come under Home Rule unless the Westminster parliament had decided otherwise in the meantime. 'Our proposals ... are put forward as the price of peace,' he declares, drawing cheers from his supporters and an audible 'hear, hear' from John Redmond.

The folly of anyone believing that temporary exclusion from the bill of some Ulster counties will be sufficient to secure peace is quickly exposed, however, when opposition leader Bonar Law rises to respond. If this really is the government's last word on the matter, he says, then the position seems to him to be very grave. If at the end of six years the Ulster counties that contract themselves out of Home Rule are required to come in, even though their hostility to Home Rule might be as strong as ever, he cannot see how this proposal can be accepted. 'It is a question of sentiment,' he says, 'of what those people in Ulster feel and are likely to feel. And no amount of argument can get over this simple fact, that if you think it is wrong to compel them to come in today, then how can you think it right to compel them to come in tomorrow?'

A sombre Redmond says the prime minister has gone to the 'extremist limits of concession', but if the government's proposal is accepted by the unionists as the basis of an agreement and of peace, 'then we on our side are prepared to accept it in the same spirit and to use all our influence with our people to induce them to work it with complete loyalty and good faith'. Only on that condition can the nationalists acquiesce to a scheme that, in truth, they do not like. 'I am perfectly well aware that in recommending that course to our people we are running the risk of misrepresentation and misunderstanding,' he says.

> All of us know well what a bitter disappointment a settlement of this kind would mean to many of the highest hopes of our people. We all recognise what a wrench it will mean to some of their inmost feelings and sentiments, what a sacrifice it will mean – and it will be bitter, let the house mark my words, it will be bitter, although the arrangement is a temporary one – to many of the ideals in which they have grown up to manhood and have cherished.

The nationalist leader then turns to Edward Carson, recalling his challenge in a recent debate to the nationalists to 'win' Ulster by demonstrating good government under Home Rule, instead of attempting to force the province into the scheme.

> Ah, sir, what a tragedy it is that the right honourable gentleman and his friends will not come in and help us to have good government in Ireland [cheers and Opposition laughter]. Well, we must deal with facts [Opposition cheers, and a voice: 'cattle driving!']. I recognise that according to his present view he will not do that; but I tell him respectfully that I believe he will live to see that he has taken a wrong course. I tell him respectfully that he will live to find that a short experience of the working of the government by

his own fellow countrymen will show him that his course has been mistaken.

The conciliatory words evaporate, however, when Redmond concludes with sharp advice for the government. The nationalists are willing to make a great sacrifice in the interests of peace, he says, but the sacrifice cannot be on one side only. If the unionists spurn this compromise, then the Irish Party must reject it too and demand that the bill goes through unaltered.

Speaking minutes later in a laboured voice because of an illness that threatened to keep him away from the debate, Carson begins with an unflinching personal attack on Redmond, further underlining the extent to which the battle over Home Rule has become a duel between the two men.

When I listened to the honourable and learned member for Waterford he will excuse me if I say that I could not take the sanguine view he professes to take as regards any compromise upon Home Rule leading to the great benefits which he professes to see; and I cannot even, I am afraid, entirely believe in his sincerity when he tries to hold out to us the great hopes and expectations of an Ireland governed with freedom when all the methods that have put him in his present position are those of violence and intimidation [cheers]. Why, he is the same honourable member who only a short time ago was telling us there was no Ulster question. He is the same gentleman who told us that, if there was a bigoted remnant, amongst whom he included myself, he would put us down with a strong arm, and he is also the gentleman who informed us in Ireland that the present opportunity which he held – meaning the number of votes he could control in the constitution of the present House of Commons – gave him the opportunity of tearing to pieces and trampling underfoot the Act of Union. I prefer to face facts rather than promises from the honourable member for Waterford [cheers].

When Carson turns to Asquith's proposals, the total failure of the government's attempt at compromise is laid bare. Ulster wants the matter settled now and for ever, he tells the house, adding, to loud cheers: 'We don't want sentence of death with a stay of execution of six years.' If the six-year time limit is not removed, Carson tells the prime minister, he is not prepared to even put the new proposal to the Ulster Unionists. Make exclusion from Home Rule permanent, however, and he would feel it his duty 'to go over to Ulster and call a convention and submit your proposals to the people'.

Some, including the next speaker, Labour leader Ramsay MacDonald, see cause for a flicker of hope in Carson's comments. If the only point of difference between the sides is the question of six years, he says, surely it is possible to come to an agreement? Writing hopefully the next day to Venetia Stanley, a young family friend with whom he has developed an infatuation, Asquith pronounces the proceedings a success, 'tho' it is too soon yet to say whether there is a real chance of *rapprochement*.

Far from bringing the sides closer together, however, Asquith's attempted compromise has made matters immeasurably worse. It has inflamed feelings in Ulster and weakened John Redmond's position, especially with the northern nationalists. The prime minister's 'settlement' is merely a precursor to further trouble.

Chapter 14 ∿

CHURCHILL TALKS TOUGH

*Let us go forward together and put these grave matters
to the proof.*

John Redmond's influential supporters in the United States are quick to tell him what they think of his decision to give up four Ulster counties – albeit temporarily – in order to get his Home Rule Bill through; Irish America, it seems, could not be more pleased with his efforts.

The telegrams for the Irish leader begin arriving at Westminster within hours of his speech on the government's county plebiscite proposal.

'The prayers of centuries and the hopes of generations have begun to be realised,' wires Cardinal William O'Connell, still in the early years of a near four-decade reign as leader of the Roman Catholic Church in Boston. The Governor of Illinois, Edward F. Dunne, is also in touch: 'Sincerely hope Bill will be successfully passed in the interest both of the British Empire and of Ireland.'

Many more such messages arrive before the evening has passed, as political and Irish community leaders salute Redmond's efforts. Gratified with the support on offer, he reads them in turn:

> From the Hon M.J. Ryan, Philadelphia, President of the United Irish League of America and Democratic candidate for the Governorship of Pennsylvania: Redmond, House of Commons, London – America will support you unflinchingly. – Ryan.
>
> The people of the State of Ohio will rejoice if the eight-centuries-old contest between England and Ireland is settled favourably to Ireland. – James M. Cox, Governor of Ohio.
>
> Congratulations upon consummation of victorious battle on behalf of justice. – James M. Curley, Mayor, Boston.

On and on come the messages of support, which are printed verbatim in the next day's *Cork Examiner*. The governors of Maine, New Hampshire, Michigan, Massachusetts, North Carolina and Nebraska, the Speaker of the Massachusetts House of Representatives, Champ Clarke, and Boston Senator Henry Cabot Lodge are others who send congratulations.

The messages of goodwill provide only a temporary respite for Redmond, who knows that the unionists' rejection of Asquith's temporary exclusion proposal has left him and his party in a vulnerable position. His strongly worded advice to the government that it must now proceed with the Home Rule Bill as it stands and face down the opposition from Ulster cannot disguise the fact that the nationalists have signed up to partition and got nothing in return.

On Wednesday, 11 March 1914 – two days after the Commons debate – Redmond and his most senior colleagues, John Dillon, T.P. O'Connor and Joe Devlin, have breakfast at 11 Downing Street with Lloyd George and Augustine Birrell. With attitudes in Ulster reported in the media to be hardening in favour of permanent exclusion from the bill, the Irish leaders are cheered to discover a corresponding determination in the government to proceed with the bill intact if the unionists persist in rejecting the compromise on offer.

In any case, amending the bill in the absence of an agreement with the unionists is not an option. Under the terms of the Parliament Act, which removed the House of Lords' veto over legislation, a bill from the Commons must go back to the Lords three times in identical form before it can be forced through against the will of the upper house. The Government of Ireland Bill – its official name – is now on its third and final journey back to the Lords; amending it at this stage would trigger a new process and reset the clock to 1912, when the bill was introduced. That is clearly not an option for the government or the Irish Party; the only way the bill can be amended now and enacted on schedule is by agreement with the opposition, which would ensure its passage through the House of Lords.

Redmond and his colleagues hold a further meeting with Lloyd George and Birrell two days later, by which time it is clear the government – stung by the unionists' cursory dismissal of Asquith's compromise offer – has been jolted into summoning some resolve to deal with the crisis head on.

A second factor, however, has also helped to force the government's hand. Police reports circulated to the Cabinet by Birrell on 11 March paint a disturbing picture of the current state of the UVF; it is now estimated to stand at eighty thousand strong and estimates of the arms at its disposal range from seventeen thousand rifles to suggestions that the entire force may be armed. Even more alarming is the disclosure of a confidential UVF circular seeking information about the strength of forces at police barracks, coastguard stations, post offices and railway stations in case these places need to be taken over; the circular also details UVF plans to sieze arms depots.

The government's response is to establish a Cabinet sub-committee, including Winston Churchill and Secretary of State for War Colonel John Seely, to deal with Ulster affairs. Among Churchill's first moves is the extraordinary decision to send a squadron of battleships from Spain to Lamlash, on the Scottish Isle of Arran, north of Belfast Lough.

With an outbreak of violence looking increasingly likely, several parties seem determined to turn up the heat. In a headline-making speech in Swansea on 13 March, Carson's fellow unionist MP for Dublin University, James Campbell – who within a decade will be the first chairman of the Free State Seanad – says that civil war is not merely a danger facing Ulster, it is 'the path of duty' for unionists.

Churchill makes an incendiary speech in Bradford the following day, in which he tells the unionists that the government has made them its final offer and if they reject it, 'it can only be because they prefer shooting to voting'. And if that is the course the Ulster loyalists want to take, well, 'there are worse things than bloodshed'.

The Ulster counties exclusion proposal involves 'the hardest sacrifice ever asked of Irish nationalists', Churchill tells his audience of nearly four thousand Liberal supporters, yet they are prepared to make it for the sake of peace.

When I think of the patience, the wisdom and the eloquence with which Mr Redmond has conducted this great, historic controversy, and when I think how dearly he and those who are working with him cherish the dream, the hope of a united self-governing Ireland, I can measure the cruel pang with which this temporary, but nonetheless serious, change has been accepted by him and the great mass of the Irish nation.

If Ulster seeks peace and fair play, 'she knows where to find it', he says, before concluding with a rallying cry that amounts to a challenge to the unionists to 'put 'em up':

If Ulstermen extend the hand of friendship it will be clasped by Liberals and their nationalist countrymen in all good faith and in all goodwill; but if there is no wish for peace, if every concession that is made is spurned and exploited, if every effort to meet their views is only to be used as a means of breaking down Home Rule and of barring the way to the rest of Ireland; if Ulster is to become a tool in party calculations, if the civil and parliamentary systems under which we have dwelt so long and our fathers before us are to be brought to the crude challenge of force, if the government and parliament of this great country and greater empire are to be exposed to menace and brutality, if all the loose, wanton and reckless chatter we have been forced to listen to these many months is in the end to disclose a sinister and revolutionary purpose, then I can only say to you: let us go forward together and put these grave matters to the proof [loud cheers].

Unionists are outraged by Churchill's 'menacing' address, as the Ulster-born Conservative MP Ronald McNeill will describe it, but Redmond is delighted. Addressing guests at a St Patrick's Day banquet in London, he lauds Churchill's 'great speech' and confidently asserts that Home Rule will be 'the law of the land' in a few weeks – and in its 'present shape', i.e. with Ulster included. Churchill, on his next appearance in the Commons, is greeted by a thunderous cheer from the Irish nationalist MPs.

Redmond also receives messages of support for his stance from local authorities all over Ireland. But almost all the motions passed at council meetings include calls to resist partition, and there are some explicit expressions of discontent. On the same day as Churchill's Bradford speech, Gorey District Council, in Redmond's home county of Wexford, unanimously passes a resolution protesting 'against the dismemberment of Ireland as an outrage against the aspirations of the Irish people' and asking the Irish Party leader to call a national convention to discuss the issue.

A motion before Mountmellick District Council in Queen's County – later County Laois – tendering 'hearty congratulations' to Redmond 'on his splendid fight for Irish freedom' provokes a row when two councillors oppose it, one of them, John Campion, declaring: 'I say that John Redmond at the present time has not the confidence of the Irish people. I say without reserve that they are the most disappointed people I know of.' This provokes indignant interruptions from fellow councillors, such as 'You must be a rancher!' and 'Go over to Carson!'

Redmond's acceptance of the government's proposal also hands a propaganda coup to his former party colleagues William O'Brien and Tim Healy, the leading figures in the rival nationalist group the All-for-Ireland League, which holds eight seats – all of them in Cork City or county – in the House of Commons.

Redmond and Healy have history that goes back to the beginning of Redmond's parliamentary career, when Charles Stewart Parnell asked him to stand aside in favour of Healy as the Irish Party's candidate for the Wexford seat vacated as a result of the death of Redmond's father, William Archer Redmond, in 1880. This delayed Redmond's entry to the House of Commons by only a few months, as he was soon – in February 1881, aged 24 – elected unopposed as the party's candidate for New Ross.

Nine years later, the two engaged in bitter exchanges as the leading protagonist on each side in the debate, played out in public in committee room 15 of the House of Commons, over Parnell's leadership after he was named in the divorce proceedings between Captain William O'Shea and his wife, Katharine, and Liberal leader William Gladstone insisted Parnell be jettisoned if his party was to maintain its alliance with the Irish nationalists.

Redmond's jousts with Healy were a feature of the proceedings. On the final day of debate, when Redmond quipped that deposing Parnell would make Gladstone 'the master of the [Irish] party', Healy came back with the rather low rejoinder: 'Who is going to be the mistress of the party?' In the uproar that followed, Parnell called Healy a 'little scoundrel' who 'in an assembly of Irishmen dares to insult a woman'.

Now, more than two decades on, Healy is at it again, in a fiery speech to an All-for-Ireland League convention in Cork, quoted verbatim in the League-supporting *Skibbereen Eagle*. Suggesting that Redmond is the worst of a succession of 'traitors' to the Irish cause, he asks: 'What man heretofore promoted the dismemberment of his country or asked for the banishment of over a million of his countrymen into a foreign state?'

> Cromwell said 'to hell or Connaught'. Redmond says 'to purgatory and Ulster' [laughter]. And we are content to vote for this infamous proposal ['Never! Never!'], that we should take it in silence and see our noble island degraded, perverted into a crippled gelding; we are to subscribe to doctrines such as these, support men who propose them [and] support a government who attempt this enormity.

Any hope that, amidst all the bombast, there might yet be scope for a settlement is soon dashed. When the matter comes back before the Commons, Asquith provokes fury on the Unionist benches by refusing to provide any further details on the government's Ulster-exclusion scheme until the opposition decides where it stands in principle. 'If our general proposal is rejected it will obviously be a waste of time to formulate for discussion all ancillary and consequential points of machinery and detail,' Asquith tells them, dismissively deflecting 26 questions on the Home Rule issue within 15 minutes.

Carson responds by describing the government's compromise proposal as 'a hypocritical sham', but a newly emboldened Asquith is unperturbed, writing to Venetia Stanley minutes after the exchange: 'We had a regular rough and tumble in the House just now at question time, which you would rather have enjoyed.'

Considered a private and inscrutable man by Cabinet colleagues, Asquith doesn't keep a personal diary. But he will continue to share his innermost thoughts and even Cabinet secrets with Stanley over the next year and a half, until she tells him of her decision to marry the Liberal MP Edwin Montagu, bringing her correspondence with the prime minister to an end.

Asquith's refusal to set out any more details of the county plebiscite proposals prompts Bonar Law to move a motion of censure against the government which, when taken on 19 March, ends any prospect of an immediate settlement. The proceedings begin on a hopeful note when Law – in a conciliatory speech at odds with his censure motion – makes Asquith an unexpected offer. Insisting that he is prepared to take 'great risks' to avert the 'calamity' of bloodshed, he says that if the government puts its Home Rule Bill to a UK-wide referendum, with the Ulster exclusion proposal included, his party will accept the verdict of the people.

Crucially, Law says that he has the support of Lord Lansdowne – leader of the Conservative and Unionist Party in the House of Lords and owner of an enormous estate in County Kerry – for this formal and 'solemn' proposal. If the British electorate votes for Home Rule, in other words, the House of Lords will do nothing to delay its enactment.

A surprised Asquith seizes on the proposal immediately, asking Law if he is saying that a referendum in favour of Home Rule would give the government the authority to coerce Ulster into an Irish parliament, and Law confirms that this is the case. The prime minister then turns to Carson, sitting adjacent to Law in the chamber: 'Would Ulster accept the decision?'

Carson parries the question: 'Does the prime minister give me a firm offer? If so I will answer it.' This draws a cheer from the opposition benches, but Asquith persists: 'This is not my offer, but I want to know what the consequences would be.'

> Carson: Is not that a hypothetical question? Where are the details? [Renewed opposition cheers]
> Asquith: I understand it is not answered. ['Wait and see!' 'Order! Order!']

The bemused prime minister – his voice hoarse as a consequence of a cold picked up at the weekend – says that the government's proposal is surely more favourable to the Ulster unionists than that just put forward by Law. It provides for two general elections to take place and for the opportunity to observe the Irish parliament in operation for six years before the Ulster counties concerned are brought under Home Rule. 'There is not a single area in Ulster that will be compelled to come in when this bill passes into law, if the opinion of the majority of the electorate is against it. Not till six years afterwards, not till twice has the electorate of the whole of the kingdom been consulted, can the inclusion, which we believe ought to take place, and will voluntarily take place as a result of that experience, become operative.'

The experience of seeing the Irish parliament in action, Asquith is arguing, will result in the Ulster unionists voluntarily joining it after the six-year exclusion period has elapsed. In making that claim, he conveniently ignores a question asked by Law moments earlier: 'If it be true, as the nationalist members tell us, that the working of the Irish parliament will make Ulster willing to come in ... what object is there in compelling them? And if they are not willing, what right have you to compel them?'

The serious debating gives way to melodrama when Carson enters the debate. Battling to overcome a mixture of boisterous interruptions and shouts of support from around the chamber, he says he intended to intervene at a later stage, 'but in consequence of many things that have happened, and not least of all in consequence of what I might call the trifling with this subject by the prime minister [opposition cheers and shouts of "oh!" "oh!" from the government benches] and the provocation which he has endorsed ["oh!" "oh!"] by the first lord of the admiralty [Churchill] last Saturday, I feel that I ought not to be here but in Belfast [cheers, laughter and a shout: "with your sword on!"].'

'We have it now,' he adds, '... from the prime minister, that this is the [government's] last word. Very well, if it is the last word, what more have we to do here?'

Carson argues that only the continuing influence of John Redmond is preventing the government from offering the Ulster counties permanent exclusion from Home Rule.

They know perfectly well that the reason they will not take away this [six-year] time limit for the exclusion, which their own press and many of their own members opposite admitted was a reasonable application, is that they have been once more called upon by the honourable and learned gentleman, the member for Waterford, to toe the line [cheers]. Yes, and they have toed it once more. It would have been just as well if they had never taken away their toe at all. Having been all this time a government of cowards, now they are going to entrench themselves behind his majesty's troops [cheers], and they have been discussing over at the War Office for the last two days how many they will require, and whether they will mobilise. They have been all this time, as I said before, manoeuvring for position [cheers].

The atmosphere in the chamber turns from fraught to poisonous when Joe Devlin, speaking for the nationalists, suggests that Carson was once a Home Ruler who became a unionist for reasons of political expediency. Challenging Carson on an assertion made during his speech that, in defending the Ulster unionist cause, he is 'not on the make', Devlin says he does not know 'what a great lawyer means by a 'politician on the make', but he will tell the house what 'an untutored layman' means by it:

When a young lawyer in a moment of youthful and generous enthusiasm follows the banner of a great cause for the sake of all that is good in it, and becomes an ardent Home Ruler, and then when the forces of honour and justice are beaten joins the forces of a powerful enemy – that is what I pronounce a man on the make [cheers].

Jumping to his feet, a visibly angry Carson says that Devlin's claim is 'an infamous lie and he knows it'. Amid disorderly scenes, Carson accedes to a request from the speaker to withdraw the unparliamentary accusation of lying. 'The statement made by the honourable member is one that has been repeated and contradicted many times. At the same time I ask leave to withdraw the words "infamous lie" and to say "wilful falsehood" [loud cheers and counter cheers].' Devlin ignores a barrage of shouts to withdraw his remark.

His comment was a cheap shot, and Carson's anger is understandable. It is true that Carson spent the greater part of his early legal career representing nationalist Irish tenant farmers in cases arising from the then newly passed 1881 Land Act, which granted smallholders the 'three FS' – fair rent, fixity of tenure and free sale. But he also took cases for landlords: given the new land legislation, it was a boom time for lawyers.

So successful was he, however, in acting for the tenant farmers that his nationalist colleagues at the bar mistook him for one of their own, inviting him to stand for parliament in Waterford – John Redmond's future constituency – as a 'no rent' candidate. They were surprised to be told by Carson that he was disqualified on two grounds: he was a unionist, not a nationalist, and in any case he had no time for politics.

Devlin's jibe persuades Carson he has had enough and it is time to make good on his assertion that he ought to be in Belfast. To jeers and shouts of 'Run away!' from the government and nationalist benches and a standing ovation and loud cheers from the opposition, he rises from his seat and makes for the nearest door, behind the Speaker's chair. As he passes the Speaker he turns, raises his right arm and waves it – whether as an act of defiance or a salute to his supporters, or a combination of both, nobody is sure.

With that, the Ulster Unionist leader is on his way to be with his people as they face whatever the coming days will bring. That may be a confrontation with the army but, in his speech a short time earlier, Bonar Law has once again raised the spectre of the army refusing to obey the government's orders should it move against the Ulster loyalists. 'And what about the army?' he asked the prime minister. 'We really have got to a stage when we must face facts. What about the army? If it is only a question of disorder, the army, I am sure, will obey you, and I am sure that it ought to obey you. But if it is really a question of civil war, soldiers are citizens like the rest of us.'

While welcoming Law's moderate tone, Asquith disagrees with his comments on the duties and functions of the army in a case of civil war. 'Who is to be the judge whether any particular contest in which the armed forces of the crown are called upon to intervene does or does not fall within the category of civil war? Is it to be left to the judgment of the individual soldier, or of the officer in command, or of the general? Such a proposition as that seems to me to strike at the very root of our society.'

What Asquith doesn't yet know is that Law is engaging in more than idle speculation in wondering aloud what the army might do in the event of a military move against the Ulster unionists. The prime minister will soon discover that senior officers in the army have been collaborating with the Conservative Party leadership over how best to respond to the threat of Home Rule. The answer to Law's question – 'What about the army?' – is soon to be delivered. And it will shake the Liberal government and the British state to their foundations.

Chapter 15

THE CURRAGH DEBACLE

The Ulster Orange plot is now completely revealed.

Since his appointment in 1911 as Commander-in-Chief of the British armed forces in Ireland, General Sir Arthur Paget has gone about his duties with a quiet efficiency, notwithstanding the occasional foray into the newspaper society columns in the company of his American-born wife. A typical example is this from the pages of the *Irish Independent* of 8 August 1913: 'General Sir Arthur Paget has returned to the Curragh. Lady Paget has been at Aix les Bains, and will join Sir Arthur Paget at the Royal Hospital for the Dublin Show at the end of the month.'

The same paper, two weeks later, reported: 'The guests at the house-party given last night by General Sir Arthur Paget and Lady Paget numbered 280. The dancing took place in the spacious hall, which was resplendent in its historic and picturesque armour trophies. The lounges and buffet rooms adjoining were lavishly decorated with palms, flowers, and draped with flags and vari-coloured drapery. Mr Clarke Barry's band supplied the music.'

Being Commander-in-Chief in Ireland is evidently not a bad life, but on 14 March 1914, Sir Arthur's equilibrium is disturbed by an unwelcome dispatch from the War Office in London.

The letter, sent on the orders of Secretary of State for War Colonel John Seely, tells him that the government has information that attempts may be made in various parts of Ireland by 'evil-disposed persons' to obtain arms and ammunition from army depots. It advises Paget to take special precautions to safeguard stores, and adds that those at Armagh, Omagh, Carrickfergus and Enniskillen in particular may be insufficiently guarded.

Paget, prone to an over-active imagination, almost certainly sees this communication as something more sinister than a routine instruction to ensure that government arms are safely locked away. More likely, he interprets the letter as something he has been dreading: the start of a military move by the government to impose Home Rule on the loyalists of Ulster.

Although Paget has largely kept himself out of the news, a remarkable speech he made a fortnight before receiving Seely's dispatch propelled him into the headlines.

In an address to members of the Corinthian Club – a men's dining club – at the Gresham Hotel in Dublin, Paget said it was 'not thinkable' for him to contemplate even being asked to move his men against the UVF. 'It may be, God forbid it should be, my lot to be ordered to move to the north,' he continued. 'I should regret it. I have no doubt that many of the officers present here tonight – many officers, friends of you all – would hate the very idea of moving one mile north of Dublin. But if the order comes they know that that order must be obeyed ["hear, hear"]. And if the order was not obeyed it means that the army is not in that state of discipline in which you would wish to see it.'

Paget fails to act on the instructions he is given, prompting an angry Seely to telegraph again on 16 March, seeking a report by 8 a.m. the next day on his plans to secure the depots, and summoning him to London. Paget replies that he has taken 'all available steps', but before leaving for London on the 17th, he writes again to Seely.

In this letter, Paget says he thinks there are sufficient troops at Enniskillen to guard the depot and he is arranging for a slight increase in the force at Carrickfergus. At Omagh and Armagh, he has decided to remove the stores of munitions rather than increase troop numbers, which will take about eight days. 'In the present state of the country,' he explains, 'I am of opinion that any such move of troops would create intense excitement in Ulster, and possibly precipitate a crisis. For these reasons I do not consider myself justified in moving troops at the present time, although I am keeping a sufficient number in readiness to move at short notice, in case the situation should develop into a more dangerous state.'

This comes as a red rag to a government seriously concerned about the security situation in Ulster as a result of the police reports circulated by Augustine Birrell to the Cabinet on 11 March. As soon as

Paget arrives in London, the government orders Major General Lovick Friend, who has been left in charge in Ireland, to send the required reinforcements to the four towns considered most vulnerable to raids. Additional troops are also to be sent to Newry and Dundalk.

To the great frustration of ministers, Friend writes back that 'it is rather doubtful if the Northern Railway will allow troop trains to travel northward.' This is too much for Winston Churchill, who dispatches two cruisers to Kingstown with orders to convey the troops to Dundalk by sea if necessary. Friend is now spurred into action, and the soldiers are moved north by rail without difficulty.

The atmosphere is already fraught, then, by the time Paget begins two days of talks in London with several ministers, including Seely and Churchill, as well as his military superiors. Asquith takes part in at least one of the discussions, which range from the immediate issue at hand – securing the depots the government is concerned about – to the wider question of army preparedness for an outbreak of hostilities in Ulster.

What exactly is said and by whom will be a matter of much controversy afterwards, but one thing is clear: Paget, with the help of the Chief of the Imperial General Staff Sir John French, secures a commitment from Seely that in the event of a conflict with the UVF, army officers living in the province will be allowed to 'disappear' and to resume their positions once operations cease. Officers not living in Ulster, though, will be required to obey orders, under threat of dismissal.

Back in Dublin, Paget manages to communicate this message to his officers, not as a concession but as an ultimatum, leaving at least some of them to think they are required to choose there and then between taking part in operations in Ulster or leaving the army. That certainly is the interpretation of General Hubert Gough, commander of the Cavalry Brigade at the Curragh, who conveys Paget's stipulation to his men, with predictable results.

At 7 p.m. that evening the War Office receives a telegram from Paget: 'Officer commanding 5th Lancers states that all officers except two, and one doubtful, are resigning their commissions to-day. I much fear same conditions in the 16th Lancers. Fear men will refuse to move.'

A second telegram follows shortly before midnight: 'Regret to report Brigadier and fifty-seven officers Third Cavalry Brigade prefer to accept dismissal if ordered north.'

It is a Friday night and Asquith is playing bridge – a favourite recreation – at the home of Venetia Stanley's father, Lord Sheffield, when he is called from the table and told the news. Seely is already in his office, where a reporter from *The Times* finds him working after midnight. He says he is aware of the 'rumours' of officer resignations and that 'appropriate steps' will be taken to deal with those concerned. He and Churchill meet in the small hours of the Saturday morning to consider what to do.

Gough and the other commanding officers involved are immediately relieved of their posts and summoned to London to explain their actions, but ministers soon get wind of the extent to which the whole affair may be down to Paget's bungled delivery of the government's message in the first place.

In a letter to Venetia Stanley later on the Saturday, Asquith indicates that a full-blown crisis may be avoidable. After telling her of the 'alarming news', he continues:

> The Brigadier – Gough – is a distinguished Cavalry officer, an Irishman, & the hottest of Ulsterians, and there can be little doubt that he has been using his influence with his subordinates to make them combine for a strike. We sent orders for him & the 3 Colonels to come here at once and they will arrive this evening. Meanwhile, from what one hears to-day it seems likely that there was a misunderstanding. They seem to have thought, from what Paget said, that they were about to be ordered off at once to shed the blood of the Covenanters, and they say they never meant to object to do duty like the other troops in protecting depots &c & keeping order. This will be cleared up in a few hours: but there have been all sorts of agitations and alarums in high quarters.

When Gough and his colleagues arrive in London to account for themselves, their first port of call is not the War Office but the home of Field Marshal Sir Henry Wilson, director of military operations at that office. Wilson, a Longford-born dyed-in-the-wool unionist and ace political agitator, sees a golden opportunity to strike a fatal blow to any government plans to move against the Ulster loyalists, and perhaps even to scupper the Home Rule Bill.

Following his Monday morning breakfast meeting with Gough at his home, Wilson then calls to the home of Conservative Party leader Bonar Law, the third such meeting between them since the Curragh controversy erupted on Friday night. Wilson has even secured from Gough a written report of what Arthur Paget told them on the previous Friday, and passed this to Law so that he might 'use it', as Wilson puts in his diary.

Law and Wilson now finalise a plan they have been hatching all weekend, agreeing that Gough must seek a guarantee in writing that he will not be called on to employ his troops in the coercion of Ulster to accept Home Rule.

Why General Gough, who has been relieved of his post and summoned to the War Office to justify himself, might be in a position to do anything more than beg for his job, might seem odd at first sight. But Wilson and Law know that the government will be anxious to put a lid on the Curragh controversy as quickly as possible and can see that Gough has an opportunity to turn the situation to his – and their – advantage.

This level of co-operation between the leader of the opposition in parliament and one of the highest-ranking officers in the army would be astonishing, were it not for the fact that it is already routine; Law and Wilson have been collaborating on their opposition to Home Rule for many months.

They have in recent times been discussing a plan that would see the Conservative Party refuse to pass the Army Annual Bill in the House of Lords in the absence of a government commitment that troops could never be used to coerce Ulster into Home Rule. Such a move by the Tories would cause the automatic disbandment of the army, leaving Britain defenceless at a time of increasing tensions between the great European powers. It is a prospect that ought to horrify Wilson, but he has given the idea his blessing in the interests of helping to defeat Home Rule.

Asquith is aware of the Tory threat to force the army to stand down – and mentioned it to John Redmond in their meeting on 2 February. Neither of them, however, is aware of the extent to which the army is prepared to be complicit in its own demise in order to further the Conservative Party's aims.

In addition to approving the Tories' plan to block the Army Bill, Wilson has felt free to offer Law advice on politics, as recorded in his diary following an earlier meeting between the two:

> I said before the Lords touch the Army Annual Act he (B.L.) should get up in the House of Commons and ask Asquith the point-blank question, 'Are you going to ask the Army to coerce Ulster or are you not?' As Asquith is sure to return an evasive answer, Bonar Law must anticipate by saying, 'There are three ways of answering the question, i.e. Yes-No-No answer. In the event of No answer, the inference will be Yes'; and Bonar Law should say that, if Asquith gives an evasive answer, it will be counted by him and his party and the country as meaning Yes.

This is far from the first time Wilson has proffered advice to Law on anti-Home Rule tactics, as this entry in his diary from November 1913 makes clear:

> We [Wilson and Law] then discussed the Linlithgow and Reading [by-]elections. Asquith was going to approach B.L. with a proposal to exclude the 4 Northern Counties [from Home Rule]. This, of course, wrecks the present Bill, and puts B.L. into an awkward position, as Ulster won't agree; and then Asquith can claim intolerance. On the other hand, Asquith is in a much tighter place, because Johnnie Redmond and Devlin can't agree to the exclusion of Ulster. The thing to do, therefore, is to make Redmond wreck the proposal.

John Redmond already knows that his opponents in the fight for Home Rule, with their explicit threats of armed resistance, are not playing by the rules of parliamentary politics. If he was aware of the secret talks between Law and Wilson, however, he would realise just how far the rules of the game are being bent. He and the government would also understand the basis for Law's and Carson's increasingly bullish statements about the likelihood of army officers refusing to take part in a mobilisation against Ulster.

Asquith does not yet know about Wilson's behind-the-scenes manoeuvrings, but within 48 hours of the Curragh incident, he has a full grasp of the consequences, writing again to Venetia Stanley on Sunday, 22 March, the day before Gough arrives for talks at the War Office, 'there is no doubt if we were to order a march upon Ulster that about half the officers in the Army – the Navy is more uncertain – would strike. The immediate difficulty in the Curragh can, I think, be arranged, but that is the permanent situation, & it is not a pleasant one.' He adds that he has spent an hour with the king that day, and found him 'a good deal perturbed'.

King George would be even more concerned if he knew that the government was set to make further blunders the following day. After the Cabinet meets at 10 Downing Street on Monday, it signs off on a memo expressing satisfaction that the resignations of Gough and his men were due to a misunderstanding, and stating that Paget's intention was only to ensure that lawful orders for the protection of lives and properties would be obeyed. This fails to satisfy Wilson, however, and both he and Gough press for a specific assurance that the army will not be required to enforce Home Rule in Ulster in the event of it becoming law.

Seely, despite being the minister directly concerned, is not present when the Cabinet agrees the wording of the memo because he had to leave the meeting to go to Buckingham Palace for an audience with the king. He returns just as the meeting is breaking up and, pressed by Gough and Wilson, agrees to add two sentences to the memo on his own responsibility. These state that the government retains the right to use the army to maintain law and order, 'but they have no intention whatever of taking advantage of this right to crush political opposition to the policy or principles of the Home Rule Bill'.

There, with the stroke of a pen, the secretary of state for war has – without consulting his Cabinet colleagues – removed the government's right to employ the army to enforce Home Rule in Ulster. The amended memo is also signed by French, the Chief of Staff, and Adjutant General Sir John Ewart, who both think it has been approved by the Cabinet.

But Gough and his fellow commanding officers are still not satisfied. They demand – and secure – a further written assurance from French that his interpretation of the additional sentences is the same as theirs, namely that under no circumstances will their troops 'be called upon to enforce the present Home Rule Bill on Ulster and that we can so assure our officers'.

Seely's miscalculation – which will cost him, French and Ewart their jobs – kills any chance of a line being drawn under the controversy at this stage. Even before word of the additional guarantees given to Gough and his colleagues gets out, the matter is a cause of uproar in parliament, with a straight-faced Law telling the House of Commons on the Monday afternoon that the army is in danger of being 'destroyed before our eyes'.

It is immediately apparent that the Conservatives are not sheltered from this storm, throwing light as it does on the party's undue influence with the armed forces. The Tories, indeed, are placed on the back foot by a devastating speech by a Labour MP, John Ward, leader of the Navvies' Union, who draws attention to the true significance of the negotiations just concluded with Gough and his colleagues.

We understand here to-day that the War Office have consulted with certain generals as to whether they will carry out orders. I am bound to say that the very first thing a recruit in the army is taught, as a common soldier, is the necessity for absolute obedience to his superiors. He never gets a lecture upon the goose step to start with, unless it is drummed into his ears that henceforth he ceases to be either a socialist, a Liberal, a Tory or a Labour man, and is, for the future, a soldier who must obey any order given to him. ...

This debate is the best illustration that we workmen have ever had in this house that all the talk about there being one and the same law for the rich and the poor is all a miserable hypocrisy. Honourable gentlemen belonging to the wealthy classes have no more intention of obeying the law that is against their interests than they have of flying to the moon. The law is for us – the poor men.

For a fleeting moment, the government appears to be off the hook, and even the unionist London *Times* declares on Tuesday, 24 March that the controversy 'may now be regarded as at an end'.

But then, on the following day, an emotional Seely tells the House of Commons that he inserted the additional sentences – which become known as the 'peccant paragraphs' – without Cabinet approval. He says he has offered his resignation to the prime minister.

Asquith, who says Seely has acknowledged an error of judgement in very trying circumstances and therefore his resignation has not been accepted, then tells the house that he first learned of the additional assurance given to Gough when he received a typewritten copy of the document on the previous night. Repudiating Seely's promise not to use the army to enforce Home Rule, he draws a standing ovation and an outburst of cheering and handkerchief-waving from the Liberal and nationalist benches with a declaration:

> So long as we are responsible for the government of this country, whatever the consequences may be, we shall not assent to the claim of any body of men in the service of the Crown, be they officers or men – it makes no difference for this purpose – to demand from the government, in advance, assurances of what they will or will not be required to do in circumstances which have not yet arisen. The new claim, as a claim, if once admitted, would put the government and the House of Commons, upon whose confidence the government depend, at the mercy of the military and navy.

The prime minister knows, though, that he is attempting to put the genie back in the bottle, and the position remains as he outlined it to Venetia Stanley three days earlier: the government has lost the authority to order the army to crush a rebellion in Ulster.

Further mis-steps by the government continue to fuel the crisis. A White Paper purporting to set out all the facts of the Curragh incident is found to have significant omissions, and the Cabinet is forced to issue a revised version weeks later. The drip-feed nature of the information coming into the public domain fuels Tory allegations of a government 'plot' to provoke an uprising in Ulster which it is now desperately trying to cover up.

A few days later, the resignations of Seely, French and Ewart are accepted. Asquith makes himself secretary of state for war, and in that office discovers the extent of Henry Wilson's collaborations with the Conservative Party. Characteristically, he decides to take no action against him, writing in his memoirs: 'I was strongly tempted to send him for a while to cool his head and heels "Where the remote Bermudas ride/In ocean's bosom unespied"; a disciplinary step he well deserved. But I was anxious to promote a temper of appeasement, and I had a genuine appreciation of his military qualities.'

In public, John Redmond and his party have kept out of the controversy, but in private he is fuming and knows how much damage has been done to the nationalist cause. He gives full vent to his anger in a cable to supporters in Australia:

> The Ulster Orange plot is now completely revealed. Carson and his army have not, and never had, the slightest intention of fighting as a fighting force. Against the regular troops they could not hold out a week. The plan was to put up the appearance of a fight, and then, by Society influences, to seduce the Army officers, and thus defeat the will of the people. The actions of the commanders of some crack cavalry regiments, officered by aristocrats, has now fully disclosed the plan of campaign. The issue raised is wider even than Home Rule. It is whether the Government are to be browbeaten and dictated to by the drawing rooms of London, seconded by officers who are aristocrats and violent Tory partisans. The cause of Irish freedom in this fight has become the cause of popular freedom, indeed, of liberty, throughout the world. It is impossible to doubt the result of such a fight.

His optimistic tone belies the reality that the government has been severely weakened by the Curragh episode. And a further blow to its authority is about to be delivered.

Chapter 16 ～

GUN-RUNNING AT LARNE

Individuals are menaced, and the nation has been outraged.

The roads of Ulster have never been as busy as on the night of Friday, 24 April 1914.

More than half the car owners in the province have, since the previous summer, placed their vehicles at the disposal of the UVF's 'motor corps', and tonight about six hundred drivers are participating in the UVF's biggest trial mobilisation to date. Unknown to the drivers and their passengers, however, this is no preparatory drill.

Only when the motorists reach the port of Larne, as directed, and find themselves driving bumper-to-bumper in an apparently endless procession of cars do they realise that a major operation is underway.

A cordon has been placed around the town by members of the volunteers and only those with a UVF-provided pass are allowed through. Wire communications to the port – and to those at Donaghadee and Bangor – have been cut off. Checkpoints have been set up on roads across the province, and police and coastguard officers have been confined to their barracks by UVF members staging 'pickets' outside.

The sight of so many cars coming downhill into the town, headlights on, provokes intense excitement in Larne. Few locals will sleep tonight. Many families turn their homes into improvised canteens, providing tea, coffee and sandwiches to those involved in this as-yet mysterious operation. The motorists wait in drizzling rain for more than two hours before a steamer, bearing the false name *Mountjoy II* in a nod to the vessel that broke the boom that ended the Siege of Derry in 1689, appears from around the Islandmagee peninsula.

The drivers are instructed to draw up their cars and then, bale by bale, the ship's cargo of 25,000 rifles fitted with bayonets, and a million rounds of ammunition, purchased in Hamburg, is unloaded. Drivers are told where to deposit their loads before coming back to repeat the exercise, and within a few hours most of the cargo has been distributed to loyalist homes and premises throughout the province. Meanwhile, a motor boat carries off a consignment to Donaghadee. Then at 5 a.m. the so-called *Mountjoy II*– its registered name is the *Clydevalley* – makes its way to Bangor, where the last of its freight is unloaded and distributed in daylight.

On board the vessel for the entire operation is its mastermind, Frederick Hugh Crawford, a retired army auxiliary officer and now head of a secret sub-committee established by the UVF to source arms. Crawford's unionist credentials are impeccable and long established: he once fostered a plan to kidnap William Gladstone on the Brighton promenade and transport him to a remote Pacific island, but had to drop it due to lack of financial support.

The successful organisation of the Larne gun-running is the outstanding achievement of his life. The 216-ton cargo has been at sea for almost a month since it departed the German port city of Kiel, and numerous obstacles have been overcome to get it to Larne, including an inspection by Danish authorities that came close to blowing the cover on the entire scheme.

Crawford's daring coup – carried out with the authorisation of Edward Carson and the Ulster Unionist Council – causes a sensation in the press and consternation in the government.

Unionist-supporting papers are breathless in their admiration of the achievement. 'For sheer audacity, perfect organisation, and determination, the gun-running exploitation carried to a complete success on Friday night and early this morning by the Ulster Volunteer Force will rank equal, if not superior, to any undertaking recorded in history,' begins the *Irish Times* report, datelined 'Belfast, Saturday night' and published on Monday, 27 April.

After a brief outline of the extent of the operation, the report says that a mere mention of the acts involved – patrolling roads, sabotaging telecommunications, seizing a railway station, etc. – is 'a serious matter, but nothing can be gained by trying to conceal the facts, and the Ulster Volunteer Force say they are "prepared to stand by their guns"'.

A shocked Augustine Birrell telegrams the news to the prime minister at his country home in Berkshire, and Asquith immediately returns to 10 Downing Street for a Saturday conference with the Irish chief secretary, at which it is agreed that the government needs to take firm steps to restore its authority. In the House of Commons on Monday, Asquith describes the gun-running as 'a grave and unprecedented outrage' and says the government will take the 'appropriate steps' without delay.

If these steps are to include prosecutions, then Edward Carson quickly puts himself at the head of the queue when, in reference to the landing of arms, he tells the Commons: 'I take full responsibility for that. You need not drag it out of me. I take full responsibility.'

This is not just a token statement. In an account of the escapade published many years later, Crawford will recall a meeting with Carson in London in early 1914 in which he impressed on the Ulster Unionist leader the risks involved for both of them in sourcing arms from Germany, warning that it could land both of them in jail.

> I so well remember the scene. We were alone. Sir Edward was sitting opposite me. When I had finished his face was stern and grim, there was a glint in his eyes which I had not seen before. He rose to his full height, looking me in the eyes, and advanced to where I was sitting. He stared down at me, shook his fist in my face, and in a steady and determined voice which thrilled through me, said 'Crawford, I'll see you through this business, even if I should have to go to prison for it.'

It very soon becomes clear, however, that neither Carson nor anybody else will be going to prison. After meeting on four successive days, the Cabinet at last decides, on Thursday, 30 April, not to prosecute anybody involved in the gun-running. It does send a cruiser and 18 destroyers to patrol the coasts of Antrim and Down, where they are saluted by UVF signallers who join them in singing 'God Save the King'.

In the meantime, an unexpected development in the Home Rule saga lightens the mood at Westminster and renews hopes of a settlement. In a Commons debate on 28 April arising from the Curragh incident,

Winston Churchill catches the opposition off guard with a surprising proposal, though not before he issues a far-sighted warning to the Conservatives about the potential consequences of their support for armed resistance in Ulster.

> Irish nationalists have always been urged by both great parties in the state to abandon unconstitutional agitation. They have not only been urged to do so, but great violence has been used against them. For a very long time they have staked their fortunes upon constitutional and parliamentary agitation [shouts of 'cattle driving!', 'moonlighting!'] and now they have brought their cause to the very threshold of success. If by an act of violence and under threats of violence the cause of Home Rule were to be shattered now, I say that the Conservative Party would themselves have taught the nationalists of Ireland the truth that there was in [the late Liberal MP] John Bright's famous saying that Ireland never gained anything but by force.

After a typically forceful defence of the government's right to use the army in Ulster as it sees fit – 'if rebellion comes, we shall put it down, and if it comes to civil war, we shall do our best to conquer in the civil war' – Churchill ends with an appeal to Carson to 'run some risk for peace', before making him an offer:

> Today I believe most firmly, in spite of all the antagonism and partisanship of our politics and our conflicting party interests, that peace with honour is not beyond the reach of all. Tomorrow it may be gone for ever. I am going to run some little risk on my own account by what I will now say. Why cannot the right honourable and learned gentleman say boldly, 'Give me the amendments to this Home Rule Bill which I ask for, to safeguard the dignity and the interests of Protestant Ulster, and I in return will use all my influence and goodwill to make Ireland an integral unit in a federal system.'

Churchill is back on old ground, suggesting that the solution to the Irish question might be a federal United Kingdom with 'Home Rule' parliaments all round, in Scotland, Wales and perhaps regions within England. Supporters of this idea believe that it offers many advantages; it would free up the imperial parliament at Westminster to focus on the business of the British Empire, while assuring unionists in Ulster that in joining a united Irish parliament their standing as citizens in a federal UK would not be diminished.

His question to Carson suggests a possible bargain: the government could agree to exclude Ulster from the Home Rule Bill if Carson in turn supported the setting up, further down the road, of a federal scheme under which Ireland would be an 'integral unit'.

John Redmond is horrified at this intimation that the government's 'last word', i.e. the offer of exclusion of some Ulster counties for six years, may not be its bottom line after all. He writes an immediate letter of protest to Asquith, saying he and his colleagues cannot go one step beyond the concession already offered.

On the following day, 29 April, Asquith makes it clear, under opposition questioning, that Churchill was speaking 'on his own account' and not on behalf of the government, but he qualifies this by saying that he is 'heartily in sympathy' with the spirit in which the offer to Carson has been made.

Carson responds in kind, telling the Commons that he is 'as anxious as any man living to find a way out of this Ulster difficulty which will avoid bloodshed'. He has always made it clear, he says, that the Ulster unionists could not complain if a federal system was introduced under which they had equal status with other citizens of the United Kingdom.

He then addresses the obvious question that arises from this stance: is he suggesting that loyalist Ulster would be happy to join an Irish parliament once a UK-wide federal scheme was introduced? Carson says it is impossible to answer without first seeing how a Home Rule parliament performs. 'Supposing the parliament is a failure? Supposing it is disastrous?' Churchill surely does not expect Ulster to commit itself in advance to joining an Irish parliament regardless of its success or failure?

No, sir, but I shall try to make an advance on what I said before. I will say this – and I hope the house will believe me, because though I do not want to be introducing my own personality into it – I am myself a southerner in Ireland – I would say this: That if Home Rule is to pass, much as I detest it, and little as I will take any responsibility for the passing of it, my earnest hope, and indeed, I would say my most earnest prayer, would be that the government of Ireland for the south and west would prove, and might prove, such a success in the future, notwithstanding all our anticipations, that it might be even for the interest of Ulster itself to move towards that government, and come in under it and form one unit in relation to Ireland. May I say something more than that? I would be glad to see such a state of affairs arising in Ireland, in which you would find that mutual confidence and goodwill between all parts of Ireland, and between all classes in Ireland, as would lead to a stronger Ireland as an integral unit in the federal scheme. While I say all that, that depends upon goodwill, and never can be brought about by force.

This intimation by Carson that there are some circumstances in which Ulster unionists might be willing to come under a united Irish parliament prompts newspaper headlines. 'A HOME RULE SURPRISE', says the *Independent*, over the sub-headline: 'Sir E Carson's new attitude'.

The Churchill–Carson exchange also brings about a sudden burst of optimism in Westminster – albeit not shared by John Redmond – that a deal may be achievable after all. The new mood in London contrasts sharply with that in nationalist Ireland, which is outraged by the recent developments. The Curragh 'mutiny', as it is perceived, and the Larne gun-running have combined to provide a huge boost to the Irish Volunteers and to those arguing for militant measures to vindicate Ireland's right to self-determination.

The new mood is exemplified by a letter to the *Freeman's Journal* from economics professor Tom Kettle, a former Irish Party MP and now a member of the provisional governing body of the Irish Volunteers. Written as Kettle was passing through Larne on the day after the gun-running, the letter calls for a 'prompt and worthy' response from nationalists.

> What is the moral, and what must be the reply? They can be stated very simply. The Government by its Arms Proclamation forbade Nationalist Ireland to undertake the task of defending itself. A corrupted army, a police and customs staff, at best hoodwinked and at worst corrupted also, have shown in a sudden flash that the government established in this country is not able to defend us.
>
> No Nationalist in Ulster can, after last night, hold his property, his civil liberties, or even his life safe. Individuals are menaced, and the nation has been outraged. A clear and instant reply must be made. The Government must withdraw the Arms Proclamation at once. A demand for that should go up forthwith from every Nationalist, and every national organisation in Ireland. Forthwith every able-bodied National Irishman should enrol himself in the Irish Volunteers. And forthwith every self-respecting man should dip his hand into his pocket to provide himself and his poorer fellow with a modern rifle.

Kettle, also a barrister and writer of note, concludes with an appeal to 'every honest, brave, unbulliable man in Ireland' to contribute generously to the volunteers' fund.

Kettle's intervention underlines the extent to which even supporters of the Irish Party are now demanding a more hardline stance in the fight for Home Rule, and Redmond soon learns that his difficulties are about to intensify, when Birrell tells him on 6 May that Asquith plans to make an 'important statement' on the government's plans. Redmond responds that any change in the government's position will have serious consequences in Ireland.

His plea is ignored, and on 12 May Asquith tells the Commons that the government plans to allow the Home Rule Bill go through as it stands, but to introduce an amending bill – providing for separate treatment of Ulster – that would become law at practically the same time. Asquith provides no details on what the amending bill might contain, but expresses the hope that an agreed settlement might still be achievable.

This fails to impress the opposition. Bonar Law responds with a warning to Asquith that passing the Home Rule Bill will lead to 'rejoicing' in nationalist Ireland and make it more difficult, not less, for the Irish Party to make concessions. In consequence, Ulster unionists will have no guarantee of the amending bill ever becoming law. 'They see the position steadily getting worse for them, and though I am sure my right honourable friend [Edward Carson] will do what he can, as he has done up to now, to prevent disorder, I really honestly believe that by the course which you are taking there is a real risk – and, if you hope for peace, an unnecessary risk – of bloodshed in Ireland which might easily have been avoided.'

Redmond is exultant at the prospect of the imminent passage of Home Rule, but worries over what further concessions might yet be offered to the Ulstermen. His state of mind is encapsulated in a letter from Asquith to Venetia Stanley: 'The Irish are in rather a panicky mood, but I think they will soon recover their nerves.'

One effect of Asquith's announcement is that the Government of Ireland Bill will, before the next recess, be sent for the final time by the House of Commons to the House of Lords, which, under the terms of Parliament Act, has no further power to delay it, having refused to pass it in 1912 and again in 1913.

This ignites new tensions in loyalist areas of Ulster, prompting Major General Sir Nevil Macready, who was sent from the War Office to take charge of military operations in the province following the Curragh incident, to seek an urgent meeting with Asquith. His subsequent discussion with the prime minister, as recorded by Macready, tells him just how much the government has been cowed by the recent near-mutiny in the army and is determined to avoid an intervention in Ulster under any circumstance.

Mr Asquith decided that in the case of serious faction fighting between Orangemen and Nationalists, troops should not intervene and run the risk of having to be extricated, but should isolate the area of fighting until reinforcements arrived. If Carson proclaimed the Provisional Government the only course was to remain on the defensive and do nothing, Mr Asquith being of opinion that a proclamation would be issued by Carson which would clear the air and give an indication as to further action. If the Lord Mayor chose to call on the UVF to restore order, a contingency he had hinted at during one of our interviews, there should be no interference, as the responsibility rested on the Lord Mayor. On a further point as to what action should be taken if special service companies of the UVF were dispatched to Londonderry or other outlying places, Mr Asquith was of opinion that there was no power to prevent it.

With notes of these heroic instructions in my pocket, I returned to Belfast that night.

A stark warning about the threat of imminent violence in the north is also issued by Bishop O'Donnell of Raphoe, who tells Redmond in a letter on 9 May that 'there is a bad 12th of July spirit even [in places] where it was not known for long years … in the [north-west] the Unionists are constantly saying they will fight; and their present hostile feeling seems to be altogether directed against Catholics and Nationalists'.

Wherever Redmond looks, there is peril. A Home Rule parliament, the fruition of his life's work, is in sight, but at a potential cost – the permanent partition of Ireland – that no Irish nationalist can tolerate. The Protestant population of Ulster is now heavily armed and, for the first time, nationalists there are living in genuine fear. The Irish Party still holds the balance of power in the House of Commons, but the government is no longer dancing to its tune.

Most worrying of all, though, is not the armed body of men in Ulster, but the dramatic rise in recent months of its counterpart in the south. The Irish Volunteers had roughly ten thousand members at the start of the year. Now it is estimated to be eighty thousand strong and members are being drilled in companies formed throughout the country. Moderate men such as Tom Kettle are urging others to arm themselves and sign up.

In this rapidly changing atmosphere, Redmond recognises that the Irish Party must reassert itself to face off a challenge to its supremacy as the voice of Irish nationalism. He resolves to do something that runs

Redmond with a copy of the Parnellite-supporting *Daily Irish Independent*. The paper was succeeded in 1905 by the *Irish Independent*, which became an arch critic of Redmond's policies. (*Image courtesy of the National Library of Ireland*)

Redmond pictured in London circa 1910 (© *Getty Images/Hulton Archive*)

January 1910 election poster for Liberal Unionist candidate Herbert Pike Pease. (© *Bridgeman Images/ Private Collection*)

Conservative Party poster from 1910 depicting Redmond as the 'Irish master' of Prime Minister Herbert Asquith and his government colleagues David Lloyd George and Winston Churchill. (© *Lordprice Collection/Alamy*)

Redmond addressing the monster Home Rule rally on O'Connell Street in Dublin on 31 March 1912. (© *Topfoto*)

Edward Carson. (*Courtesy of the Library of Congress Prints and Photographs Division*)

Bonar Law. (*Courtesy of the Library of Congress Prints and Photographs Division*)

Carson addressing his first major anti-Home Rule rally, at Craigavon on 23 September 1911. (*Courtesy of the Library of Congress Prints and Photographs Division*)

An illustration of the scenes in Belfast when Winston Churchill, his car surrounded by angry loyalists, arrives to deliver a speech in favour of Home Rule. (© *Topfoto*)

Herbert Asquith. (*Courtesy of the Library of Congress Prints and Photographs Division*)

David Lloyd George. (© *Getty Images/Mansell/Time & Life Pictures*)

Churchill on 10 February 1912, two days after he delivered his Belfast speech. (© *Topfoto*)

Augustine Birrell. (© *Getty Images/ Hulton Archive*)

Venetia Stanley, with whom Herbert Asquith carried on an intense correspondence, sharing intimate thoughts and cabinet secrets. (© *Mary Evans Picture Library/Illustrated London News*)

John Redmond with his wife, Amy, and his daughter, Johanna. (*Image courtesy of the National Library of Ireland*)

Redmond's home in Aughavanagh, in the Wicklow Mountains, a former military barracks previously used by Charles Stewart Parnell as a shooting lodge. (*Image courtesy of the National Library of Ireland*)

Redmond with Amy and their dog at Aughavanagh. (*Image courtesy of the National Library of Ireland*)

Redmond in his study at Aughavanagh. (*Image courtesy of the National Library of Ireland*)

Redmond fishing at Aughavanagh. (*Image courtesy of the National Library of Ireland*)

Edward Carson inspecting the Ulster Volunteers. (*Image courtesy of the National Library of Ireland*)

The crowds waiting on O'Connell Street in Dublin on 18 July 1912, for the arrival of British Prime Minister Herbert Asquith. (© *Getty Images/Topical Press Agency*)

Mary Leigh, the English suffragette who threw a hatchet at Asquith outside the GPO, missing him but grazing John Redmond on the ear. She is pictured in 1909 wearing her musical band uniform. (© *Heritage Image Partnership Ltd/Alamy*)

Redmond's memo of a meeting with the government chief whip (Alexander Murray, the Master of the Elibank) on 24 February 1910, in which he warned that the Irish Party would withdraw its support for the Liberals unless they moved at once to abolish the House of Lords veto over legislation. The government's reply, that it has 'nothing to say', is also noted. (*Image courtesy of the National Library of Ireland*)

Redmond with John Dillon (*left*) and Joe Devlin (*right*). (*Image courtesy of the National Library of Ireland*)

A crowd gathering outside Buckingham Palace during the failed talks of July 1914 between the nationalists, the unionists and the British government. (© *Getty Images/ Topical Press Agency*)

Willie Redmond and his wife, Eleanor. (*Courtesy of the Library of Congress Prints and Photographs Division*)

Willie Redmond, John Redmond and John's son, William, attending a centenary celebration at their old school, Clongowes Wood College, in June 1914. (*Image courtesy of the National Library of Ireland*)

The funeral cortege of the victims of the shootings by British soldiers on Bachelors Walk in July 1914 passing the scene of their deaths. (© *Getty Images/Topical Press Agency*)

THE DEAD IRISH LEADER: AT THE FUNERAL OF MR. JOHN REDMOND.

PHOTOGRAPHS BY VANDYK, BALDWIN, ILLUSTRATIONS BUREAU, AND FARRINGDON PHOTO. CO.

AT NIGHT IN WESTMINSTER CATHEDRAL: THE REMAINS OF MR. REDMOND LAID BEFORE THE ALTAR.

DURING THE REQUIEM MASS IN WESTMINSTER CATHEDRAL: WHILE THE CELEBRATION WAS TAKING PLACE.

AT THE CHURCH OF THE IMMACULATE CONCEPTION AT WEXFORD: MRS. REDMOND LEAVING.

WREATHS THAT WERE LAID ON THE GRAVE: AMONG THE CROWD IN WEXFORD CEMETERY AFTER THE INTERMENT.

AFTER THE LOWERING OF THE COFFIN: CAPTAIN JOHN REDMOND, D.S.O.

IN THE STREETS OF WEXFORD: THE DRAPED MONUMENT TO THE MEMORY OF THE LATE MR. JOHN REDMOND'S GRANDFATHER.

ACCORDING TO OLD IRISH USAGE: THE HEARSE; WITH ATTENDANTS WITH WHITE SASHES AND HAT-BANDS, AND IN IRISH FUNERAL COSTUME.

The remains of the late Leader of the Irish Parliamentary Party, Mr. John Redmond, who died in London on March 6, after an operation, rested on the following night in Westminster Cathedral, where next morning a Requiem Mass was celebrated. Thence the body was conveyed to Ireland and laid to rest in the ancient graveyard at Wexford, where many of the late Irish leader's ancestors lie buried. An immense gathering followed the funeral procession, the coffin being covered with the same green flag that, twenty-seven years before, had formed the pall of Parnell's coffin. Mrs. Redmond; her son, Capt. Redmond, of the Irish Guards; her daughter, Mrs. William Redmond; and several Nationalist M.P.'s accompanied the remains. At Wexford, the band and a detachment of the Royal Irish Regiment headed the procession of 30,000 people, all wearing black-and-white tokens. Among those following were Mr. Duke, Chief Secretary for Ireland, who was with Capt. Redmond immediately behind the coffin; delegates of the Irish Convention; Sir Bryan Mahon, Commander-in-Chief in Ireland; and Mr. John Dillon. The first part of the funeral service took place in the Church of the Immaculate Conception, Wexford.

A page from the *Illustrated London News* of 16 March 1918, on John Redmond's funeral. (© *Mary Evans Picture Library/Illustrated London News*) counter to the principles he has stood for in his 33 years in constitutional politics. Realising that he cannot beat the Irish Volunteers, he decides to take them over.

Chapter 17 ∿

A HOSTILE TAKEOVER

The Union as we have known it is dead.

Six months before Herbert Asquith brings forward his plan to accompany the Government of Ireland Bill with an amending bill dealing with Ulster, a small group of men meet in a private room in Wynn's Hotel in Dublin.

Up to half of the ten or 12 present – most likely unbeknownst to the other half – are members of the secret revolutionary body, the IRB, which has been considering the possibility of forming an armed organisation to counter the threat to Home Rule posed by Edward Carson's 'army' in the north.

They have succeeded in persuading Eoin MacNeill, professor of early Irish history at University College Dublin, to lead their new organisation, following the publication of his article, 'The North Began', calling for the establishment of an armed organisation to mirror Carson's movement in Ulster.

MacNeill's article, in the Gaelic League's organ, *An Claidheamh Soluis*, is followed a week later by another opinion piece in the same publication, by Patrick Pearse, supporting the professor's suggestion. 'I am glad then that the North has "begun"', states Pearse, continuing:

I am glad that the Orangemen have armed, for it is a goodly thing to see arms in Irish hands. I should like to see the A.O.H. [Ancient Order of Hibernians] armed. I should like to see the Transport workers and I should like to see any and every body of Irish citizens armed. We must accustom ourselves to the thought of arms, to the sight of arms, to the use of arms. We may make mistakes in the beginning and shoot the wrong people; but bloodshed is a cleansing and a sanctifying thing, and the nation which regards it as the final horror has lost its manhood. There are many things more horrible than bloodshed; and slavery is one of them.

Pearse, the founder of St Enda's School in Rathfarnham, is among those present at the first meeting of the Irish Volunteers, chaired by MacNeill, in Wynn's on 11 November 1913. He is not yet a member of the IRB, but will later join. IRB members there include Seán Mac Diarmada (Seán MacDermott), Éamonn Ceannt and Piaras Béaslaí, a journalist with the Redmond-supporting *Freeman's Journal*.

The publisher of *An Claidheamh Soluis*, Michael Joseph O'Rahilly – better known as The O'Rahilly – is also present. He is also not a member of the IRB but MacNeill is aware that most of the men in the room have been invited because they are involved in or allied in some way to the old physical force movement and that they see him – who has had no connection with it – as a respectable figurehead.

Despite the deep antagonism of the majority at the meeting to John Redmond and the constitutional politics he espouses, they recognise that without Irish Party support the new volunteer body will lack credibility and will struggle to recruit large numbers. They resolve to try to get some known Redmondites on to the committee and, by the time of the group's next meeting three days later, it has secured the involvement of two such men: solicitor John Gore and Dublin Corporation electrical engineer Laurence Kettle.

Kettle's brother Tom – whose letter to the *Freeman's Journal* following the Larne gun-running will later help boost recruitment to the Volunteers – also comes on board, joining the new organisation's 25-member provisional governing committee. Despite the active support of a small number of Redmond supporters, however, the relationship between the leaderships of the Irish Party and the newly formed Irish Volunteers is one of mistrust and suspicion.

Nevertheless, some contacts are maintained, and in late April 1914 – while Fred Crawford's Larne-bound cargo of guns and ammunition is still at sea – MacNeill travels to London with Tom Kettle and Sir Roger Casement, who has also joined the Volunteers' committee, for a meeting with Redmond and John Dillon. Casement is well known and respected for his work in exposing human rights abuses by colonial powers in the Congo and Peru.

No accommodation is reached, but there is further correspondence between the sides, and on 13 May MacNeill writes to Joe Devlin

suggesting that Willie Redmond – the Irish Party MP for Clare East
and John's younger brother – join the new directorate of the Irish
Volunteers, which is to supersede the existing provisional committee.

MacNeill says that it has been agreed that the existing treasurers and
secretaries of the Volunteers – namely himself, Gore, Laurence Kettle
and The O'Rahilly – would also sit on the executive committee, and he
intends to use all his influence to have Casement included too. Adding
Willie Redmond's name to the list would be the best possible way of
signalling John Redmond's backing for the Volunteers, he suggests.

'The spirit of the country is rising rapidly,' MacNeill adds, 'and I
have daily evidence that money will be forthcoming in thousands of
pounds for the purchase of arms ... Assure Mr John Redmond from me
that we will stand by him to a man and strengthen him, maintain all he
has won, and back him to victory, if he only trusts us.'

Redmond decides it is time to act, and he writes to MacNeill to say he
is 'extremely anxious' that the two sides should come to agreement on
the organisation of a united volunteer body which has the confidence
of nationalist party supporters throughout the country. It would be
a grave misfortune, he adds, 'if a disagreement should result in the
formation of a second body of Irish Volunteers'.

He understands MacNeill to be suggesting an executive committee
of six to run the Volunteers, i.e. the four existing officers as well as Willie
Redmond and Roger Casement. Redmond says he has no objection
to any of the names mentioned, but he cannot sanction his brother's
appointment unless the executive is enlarged to eight members 'by the
addition of two men possessing our confidence'.

He concludes with a repeated implied threat to set up a rival
volunteer body if the two sides cannot come to an agreement: 'I consider
the matter extremely urgent as members of our Party in various parts
of the country are being pressed by their constituents to assist in the
formation of Volunteer bodies under local county authority, and it will
be necessary for us to take action without much further delay either in
conjunction with you or otherwise.'

This draws an angry response from MacNeill, who says that
Redmond's letter suggests that if the executive committee is not
reconstructed along the lines he requires, the Irish Party will form its

own volunteer force. 'I cannot conceal from myself that a proposal in this form, offering this alternative, amounts to a condemnation of the line of action with which I have been associated, and that my acceptance of a proposal in this form must stand as an admission on my part that I have acted wrongly and that all the assurances which I have given, publicly on many occasions and privately to yourself, Mr Dillon, and Mr Devlin, are judged and admitted to be worthless.'

MacNeill goes on at some length to assure Redmond of his personal loyalty and to defend the Volunteers against any suggestion that the organisation might be hostile to the Irish Party. 'My aim has been to unite and strengthen the forces of the Nation against the conspiracy which threatens, through violent and unconstitutional action, backed up by the money of wealthy English partisans, to ... bring all your efforts to nothing ... I have worked for confidence, I have asked for confidence, and I now appeal to you, as my political leader, and to all your colleagues, for confidence.'

Redmond responds in exasperation, telling MacNeill that he has received this letter, 'but I must confess to some difficulty in understanding its meaning'.

The two men, he reminds MacNeill, were in agreement on all points when they met recently in London in the company of Dillon, Casement and Kettle. At that meeting, Redmond says, he expressed his support for the Volunteer movement and MacNeill in turn confirmed that the purpose of the organisation was to assist the Irish Party in securing Home Rule. Redmond adds that he made it clear at the meeting that if the Volunteers were to command the support of the Irish people, it was necessary that the Irish Party should have adequate representation on its executive committee. 'The present Committee is purely provisional, self-elected, and includes no representative of the Irish Party ... Why this moderate demand of ours is not conceded at once, I cannot understand.'

Redmond says his proposal, as outlined in his previous letter though now slightly reformulated, is that the governing body of the volunteers should have no more than eight members, three of whom should be nominated by the Irish Party. As the matter is now 'very urgent' he asks for a 'definite reply' by return or, even better, a further meeting with MacNeill in London.

The distrust between the two men is understandable. Redmond undoubtedly knows that many of those involved in the new movement are not supporters of his party but rather are adherents to the old physical force tradition, favouring an armed rebellion to drive Britain out of Ireland. He may even be aware that the initial approach to MacNeill was instigated by Bulmer Hobson, an IRB member considered so extreme in his views that Pearse warns MacNeill to have nothing to do with him.

MacNeill, on the other hand, realises that there is a large element of expediency in Redmond embracing this radical new movement. Nevertheless, he replies in a friendly spirit, indicating general agreement with Redmond's proposal, but pointing out that the particular men nominated to represent the Irish Party on the executive committee must be 'thoroughly in favour of the Volunteer movement' and prepared to co-operate fully in its work, and not merely placed there 'to watch over the others'. He also proposes Colonel Maurice Moore – a prominent activist in the Irish language revival movement – as a ninth member of the committee.

In the meantime, there is no let up in the pace of political developments following Asquith's announcement on 12 May of his intention to bring in an amending bill to deal with the Ulster question. Redmond immediately expresses concern in the Commons, and three days later he sets out the Irish Party's position in a formal memo to Birrell. He acknowledges the situation in Ulster has become 'much more serious' but again insists there is 'no real danger of civil war' when the Home Rule Bill goes through. He also predicts that Carson's provisional government, if it is established, will 'crumble to pieces in ridicule' without a 'single drop of blood' having to be shed.

Redmond adds that his party is taking two things for granted: that no further statement will be made about the amending bill before the Home Rule Bill proper is voted on, and that, in the absence of an agreement, the amending bill will involve no further compromise on what is already on offer, i.e. the right of Ulster counties to vote themselves out of Home Rule for six years.

When the matter comes before the Commons again on 21 May, Asquith refuses to comply with opposition demands to provide details of the amending bill, other than to say that it will be introduced – at an unspecified date – in the House of Lords. Conservative and Unionist MPs react by chanting, for several minutes, 'Adjourn! Adjourn!', forcing the Speaker to suspend the session amid scenes of disorder.

Then, on Saturday the 23rd, Redmond receives good news from Birrell. When parliament sits again on Monday, the final vote on the Home Rule Bill will be taken, without further debate. The prime minister will also say that in the absence of agreement on the amending bill, the government's measure will encompass the county exclusion proposal as already outlined 'and *nothing* more' – just as Redmond has demanded.

∿

Monday, 25 May 1914, is an auspicious day in the lives of John Redmond and the Irish Party.

At 3.20 p.m. Prime Minister Herbert Asquith enters the House of Commons to the characteristic cheers of his supporters and shouts of 'Ipswich!' from the opposition benches, in reference to the loss of a Liberal seat to the Tories in a by-election at the weekend. Although the chamber is packed and there is a strong sense of history being made, the proceedings are calm and purposeful and there is no hint of the chaos that reigned in the house just four days previously.

Asquith begins by confirming that the amending bill will be introduced in the House of Lords at a later date. He still hopes it will be the product of an agreed settlement, but if this proves impossible, then it will embody the proposals made by the government on 8 March, i.e. the exclusion from Home Rule of some Ulster counties for six years.

This failure of the prime minister to advance on the offer already on the table is greeted with groans of disapproval from the opposition benches. Bonar Law, responding, acknowledges the conciliatory tone of the prime minister's contribution, but says that the essential facts haven't changed. He then advises his followers to allow 'the thing' to end and for a vote on the Home Rule Bill to be taken without delay. 'Let the curtain be rung down, and the sooner the better on what is a contemptible farce.'

When the vote is taken, the Government of Ireland Bill – providing for a Home Rule parliament in Ireland – is passed by 351 votes to 274, prompting cheers on the Liberal and nationalist benches. As the Liberal MPs retake their seats and the cheering among them subsides, Redmond and his Irish Party colleagues remain standing and increase the volume, waving hats, handkerchiefs and order papers in the air.

As the Clerk of the Commons, Sir Courtenay Ilbert, takes the bill to the House of Lords, a number of nationalist and Liberal MPs, headed by the member for Kildare North, John O'Connor, form a procession behind him. Arriving in the central lobby on the way to the upper house, Sir Courtenay is surprised to be greeted by a crowd of Irish nationalist supporters, cheering and waving hats and umbrellas in the air. As the MPs return to the Commons moments later, they are again greeted with cheers from their followers, who break into renditions of 'God Save Ireland' and 'A Nation Once Again'. In the upper chamber, the Marquis of Crewe moves that the bill be read a first time, with the celebrations of the Irish supporters audible to himself and his fellow peers.

The passing of the bill prompts spontaneous public celebrations. In Cork, the stronghold of William O'Brien's All-for-Ireland League, which abstained from the vote on the bill, bonfires are lit in the streets and a great crowd gathers to hear speeches made by prominent supporters of the Irish Party from a window of the Victoria Hotel on Patrick Street. Several local bands come out to give the proceedings a festive air, reports the *Cork Examiner*.

The bill is now before the House of Lords for the final time and, under the terms of the Parliament Act, it must be passed within a month. But the extent of the Home Rule parliament's jurisdiction in Ireland will not be known until the promised amending bill has also been brought forward and passed.

Nevertheless, Redmond issues a triumphal statement to the *Freeman's Journal*, the newspaper most closely identified with his party:

> The Union as we have known it is dead. That much at any rate is beyond doubt or question after today's division. There are only two eventualities, and both of them are impossible, which could

possibly prevent the Home Rule Bill actually becoming a statute in a few weeks' time. The first is that the present Session of Parliament should come to an abrupt end before one month from this date – an utterly unthinkable proposition; and the other is that the House of Commons should suddenly go mad and pass a resolution to the effect that the Bill should not be presented for the Royal Assent. In the absence of these two absurd contingencies, the Bill *must* automatically become law.

The passing of the bill is reported enthusiastically by newspapers supportive of Redmond and his party.

'IRELAND'S DAY OF TRIUMPH', runs the banner headline in the *Freeman's Journal*, over sub-headlines running across several columns: 'HOME RULE BILL THROUGH' – 'MEMORABLE SCENE IN COMMONS' – 'IRISH LEADER'S MESSAGE'. O'Brien's contribution is given a headline of its own: 'THE DISAPPOINTED WRECKER'S LAST EFFORT'.

The *Cork Examiner*, which reports the extraordinary scenes as the bill is conveyed to the House of Lords, is no less ecstatic. 'AT LAST!' screams its main headline in large type, over the sub-headings: 'HOME RULE TRIUMPHS' – 'PRACTICALLY LAW' – 'TORY COLLAPSE' , and, in reference to O'Brien, 'FACTIONIST TREACHERY' – 'REFUSE TO VOTE'.

The 'Healyite' *Irish Independent*, as it is dubbed by the *Freeman* in reference to its consistent support for Tim Healy, is underwhelmed, reporting the passage of the bill with the rather understated headline and sub-headings 'FROM COMMONS TO LORDS' – 'HOME RULE BILL'S THIRD READING' – 'A MAJORITY OF 77'.

The *Independent*'s cool response notwithstanding, the passage of the bill from the House of Commons bolsters Redmond's status in nationalist Ireland as he turns again to the thorny issue of the Irish Volunteers. Eoin MacNeill's most recent letter, on 23 May, in which he appears to acquiesce to the request that two additional Irish Party nominees be appointed to the Volunteer executive, has helped to lighten the mood, and Redmond writes back on 26 May to tell MacNeill that he is 'greatly gratified'.

He says that in addition to Willie Redmond, he would like to nominate Joe Devlin and Michael Davitt to the Volunteers' governing body. Davitt, the son of the late Land League founder of the same name, is a supporter of the Irish Party who spoke from the main platform with Eoin MacNeill and Patrick Pearse on the night the Volunteers were launched at the Rotunda Rink.

Redmond also tells MacNeill that he approves of the suggestion to add Colonel Maurice Moore to the executive, as a ninth member. As matters stand, then, he writes, the proposed new governing body of the Volunteers would consist of MacNeill, Devlin, Davitt, Willie Redmond, Moore, Roger Casement, Laurence Kettle, John Gore and The O'Rahilly. He suggests that MacNeill meet John Dillon in Dublin to finalise the arrangements, as the matter is now urgent and he would like to publish the names of the new governing body within a few days.

But the deal Redmond thinks is in place immediately unravels. On 28 May Dillon writes to Redmond, now at home in Aughavanagh as the House of Commons is in recess, to inform him that he has had two long interviews that day with MacNeill, 'during which he smoked many pipes'.

'To my amazement he raises an objection to Davitt's name – says he could not carry him with his committee,' writes Dillon, who then raises a potential new worry for Redmond, concerning MacNeill's ability to deliver on any deal reached: 'During our interviews, it became plain he had not consulted any members of his Committee except Casement, Moore and (today, for the first time) O'Rahilly.' MacNeill, he adds, is 'a most exasperating man to deal with'.

On the same evening Davitt calls on Dillon at his Dublin home on North Great George's Street and explains the likely reason for MacNeill's hostility. He says that on the night he spoke at the formation of the Volunteers at the Rotunda, he came to the conclusion that the movement was 'in bad hands' and resolved to have nothing more to do with it. He subsequently succeeded in preventing a formation of a corps of the Volunteers by about fifty 'violent Gaelic Leaguers' at the university college, and MacNeill had been very angry with him.

Dillon, who relays this to Redmond in a follow-up later the same day, concludes: 'It is a very difficult situation. But I think that if you take a firm stance with him, MacNeill will get a settlement through.'

MacNeill follows with another long letter to Redmond, saying that even if he were to recommend 'young Dr Davitt' as a member of the governing council he would not be able to get anybody to accept him. 'The impudence of this communication is really sublime,' is Dillon's response on being shown this letter, but he says that it is much better that the party should know 'where we really are'.

The prolific MacNeill follows up a few days later, on 2 June, with another long letter to Redmond explaining his position and concluding: 'I trust at least, that, on the part of the Irish Volunteers, we shall be able to proceed with our work free from any counter move or interference, and that you will not countenance any departure that would tend to impair the unity of National effort at this crisis.'

By now Redmond has had enough. On 3 June he writes MacNeill a curt note:

Dear Mr MacNeill,
You have made the position perfectly clear to me. As you say in your letter you invited me to nominate, in addition to Mr William Redmond, two other persons to serve on the new governing body along with yourself, Mr Gore, Mr L Kettle, The O'Rahilly, Sir Roger Casement and Col Moore.

In response to your invitation I nominated Mr Joseph Devlin, MP and Mr Michael Davitt.

You now veto Mr Davitt for what reason I know not. I understand from this that you no longer desire my co-operation or that of my friends in the control of the movement and I must now act accordingly.

Very truly yours,
J.E. Redmond

By now rumours of the tensions between the Volunteers and Redmond have begun to surface in the national press. The unionist *Irish Times* sees an opportunity to embarrass the Irish Party leadership and on 6 June runs an unlikely editorial in praise of the new organisation and criticising Redmond and Dillon for trying to 'capture' it and 'kill it'.

If the National Volunteers are left alone, they may 'help to mould the national destiny to great ends', the paper argues, concluding: 'If the politicians win, the passions and prejudice which now divide Unionist and Nationalist will take a new lease of life. Nationalist Ireland is at a parting of the ways.'

If John Redmond reads this editorial, he might be forgiven a puzzled scratch of his head. In any case, he finally moves to seize control of the Volunteers in a letter published in the nationalist newspapers on 10 June.

Sir,

I regret to observe the controversy which is now taking place in the Press on the Irish National Volunteer movement. Many of the writers convey the impression that the Volunteer movement is, to some extent, at all events, hostile to the objects and policy of the Irish Party. I desire to say emphatically that there is no foundation for this idea, and any attempts to create discord between the Volunteer movement and the Irish Party are calculated, in my opinion, to ruin the Volunteer movement, which, properly directed, may be of incalculable service to the National cause.

Up to two months ago I felt that the Volunteer movement was somewhat premature, but the effect of Sir Edward Carson's threats upon public opinion in England, the House of Commons, and the Government; the occurrences at the Curragh Camp; and the successful gun-running in Ulster vitally altered the position, and the Irish Party took steps about six weeks ago to inform their friends and supporters in the country that, in their opinion, it was desirable to support the Volunteer movement, with the result that within the last six weeks the movement has spread like a prairie fire, and all the Nationalists of Ireland will shortly be enrolled.

Within the last fortnight I have had communications from representative men from all parts of the country inquiring as to the organisation and control of the Volunteer movement, and it has been strongly recommended to me that the Governing Body should be reconstructed and placed on a thoroughly representative basis, so as to give confidence to all shades of National opinion.

So far as my information goes, the present Provisional Committee is self-elected. It consists of some twenty-five members, all of whom are resident in Dublin, and there appears to be no representation on it from any other part of the country. It only claims to be a strictly provisional and temporary body, and holds office only pending the constitution of a permanent Governing Body.

In deference to the representations that have been made to me, and in the best interests of the Home Rule cause, which the Volunteer movement has been called into existence to vindicate and safeguard, I suggest that the present Provisional Committee should be immediately strengthened by the addition of twenty-five representative men from different parts of the country nominated at the instance of the Irish Party and in sympathy with its policy and aims.

The committee so reconstituted would enjoy the confidence of all Nationalists, and could proceed with the work of completing the organisation of the movement in the country, so that, at the earliest possible moment a conference of Volunteer representatives might be held by which the permanent Governing Body could be elected. If this suggestion is accepted the National Party and I myself will be in a position to give our fullest support to the Volunteer movement, but, failing the acceptance of some such arrangement as that above suggested, I fear it will be necessary to fall back on county control and government until the organisation is sufficiently complete to make possible the election of a fully representative Executive by the Volunteers themselves.

Very truly yours,

J.E. Redmond

The letter comes as a shock to the Volunteer committee, many of whom were unaware of the discussions between Redmond and MacNeill. A meeting is immediately called and after a late night conference at its office on Brunswick Street – later to be renamed Pearse Street, after one of those present – the committee issues a statement in the early hours of 11 June that amounts to a rejection of Redmond's proposal.

This provokes a further letter to the papers from Redmond in which he gives the Volunteers an ultimatum: reconsider his proposal or face being sidelined by an alternative movement organised by the Irish Party.

The issue dominates the nationalist newspapers for several days and there is criticism of Redmond over what some see as his 'divisive' intervention, but the weight of opinion is very much behind the Irish Party leader. Several county councils pass resolutions in support of Redmond, as do a large number of local companies of the Volunteers, and on 16 June the provisional committee reluctantly gives way, accepting Redmond's proposal as 'the lesser evil' in order to avoid a split in the movement. But the resolution reached is far from amicable, as the committee makes clear in a statement: 'In the interests of National unity, and in that interest only, the Provisional Committee ... accede to Mr Redmond's demand to add to their number 25 persons nominated at the instance of the Irish Party.'

Several members of the committee, including Pearse, Éamonn Ceannt, Con Colbert, Seán Mac Diarmada and Piaras Béaslaí, dissent from the committee's decision, but they later decide to accept it, under protest, and remain involved in the Volunteers.

Redmond has won his battle with the Volunteer founders and fortified his position as the sole recognised leader of nationalist Ireland. But he is soon beset by difficulties emanating from events abroad.

Chapter 18

AN INVITATION TO THE PALACE

Your responsibilities are great. The time is short.

On 29 June 1914, a motor car carrying the heir to the throne of the Austro-Hungarian Empire, the Archduke Franz Ferdinand, and his wife, Sophie, takes a wrong turning as it leaves the centre of the Bosnian capital, Sarajevo, where the couple have survived an assassination attempt earlier in the day.

As their convoy attempts to reverse out of Franz Josef Street and resume its journey to the outskirts of the city, 19-year-old Serb Gavrilo Princip, one of those involved in the failed attempt to kill the archduke a couple of hours earlier, emerges from under the awning of a shop with a bomb tied to his waist and a revolver in his hand.

Unable to free the bomb, he draws his revolver and points it towards the car carrying the royal couple. More than one of those present will later recall experiencing a strange sense both of time slowing down and a silence descending, as Princip keeps his revolver raised and fires two shots. Neither seems to cause any harm, as both the archduke and his wife remain sitting upright while their car speeds away towards Appel Quay and across the city's river.

But then the duchess, who has been shot in the abdomen, slumps sideways, her head falling between her husband's knees. The archduke, blood pouring from his neck, speaks to her in a soft voice: 'Sophie, Sophie, don't die, stay alive for our children.' His plea is in vain, and moments later he too is dead.

⌒

Every known detail of Princip's act is conveyed in the following day's Irish and British newspapers, the *Cork Examiner* lamenting the 'terribleness' of the crime (though its main headline, 'UNHAPPY HAPSBURGS', may fairly be described as an understatement) and the *Freeman's Journal* terming it an 'appalling tragedy'. But there is no immediate concern that this faraway event might yet have disastrous global consequences, the London *Times* noting merely: 'No one has yet attempted to gauge its possible effect upon the stability of Europe, and the diplomatic world is almost stunned.'

The *Journal*, the *Examiner* and the *Irish Independent* all give near equal prominence to a domestic story, the news that John Redmond has written to Eoin MacNeill and Laurence Kettle to provide them with the list of 25 Irish Party nominees to the provisional governing committee of the Irish Volunteers. The list includes three nationalist MPS – Joe Devlin, Willie Redmond and T.J. Condon – as well as two parish priests, a couple of other clergymen, local politicians and several members of the legal profession.

Redmond has every reason to be satisfied with developments since the passing of the Government of Ireland Bill in the House of Commons a month earlier. His decisive manoeuvre to take over the Volunteers has been welcomed at home and earned him praise in Britain, even in some sections of the Conservative press. And the government has held the line on Home Rule, offering no new concessions to the Ulster unionists.

In the midst of these events, Redmond – in the company of his brother Willie and son William – attends a centenary celebration at his old school, Clongowes Wood College in County Kildare, where he is greeted ecstatically as, in effect, Ireland's prime minister-in-waiting. In an address in his honour a student declares: '[The] long struggle for freedom, which was begun by O'Connell and brought forward by Butt and Parnell, has, at last, through your skill, perseverance, and eloquence during fourteen years of brilliant leadership, been brought to a glorious triumph.'

Redmond responds by telling the students that they are all engaged in a struggle for the regeneration and happiness of Ireland.

For my part all I claim is this: that I and my friends have done something, have done our best at any rate, and with some success [applause] to open for the coming generations of the Irish race, at long last, an honourable career in the service of their own country [applause]. The future is with the young men of Ireland. Our day will soon be passed. But, boys, when you grow up, when you leave this college and go forth into the world, and into the public life of Ireland, it is you who will have put upon your shoulders the duty of making good the work that we have endeavoured to perform.

For the next several weeks, tensions remain high, particularly in Ulster, as the government's amending bill is awaited. On 20 June, in a speech at Bessemer House, a mansion in the London suburb of Camberwell, David Lloyd George confirms the unionists' fears, indicating by way of a forceful defence of the government's existing position that there will be no new offer made to Ulster. He is twice interrupted by male supporters of the suffragette movement, including a clergyman, who are forcibly removed from the audience and thrown into the large pond on the estate grounds. There, the clergyman engages in a fight with a supporter of the chancellor, who tries in vain to duck him in the water.

Three days later the opposition receives a metaphorical ducking when Lord Crewe – the leader of the house – introduces the amending bill in the House of Lords. Not since the debates over Lloyd George's 'people's budget' in 1909 and the subsequent Parliament Act have the benches and galleries of the upper house been so crowded. Nobody is surprised to learn that the government has not moved from the offer made by prime minister Herbert Asquith on 9 March, namely provision for Ulster counties to vote themselves out of Home Rule for a period of six years.

But the government has not given up hope of a negotiated settlement. On 30 June, a week after the amending bill is introduced, Redmond is told by the former Liberal chief whip Alexander Murray, now Lord Murray of Elibank, that he has been 'unofficially asked to intervene' to try to bring about a settlement of the Ulster question. He tells Redmond that he has already had 'long conferences' with Carson and Law, and that they and Lord Lansdowne have assured him they earnestly desire a settlement. Asquith, he adds, is aware of the discussions and approves of them.

Murray then gives Redmond a document outlining what he says is the opposition's view on a possible agreement. It proposes exclusion from Home Rule of an artificial area within Ulster comprising approximately five counties for a period of six years. After that, a statutory poll would take place every six years on whether the area would remain outside or come under the jurisdiction of a Home Rule parliament.

Redmond dictates a memorandum of the meeting, which records his own response as well as an intriguing statement from Murray.

> I informed him that my position must remain unchanged on the two essential points – that is to say, the time limit and the area; but that, of course, if I received a firm offer, I would then carefully consider it in all its bearings with my colleagues. Beyond that I could not go.
>
> He then left me, with the understanding that he would see me again to-morrow morning.
>
> He informed me that Sir Edward Carson had stated to him, in the presence of Mr Bonar Law, and with his approval, that it was the opinion of them all that Home Rule was inevitable, and that the inclusion of Ulster in a comparatively short time was, in their judgment, inevitable also.

Law's record of the talks he and Carson have had with Murray, however, gives a different perspective. The Tory leader's account suggests it was not the opposition, but Murray himself – acting on behalf of Asquith – who proposed taking an artificial slice of Ulster out of the Home Rule Bill.

The substance of Murray's suggestion, writes Law, 'was that a Protestant area should be created in Ulster, which would be excluded from the Home Rule Bill as a unit. The area suggested included the four Counties [Antrim, Armagh, Down and Derry], with the exception of a part of South Armagh and a strip of South Down. It included also a strip of Donegal, and the discussion showed that if it were possible they were willing also to put within the excluded area a strip of Monaghan and possibly of Cavan.'

Murray, Law's memo adds, pointed out that Tyrone would be the main difficulty, but the government would, he believed, 'be prepared to make a partition of it'. He received a definitive response on that suggestion: 'Carson intimated at once and in such a way as to make it clear that there could be no change in his view, that the whole of Tyrone must be in the excluded area.'

At a later meeting with Asquith, Law finds the prime minister 'less yielding' than Murray, which suggests that the former chief whip has at least to some degree been acting on his own initiative in trying to find potential grounds for a deal.

At a second meeting with Redmond, Murray – who has just met Law separately – again paints an over-optimistic picture of the opposition's stance. Redmond records:

> He said that Mr Bonar Law was still most anxious to find a way out of the difficulty, and apparently the real crux of the situation is Tyrone. Bonar Law said that Carson must take the responsibility of deciding this point about Tyrone. Lord Murray is of opinion that this is the only real obstacle. He tells me that Mr Bonar Law was most conciliatory.
>
> He informed me that [Dublin-born newspaper magnate] Lord Northcliffe was not aware of what was going on, but that he could be relied upon to support, through [his publications] the *Daily Mail* and the *Times*, any settlement that was arrived at.
>
> He informed me that the Archbishop of Canterbury was also busy interviewing Unionist leaders in the interests of peace.
>
> Lord Murray said he would communicate with me to-morrow the result of his conversation with Sir Edward Carson to-day.

Two further memos by Redmond on the next day, 2 July, point to the frantic pace of discussions now under way.

> Lord Murray called on me this morning at 9.30; informed me that he had lunched yesterday with Sir Edward Carson and had a long interview afterwards with Mr Bonar Law.
>
> He had nothing further of substance to communicate to me except to say that he was quite convinced that the only point which at present could be truthfully regarded as an absolute deadlock

was the question of the inclusion or exclusion of Tyrone. Carson and Bonar Law profess to regard this as impossible to give up, and of course he recognised and informed them of my absolute *non possumus* attitude upon the point.

He informed me that he was in communication with the King, and that he had reason to believe that it might be possible to induce the King to bring very serious pressure on this point on Carson and Bonar Law.

He told me also that Carson and Bonar Law assured him most emphatically that if any arrangement were come to they would make one of the conditions a guarantee that the entire Tory Press in England would demand for the new Irish Parliament absolute fair play and every chance.

I asked him whether they would include a guarantee that the Unionist Party, if they came back to power at the next General Election, would not attempt to interfere with the Home Rule Bill. He told me that he thought I might take that for granted.

Despite the apparent improvement in the atmosphere, Redmond's second memo of the day records that the talks have run into deadlock.

I had a further interview with Lord Murray, who was accompanied by [co-owner of the *Daily Mail* and brother of Lord Northcliffe] Lord Rothermere, at 24 Queen Anne's Gate. They reported to me that they had just concluded a two hours' interview with Sir Edward Carson and Mr Bonar Law, and that they had got no farther at all in the direction of a settlement.

I asked them to let me know, in so many words, what exactly the proposal or suggestion tentatively put forward by the Opposition was.

They said it was as follows:

1. Plebiscite by counties to be abandoned. A [single] plebiscite to be taken in an area consisting of Antrim, Down, Derry, Tyrone, North and Mid Armagh, and North Fermanagh, and Derry City. *Note*: With reference to Down, some possible arrangement as to Catholic area.

2. Time limit to be so changed as to leave the option to this area of deciding by plebiscite when they would come in.

3. Part of the agreement would be an undertaking by the Opposition and by Sir Edward Carson on behalf of his friends, both by speeches in the country and through the entire Tory Press in Great Britain, to support and assist and encourage the Irish Parliament in every way possible. The settlement would be regarded as practically final. No attempt would be made by the Tory Party, if they came back into power, to repeal it, and the demand for a General Election on the question of Home Rule would be absolutely given up.

Lord Murray stated that he understood that Sir Edward Carson himself would be willing to attend the opening of the Irish Parliament.

I informed Lord Murray and Lord Rothermere that these suggestions were quite impossible, and that I could not even discuss the question of the time limit, unless the plebiscite by counties were accepted.

They suggested that some other influence might be put in motion to bring pressure to bear on Mr Bonar Law and Sir Edward Carson, and that they did not abandon the hope of arriving at some settlement.

Redmond's chief objection to the scheme relayed by the two peers is that it involves the north-eastern counties voting as a bloc – what Edward Carson has described as a 'clean cut' – on whether they opt into or out of Home Rule. Redmond wants a separate vote for each county, knowing that Tyrone and Fermanagh, with their small Catholic majorities, would probably elect to come under the Irish parliament.

As the annual loyalist celebrations of 12 July approach, there are increasing fears of an outbreak of violence. These are not assuaged by the sound of hundreds of revolver shots being fired into the air as Carson prepares to address an estimated crowd of seventy thousand at the main 'Twelfth' rally in Drumbeg, County Down. Neither does his warlike speech, reported in full in *The Times*, do anything to defuse the continuing crisis. Reflecting on the large crowds who have cheered him to Drumbeg on his journey from Belfast, Carson rhetorically asks what lesson he has learned from all he has seen today.

> I think I can sum it up in the old two words you all wish to say to me – 'no surrender!' [great cheers]. Do not let us be under any delusion when we use the words 'no surrender' at the present moment. They mean, if they are to have any reality at all, that you are prepared to do within the next few weeks, if necessary, what your forefathers did upon the day you are now celebrating, when William crossed the Boyne [cheers], and also when behind the Walls of Derry the British connection was maintained and your civil and religious liberties were secured. Do not think lightly of 'no surrender', and do not imagine that you can carry out a policy of 'no surrender' by merely going to meetings. Do not imagine you must not suffer.

The government seems to be in great difficulties about what to do with its amending bill, he continues, but he can help it out by stating clearly the alternatives open to it: 'Give us a clean cut for Ulster or come and fight us.'

The amending bill is due to come back before the House of Commons on 20 July. In the meantime the Lords has passed an amendment to it, proposed by Lord Lansdowne, replacing the county-by-county vote and six-year time limit with the permanent exclusion from Home Rule of the entire nine counties of Ulster. If the amending bill is presented in the Commons in this form, the Irish Party will have no choice but to vote against it, forcing the defeat of the government on one of its own bills and most likely causing the administration's collapse.

The week beginning Monday, 13 July, is set to be make or break, and for the prime minister it begins with a meeting with Lord Northcliffe, who is just back from a visit to Ulster. Asquith is no fan of the press baron, telling Venetia Stanley in a letter days earlier: 'I hate & distrust the fellow & all his works.'

Nevertheless, he agrees to hear what Northcliffe has to say, and he brings Stanley – with whom he is now in daily contact about the most sensitive political matters – up to date: 'I have had two interesting if not very enlivening interviews. The first (which is most secret) was with Lord Northcliffe – of all people – at the Master's [Lord Murray's] flat in Ennismore Gardens. He has been "doing" Ulster, & is much struck with the Covenanters, whom he regards (what with fanaticism & whisky) as a very formidable tho' most unattractive crew. I talked over the question of areas &c with him, & tried to impress upon him the importance of making *The Times* a responsible newspaper. After I got back to the House I had half an hour with Redmond & Dillon – also mainly about areas. I found them in a decidedly impracticable mood, and I foresee great difficulties in the coming week, which will practically decide whether we can come to an agreement.'

Asquith – still focused on the Irish crisis and unaware that Britain is within weeks of being plunged into a catastrophic continental war – has entered what he describes to Stanley as 'the most critical time of my life'. Frantic efforts in the following days to secure a deal bring no result, however.

The prime minister is under pressure from all sides, and faces the prospect that King George could refuse to sign the Government of Ireland Bill in the absence of an agreement on Ulster. Asquith acknowledges as much in a meeting with Law, conceding – according to Law's record of the discussion – that if the government failed to produce its promised amending bill, the king would be within his rights to refuse to assent to Home Rule. That, in turn, could trigger an election and undo all the progress made by Redmond and his colleagues.

On Thursday, 16 July, Asquith again meets Redmond and Dillon and tells them that Murray has been continuing his discussions with Law and Carson, but without success. The prime minister says that he too has met Law, who told him he could see no hope of persuading Carson 'to give up Tyrone'.

For some time Asquith has been resisting pressure from the king to call a conference of the relevant party leaders to try to negotiate a settlement to the Irish question, judging the idea premature. Law tells him, indeed, that such a conference would be 'useless'. But the prime minister now decides the time is right. The news is leaked to *The Times* and the *Daily Mail*, so it is no surprise when Asquith tells the

Commons on Monday, 20 July that he has been authorised by the king to announce to the house that in view of 'the grave situation which has arisen he has thought it right to summon representatives of parties, both British and Irish, to a conference at Buckingham Palace'.

News of the conference, to begin the next day, generates intense political excitement. Redmond and Dillon arrive at the palace by taxi and are cheered, in common with the other leaders, by a large crowd gathered at the entrance. The government is represented by Asquith and Lloyd George, the Conservative Party by Law and Lansdowne, and the Ulster Unionists by Carson and James Craig.

King George begins proceedings at 11.30 a.m. with a short statement that his intervention, though a 'new departure', is justified by the circumstances. 'Your responsibilities are great,' he tells the negotiators. 'The time is short. You will, I know, employ it to the fullest advantage, and be patient, earnest and conciliatory, in view of the magnitude of the interests at stake.'

The king then withdraws to let the conference, chaired by the Speaker of the Commons James Lowther, go on in his absence. The talks take place in secrecy, although Redmond and Law both keep a record of the proceedings.

They begin with a row over whether the area to be excluded from the Home Rule Bill, or the time limit to be applied to the exclusion, should be discussed first. After Redmond and Dillon get their way in demanding that the area be the first item on the agenda, Carson argues for taking the whole of Ulster out of Home Rule.

'He gave it as his opinion that if this were done generously, then there would be a likelihood within a reasonable time of Ulster being willing to come into a united Ireland, whereas if any attempt to coerce any part of Ulster were made a united Ireland within the lifetime of anyone now living would be out of the question,' Law states in his record. Redmond notes that he told Carson and Law it would be impossible for his side to accept this proposal, though Law's memo adds: 'Both Redmond and Dillon admitted that if they were free agents that is a plan which they would adopt, but both of them said that it was absolutely out of the question, and that if they were to propose it it would mean they would be without a party either in Ireland or anywhere else.'

With no progress made on the area question, the talks break up for the day at 1 p.m.

Hours later, Galway MP Stephen Gwynn is sitting alone on the House of Commons terrace when Redmond comes out to join him. It is a warm July night and Redmond, enlivened by the day's events, is unusually talkative. He tells Gwynn how visibly nervous the king, whom he was meeting for the first time, appeared to be about the Irish situation. 'When I think over Redmond's description of the Sovereign's personality,' Gwynn will write in his biography of Redmond, 'it seems to me he was describing one so paralysed, as it were, by anxiety as to have lost the power of easy, genial and natural speech.'

Redmond also tells Gwynn that the participants sat facing each other across a long table – the Irish Party and government leaders on one side, the Conservatives and Ulster Unionists on the other – but that among all those present, Carson stood out. 'As an Irishman, you could not help being proud to see how he towered above the others. They simply did not count. He took charge absolutely.'

But what made the deepest impression on Redmond was the information displayed in a great map in relief that was constructed for the conference, showing the distribution of the Protestant and Catholic populations. It showed, Redmond tells Gwynn, the astonishing extent to which the Catholics lived mainly on the mountains and hilltops, and the Protestants among the valley lands.

The following day the parties return to the palace for a further 90 minutes of talks. Again the focus is on the area to be excluded from Home Rule. Carson drops his demand for all of Ulster to be left out and proposes instead that six counties – all those in the province except Donegal, Cavan and Monaghan – be allowed to vote as a bloc on whether they wish to be omitted or not. Redmond responds that this is no more acceptable than the exclusion of the entire province. There is much talk about Tyrone and Fermanagh, to which both sides lay claim, but no agreement.

Carson's argument for Tyrone's exclusion from Home Rule, in spite of it having a small nationalist majority, is essentially this: as the status of the counties being excluded will not change – they will remain under the jurisdiction of Westminster – there needs to be an overwhelming case to make such a radical change as to force them out of the jurisdiction in which they exist. '[Carson] pointed out [that] if there were the same division of parties throughout the whole of Ireland as existed now in Tyrone, any suggestion of Home Rule would be considered altogether absurd,' notes Law.

Walking back to the House of Commons after the talks again adjourn at 1 p.m., Redmond and Dillon are followed by supporters who cheer them and sing 'A Nation Once Again'. As they pass the Wellington Barracks the soldiers in the Irish Guards recognise the nationalist leaders and join in the cheers of support, some waving their caps and shouting, 'Home Rule for ever!' and 'Redmond for ever!'

In the afternoon an exasperated Asquith writes to Venetia Stanley to express his deep frustration at the lack of progress.

> We sat again this morning for an hour & a half, discussing maps & figures, and always getting back to that most damnable creation of the perverted ingenuity of man – the County of Tyrone. The extraordinary feature of the discussion was the complete agreement (in principle) of Redmond & Carson. Each said 'I must have the whole of Tyrone, or die; but I quite understand why you say the same'. The Speaker who incarnates bluff unimaginative English sense, of course cut in: 'When each of two people say they must have the whole, why not cut it in half?' They wd. neither of them look at such a suggestion. L.G. & I worked hard to get rid of the county areas altogether & proceed on Poor Law Unions, wh. afford a good basis of give & take. But again both Irish lots would have none of it. Nothing could have been more amicable in tone, or desperately fruitless in result. We agreed to meet once more to-morrow, when we shall make a final – tho' I fear futile – effort to carve out a 'block'. I have rarely felt more hopeless in any practical affair: an impasse, with unspeakable consequences, upon a matter which to English eyes seems inconceivably small, & to Irish eyes immeasurably big. Isn't it a real tragedy?

As the parties arrive at the palace for a third successive day, the crowd outside is more muted than on the previous days and, the Press

Association reports, there is no cheering for any of the political leaders. The only excitement is caused by a woman who makes a rush towards the palace and throws a section of lead piping in its direction. As she is taken away by police she is heard to shout something about the king receiving rebels but declining to receive women. She draws a hostile response from the crowd, and there are cries of 'Duck her in the fountain!' and 'What about your husband's dinner?! You ought to be ashamed of yourself!'

There is no such drama inside the palace walls, where the parties have still not moved on from the first matter for discussion – the area to be excluded from Home Rule. Asquith suggests dividing Ulster by its parliamentary constituencies, with the exception that nationalist West Belfast and Derry City would be in the excluded area. This proposal, however, would leave three-quarters of Tyrone under the jurisdiction of the new Irish parliament and is therefore rejected by Carson.

After other permutations are suggested, and dismissed, Redmond makes a final plea for all of Ulster to come under Home Rule, in return for 'very large concessions' by the nationalists, but this too is turned down by the unionist side, and soon all the participants must face the inevitable: the conference has failed. They return to the palace the following day, Friday, but only to agree on the terms of a statement announcing the conclusion of the talks without agreement.

Asquith delivers the news to the House of Commons later the same day and announces that the second reading of the amending bill will now be taken on Tuesday of the following week. The day of reckoning has come and the government must now decide whether it is prepared to coerce the Ulster Unionists into a Home Rule parliament, albeit after a delay of six years, or face down John Redmond and his party and bring in a law providing for the partition of Ireland with no time limit.

Before Asquith is required to act, however, momentous happenings intervene at home and abroad. When the House of Commons reconvenes on Monday, all thoughts of the amending bill will have been swept aside by the previous day's events in Dublin. And the British political establishment will – incredibly late in the day – be waking up to the fact that their country is in danger of being dragged into a Europe-wide war triggered by the chain of events set off by the murderous action of Gavrilo Princip in Sarajevo on 29 June.

Chapter 19

A BLOODY SUNDAY ON BACHELORS WALK

The Irish people will not submit any longer to be bullied, or punished, or penalised, or shot.

The Buckingham Palace conference has ended in failure but all sides agree on one thing: the talks were held in a great spirit and there is renewed hope that an agreed settlement may yet be achieved.

Before the party leaders depart the palace, the king asks for a private audience with each of them, and he tells Redmond of his delight at the 'amicable and conciliatory manner' in which he and Carson dealt with each other. The conference, he adds, is bound to have done some good.

The talks have undoubtedly helped to improve relations across the nationalist–unionist divide. Carson will later recall that, as the two of them were leaving through the palace gates, Redmond approached him and said, 'For the sake of the old times on the Leinster [legal] circuit, let us have a good shake hands,' which the two men did.

It is all too much for Asquith, who writes to Venetia Stanley on Friday, 24 July, following the break-up of the conference: 'Redmond assured us that when he said good-bye to Carson the latter was in tears, and that Captain Craig, who has never spoken to Dillon in his life came up to him & said: "Mr Dillon will you shake my hand? I should be glad to think that I will be able to give as many years to Ulster as you have to the service of Ireland." Aren't they a remarkable people? And the folly of thinking we can ever understand, let alone govern them!'

The prime minister, having let the situation drift for the past two years – the policy derided by his opponents as 'wait and see' – in the hope that these unfathomable Irishmen would eventually reach an accommodation, now needs to act. He calls a meeting at 10 Downing

Street with Redmond and Dillon – with Lloyd George and Birrell also in attendance – immediately after the collapse of the talks.

Asquith tells the Irish leaders that he intends to remove the time limit from the amending bill; in other words, there will be no automatic requirement for Ulster to come into a Home Rule parliament after six years. But Carson will not be getting his 'clean cut'; rather, each county will be given the option of voting itself into or out of Home Rule. This leaves the Irish leaders facing the threat of partition for an indefinite period, but with the likely loss of four counties instead of six, as Tyrone and Fermanagh would be expected to vote themselves into the new Irish parliament.

It is a bitter pill nevertheless, and Asquith tells Stanley, in the same letter of 24 July, that 'after a good deal of demur' the Irish leaders 'reluctantly agreed to try & persuade their party to assent'. A meeting of the Irish Party to consider the situation is called for the following Monday, but shocking events in Dublin at the weekend will push a new item to the top of the agenda.

The Irish Volunteers, boosted by Redmond's public declaration of support, now boasts a membership of 180,000 and its rapid rise is making a marked impression on the British political establishment. The House of Lords debate on the amending bill has, indeed, been characterised by frequent references to the perils posed by the existence of two large bodies of armed men in Ireland.

Redmond appreciates, however, that the southern Volunteers – while now much greater in number than their 100,000-strong Ulster counterpart – are not nearly as well armed, and he sends Tom Kettle and the Kildare North MP John O'Connor to Belgium to buy guns and ammunition. Unknown to the Irish Party leader, however, a gun-running plot by another group of volunteers – including Roger Casement – has been in place since May and is at a much more advanced stage.

The London-based novelist Erskine Childers and other Anglo-Irish supporters of the nationalist cause help to finance the scheme, and on the afternoon of 26 July Childers skippers his yacht the *Asgard* into Howth harbour, with nine hundred German Mauser rifles and nineteen thousand rounds of ammunition, bought in Hamburg, on board.

A contingent of eight hundred members of the Volunteers, unaware, like their northern counterparts in Larne three months earlier, that they are taking part in anything more than a routine drill, march into the port just in time to unload the cargo. They are instructed to march back to the city centre with the unloaded rifles, while the ammunition is transported separately in a fleet of waiting motor cars.

In Clontarf, the Volunteers, who sing 'A Nation Once Again' and other nationalist songs as they march, are confronted by the assistant commissioner of the Dublin Metropolitan Police, William Harrel, and members of his force, backed up by a company of the King's Own Scottish Borderers, whom Harrel – acting beyond his legal powers, as a subsequent inquiry will establish – has called out from its barracks in Kilmainham.

After Harrel orders the police to seize the rifles, a brief fight takes place before the police withdraw, resulting in a standoff. While two of the leaders of the Volunteers – Thomas MacDonagh and Darrell Figgis – then engage Harrel in an argument about the legalities of the matter, the men standing behind the front rows of the Volunteers scarper across the nearby fields with rifles in hand.

Harrel, having succeeded in seizing only 19 rifles – which will later be returned to the Volunteers as they are deemed to have been taken illegally – stands down the soldiers. Word of the incident quickly reaches town, however, and on their return to barracks, the soldiers are pelted with stones and bottles by a crowd of spectators on O'Connell Street. As the men turn right on to Bachelors Walk, a crowd – many of them juveniles – continues to pursue them and shout abuse. As they near the Ha'penny Bridge, some of the soldiers turn and fire on the crowd, killing three people and injuring 38. A fourth person dies later from a bayonet wound.

Newspaper accounts of the shootings the following day underscore the deep shock and anger at what has happened. An *Irish Independent* report, under an eight-column banner headline, 'SOLDIERS SHOOT DOWN DUBLIN CITIZENS', describes a 'heartrending' spectacle on Bachelors Walk as, moments after the shootings, the groans of the seriously wounded mix with 'hysterical cries' and 'piteous wailings'. It also details scenes of 'excruciating horror' at Jervis Street hospital, where most of the injured are treated.

'Pedestrians who were not in the crowd at all received bullet wounds,' the report continues. 'A more cruel, heartless outrage could not have been perpetrated. The little harassing the soldiers were receiving at the hands of their pursuers could have no possible justification for the deadly onslaught. Some of the bullets actually struck Carlisle Building about 400 yards distant.'

The ensuing outrage in nationalist Ireland is compounded by the fact that on the Saturday of the same weekend some five thousand armed members of the Ulster Volunteers were allowed to march, unmolested by the authorities, through the streets of Belfast. The discrepancy between the official response to the Irish Volunteers arming themselves and the stance taken towards their Ulster counterparts, who have been openly drilling with guns for two years, could not be more transparent.

The Dublin shootings dominate proceedings in a shocked House of Commons on the Monday, and when Augustine Birrell announces that Harrel, the assistant police commissioner, has been suspended from his post, Willie Redmond declares in response: 'He should be hanged!'

John Redmond, in a lengthy speech on the affair, says that the issues involved are 'not only grave legal and constitutional questions, and not only the question of the impartial administration of the law between different sections of his majesty's subjects, but, I am sorry to say, questions of human life'.

> In this matter blood has been shed and life has been lost, and it seems to me that unless the most definite and drastic steps be taken to prevent a recurrence of events of this kind, disastrous consequences must certainly ensue.

He calls for the immediate suspension of Harrel's superior, Sir John Ross; an independent inquiry into the events of the previous day; a separate judicial and military inquiry into the actions of the troops and for those found guilty to be punished; for the regiment concerned to be removed from Ireland; and for a lifting of the ban on the importation of arms.

I ask that the law shall be administered impartially, and that what is regarded as lawful in Ulster shall not be regarded as a crime in Munster, Leinster or Connaught. I ask that so long as the Ulster volunteers are allowed to arm and drill and march with fixed bayonets and machine guns, nationalist volunteers must be given the same freedom, and I conclude by saying, let the house clearly understand that four-fifths of the Irish people will not submit any longer to be bullied, or punished, or penalised, or shot, for conduct which is permitted to go scot-free in the open light of day in every county in Ulster by other sections of their fellow countrymen.

The funerals of the three immediate victims of the shootings – Mary Duffy, aged 50, who has a 19-year-old son in the Royal Dublin Fusiliers; Patrick Quinn, a 46-year-old father of six; and James Brennan, an 18-year-old messenger boy – are an occasion of national mourning. Requiem Mass for the three is celebrated in the Pro-Cathedral by the Archbishop of Dublin, William Walsh, and followed by scenes described by the *Cork Examiner* as the type witnessed once in a generation.

Led by an armed company of the Irish Volunteers, the funeral procession is of such dimensions, the paper reports, 'that the first portions of it must have very nearly reached Glasnevin Cemetery when the last part had passed the O'Connell Monument' (two miles away). Several bands walk in the cortège, playing funeral marches. Blinds are drawn along the route and one shop on Earl Street is draped in a black flag bearing the inscription 'R.I.P.' The only soldiers in uniform to be seen are Mrs Duffy's son and nephew, also a member of the Dublin Fusiliers, walking behind her coffin.

In the prevailing atmosphere, rational discussion of the amending bill would be impossible, and Asquith decides to postpone the second reading of the bill for two days, until Thursday, 30 July. As the days pass, however, the realisation that the unfolding European crisis is leading to a war that will involve the continent's great powers belatedly dawns on the British political establishment.

Almost incredibly, the Ulster crisis has become so all-consuming for the government that Asquith has come to view the prospect of a European conflict as a welcome way out of the Irish quagmire. He tells

Venetia Stanley, in a letter of 26 July: 'no-one can say what is going to happen in the East of Europe ... it is the most dangerous situation of the last 40 years, and may incidentally have the good effect of throwing into the background the lurid pictures of "civil war" in Ulster.'

Stanley obviously replies to the effect that the prime minister may be missing the bigger picture, because, writing to her again on 28 July, the day he was supposed to bring the amending bill back before the Commons, he says: 'What you say à propos of the War of cutting off one's head to get rid of a headache is very good. Winston [Churchill] on the other hand is all for this way of escape from the Irish troubles, and when things looked rather better last night [in relation to the European crisis], he exclaimed moodily that it looked after all as if we were in for a "bloody peace".'

On Thursday, 30 July, exactly a week before Britain will go to war with Germany, Asquith continues to be more troubled by the Irish question than the looming international catastrophe. Sitting in the Cabinet Room with a map of Ulster and 'a lot of statistics about populations and religions' – as he puts it in a letter to Stanley later in the day – he receives a telephone call from Bonar Law asking him to come to Law's home in Kensington for a meeting with himself and Edward Carson. Law sends his car, and on the way to the house on Bayswater Road Asquith wonders – as he will later confide to Stanley – if he is about to be kidnapped by the UVF.

Law and Carson, however, appear to have a rather more statesmanlike objective in mind. They propose to Asquith that, in view of the European situation and the need to present a united front, he postpone the amending bill for the time being. The prime minister goes at once to consult Lloyd George, Foreign Secretary Edward Grey and John Redmond, all of whom concur with the plan.

'Redmond', Asquith writes to Stanley, '... thought it an excellent chance of putting off the Amending Bill, & for the first time in my experience of him made a really useful suggestion: namely, that if we wd. put off the Amending Bill till next session, he would agree that the operation of the Home Rule Bill (to be put of course on the Statute Book now) should be suspended until the Amending Bill became law. He said that under those conditions he could make much larger concessions than he can now.'

Redmond's gamble is that if he can get the Home Rule Bill placed on the statute book without delay, a short postponement in bringing it into effect will be of no great consequence. In making this conciliatory gesture, he has also on this occasion outmanoeuvred the unionists, who banked on Redmond not being able to match their ostensibly patriotic offer to have the amending bill postponed.

This is confirmed in a letter from James Craig to Edward Carson on 30 July, which shows that the unionists believed, in proposing to Asquith that he postpone the amending bill, that they would put one over on their nationalist opponents. The offer to allow a postponement of the bill in the face of war, writes Craig, 'may very greatly disconcert the Coalition, especially the Nationalists. They would find it extremely difficult to follow on with a similar effort from their side; and surely the country would be able to read between the lines and store up that much to our credit when the issue is finally fought out.'

By matching their offer and, in a sense, trumping it with a further suggestion of his own, Redmond has ensured that the credit remains at least equally stored on his side.

With the Irish crisis now parked, the government is free to train its sights on the developing international crisis. Only six days earlier, on 24 July, Asquith was confident that Britain could be kept out of any continental war, writing to Stanley, 'we are within measurable, or imaginable, distance of a real Armageddon, which would dwarf the Ulster & Nationalist Volunteers to their true proportion. Happily, there seems to be no reason why we should be anything more than spectators. But it is a blood-curdling prospect, is it not?'

By the time the prime minister rises in the Commons on the afternoon of Thursday, 30 July – following his consultations with Law, Carson and Redmond – to make a statement on the Government of Ireland (Amending) Bill, the Austro-Hungarian Empire has declared war on Serbia, bombs have been dropped on Belgrade and the German and Russian armies have been mobilised. He tells the house that consideration of the bill is to be put off for the present, 'in the hope that by a postponement of the discussion the patriotism of all parties will contribute what lies in our power, if not to avert, at least to circumscribe, the calamities which threaten the world'.

Asquith remains hopeful that, whatever disasters come to pass, his country can be spared direct involvement in them. Within days, that hope will be extinguished as Britain stands on the brink of war.

Chapter 20 ∼

BRITAIN GOES TO WAR

The one bright spot in the whole of this terrible situation is Ireland.

Not since the day in 1886 when William Gladstone introduced his first Home Rule Bill for Ireland has the House of Commons been as packed – and as buzzing with expectancy – as it is on the bank holiday Monday of 3 August 1914.

With every space filled on the green benches and side galleries, chairs are placed in the gangway of the chamber to accommodate about twenty members who have been unable to secure a seat, the first time that this has been necessary in the 28 years since Gladstone famously introduced his bill 'to amend the provision for the future government of Ireland'.

All eyes today are on the anxious face of the foreign secretary, Sir Edward Grey, who rises shortly after 3 p.m. to make a statement to the house on Britain's attitude to the war now under way between Germany and Russia. 'Last week I stated that we were working for peace not only for this country, but to preserve the peace of Europe,' he begins. 'Today events move so rapidly that it is exceedingly difficult to state with technical accuracy the actual state of affairs, but it is clear that the peace of Europe cannot be preserved.'

A solemn Grey spends over an hour explaining the extent of Britain's entanglements with the parties to the war. France is involved in the crisis because it has a definite obligation to Russia, he says. Britain is not party to the Franco-Russian alliance and therefore not bound by it, but it has a 'longstanding friendship' with France. As a consequence, he has assured France that should the German navy undertake hostile operations against French coasts or shipping, the British fleet 'will give all the protection within its power'.

This draws loud cheers from the house, but Grey goes on to say that an even more serious consideration is the neutrality of Belgium, which is under threat from Germany and which Britain is bound to defend under a treaty of 1839.

John Redmond, listening intently in common with every other MP in the house, many of whom are learning at this moment that Britain is on the threshold of war, has no intention of speaking. But then the foreign secretary says something unexpected: 'The one bright spot in the whole of this terrible situation is Ireland. The general feeling throughout Ireland – and I would like this to be clearly understood abroad – does not make the Irish question a consideration which we feel we have now to take into account.'

Grey is sending a belated message to Germany and Austria-Hungary that it will not be deflected by the Irish crisis from entering the war if necessary. In later years some historians will speculate that, had the British government been able to make such an unequivocal statement a week or two earlier, the First World War might have been averted. Evidence will certainly emerge that, in making their plans for war, elements within the Axis powers were convinced that Britain was too distracted by its Irish problems to interfere. The sight of a government apparently not in full control of its army following the Curragh incident and the rapid rise of a nationalist volunteer force thought capable of revolting against the British Empire has also fed German thinking in the run-up to the war.

Grey's positive words about Ireland, then, may be intended primarily for German ears, but Redmond is moved by them. He turns to one of his closest confidantes within the Irish Party, the Roscommon South MP John Hayden, and says, 'I'm thinking of saying something. Do you think I ought to?' Hayden replies that that depends on what Redmond intends to say. 'I'm going to tell them', says the party leader, 'that they can take all their troops out of Ireland and we will defend the country ourselves.' In that case, replies Hayden, 'you should certainly speak.'

Redmond then consults T.P. O'Connor, who is sitting immediately below him. O'Connor disagrees with Hayden, advising his party leader not to take such a big political risk. Nationalist Ireland is still raw with the wounds of the Bachelors Walk shootings and discriminatory treatment of the Irish Volunteers, and Redmond is already conscious that its people may not be in the mood for magnanimous gestures.

Nevertheless, he goes with his instincts. After Grey finishes his speech, Bonar Law speaks briefly, assuring the government of the opposition's unhesitating support in whatever steps it considers necessary. Redmond then stands up to deliver, impromptu, the defining speech of his parliamentary career.

I hope the house will not consider it improper on my part, in the grave circumstances in which we are assembled, if I intervene for a very few moments. I was moved a great deal by that sentence in the speech of the secretary of state for foreign affairs in which he said that the one bright spot in the situation was the changed feeling in Ireland. In past times when this empire has been engaged in these terrible enterprises, it is true – it would be the utmost affectation and folly on my part to deny it – the sympathy of the nationalists of Ireland, for reasons to be found deep down in the centuries of history, have been estranged from this country.

Allow me to say that what has occurred in recent years has altered the situation completely. I must not touch, and I may be trusted not to touch, on any controversial topic. But this I may be allowed to say, that a wider knowledge of the real facts of Irish history have, I think, altered the views of the democracy of this country towards the Irish question, and today I honestly believe that the democracy of Ireland will turn with the utmost anxiety and sympathy to this country in every trial and every danger that may overtake it.

There is a possibility, at any rate, of history repeating itself. The house will remember that in 1778, at the end of the disastrous American war, when it might, I think, truly be said that the military power of this country was almost at its lowest ebb, and when the shores of Ireland were threatened with foreign invasion, a body of 100,000 Irish volunteers sprang into existence for the purpose of defending her shores. At first no Catholic – ah, how sad the reading of the history of those days is! – was allowed to be enrolled in that body of volunteers, and yet, from the very first day the Catholics of the south and west subscribed money and sent it towards the arming of their Protestant fellow countrymen.

Ideas widened as time went on, and finally the Catholics in the south were armed and enrolled as brothers in arms with their fellow countrymen of a different creed in the north. May history repeat itself. Today there are in Ireland two large bodies of volunteers. One of them sprang into existence in the north. Another has sprung into existence in the south. I say to the government that they may tomorrow withdraw every one of their troops from Ireland. I say that the coast of Ireland will be defended from foreign invasion by her armed sons, and for this purpose armed nationalist Catholics in the south will be only too glad to join arms with the armed Protestant Ulstermen in the north.

Is it too much to hope that out of this situation there may spring a result which will be good not merely for the empire, but good for the future welfare and integrity of the Irish nation? I ought to apologise for having intervened, but while Irishmen generally are in favour of peace, and would desire to save the democracy of this country from all the horrors of war, while we would make every possible sacrifice for that purpose, still if the dire necessity is forced upon this country we offer to the government of the day that they may take their troops away, and that if it is allowed to us, in comradeship with our brethren in the north, we will ourselves defend the coasts of our country.

As Redmond speaks, standing at the top of the gangway with his head thrown back, intermittent cheers give way to unanimous roars of approval from all sides of the house. When he sits down, many of his perennial opponents on the Conservative and Unionist benches are standing and cheering and supportively waving their papers in the air. A notable exception, however, is Edward Carson, who – the *Irish Independent* notes the next day – shows 'not the slightest emotion' while Redmond has the floor.

A short time later the parliamentary correspondent of the *Freeman's Journal*, P.J. Hooper, is surprised to find Redmond alone in the corridor near the press gallery where the teleprinters are transmitting the news of the day. 'Well, what's the news?', Redmond enquires, to be told by Hooper that the Irish Party leader himself will be the focus of the headlines at home. This prompts Redmond to ask: 'How do you think they will take it?'

He will soon find out that he has no cause for concern, as his daring intervention is warmly welcomed in the following day's nationalist press. By acting so swiftly and decisively he is seen to have boldly retaken the initiative from Carson and boosted the case for a prompt enactment of the Home Rule Bill. 'The enthusiasm shown by Unionists both in the House and in the Lobby for Mr Redmond's statesmanlike speech has given rise to hopes on both sides that his utterance may have a far reaching influence for good on the future of Home Rule,' comments the *Independent*, whch is not a consistent supporter of the nationalist leader.

English newspapers take a similar view, with the Liberal-supporting *Daily Chronicle* leading the chorus of approval: 'For the first time for many long years an Irish leader has associated himself heart and soul with the patriotic feelings of the average Englishman in face of a great national emergency. Mr Redmond spoke briefly, but with an affecting eloquence that thrilled the House ... The battle of Home Rule is already won.'

Carson's failure to follow Redmond with a similar gesture of support on behalf of the Ulster Volunteers is much commented upon, the *Liverpool Daily Post* noting, 'A few generous words from Sir Edward Carson would have been appropriate, but Sir Edward remained silent. Perhaps he was overcome by the prospect of the Home Rule Bill passing by common consent.'

Redmond's stance is also immediately endorsed by the standing committee of the Irish Volunteers which, meeting on the day after his Commons speech, passes a resolution expressing 'complete readiness to take joint action with the Ulster Volunteer Force for the defence of Ireland'.

Over the following days messages of support for Redmond's position come in from all over Ireland, as a view takes hold that in one short speech he has taken a giant step towards uniting the nationalists and unionists of the country.

An editorial in the *Cork Examiner* on 4 August – the day Britain officially joins the war – exemplifies the mood: 'It would, of course, be ridiculous to suggest that as a result of [Redmond's speech] Unionists will become Home Rulers, or that political differences will cease to exist between North and South. Yet it is easy to discern that while the political convictions of no Irishman will be altered by Mr Redmond's speech, it is at the same time safe to assume that all Irishmen will be brought closer together, and that many misunderstandings will be removed. Mr Redmond's memorable offer marks a turning point in Irish history, and it may well be that at last a way has been found to bridge over the dissensions which have kept Irishmen apart for so long.'

A telegram to Redmond the following day, from the former Unionist MP for Dublin South, Bryan Cooper, suggests that the *Examiner*'s view is, if anything, too cautious: 'Your speech has united Ireland. I join National Volunteers to-day, and will urge every Unionist to do the same.'

In Omagh, County Tyrone, unprecedented scenes unfold when the Irish Volunteers and Ulster Volunteers jointly escort to the town's train station units of the Iniskilling Fusiliers, mobilised for the war, through streets lined with people cheering in support. At one point torch-bearing members of the UVF encircle a nationalist band to give the musicians extra light. 'It was indeed a revelation for those who thought that such a thing could not have happened,' the *Ulster Herald* notes in its report of the incident.

With Carson apparently on the back foot and Redmond's standing in Ireland and Britain higher than perhaps it has ever been, the nationalist leader moves to press home his advantage, writing to Herbert Asquith and other Cabinet members to urge that the Home Rule and amending bills be immediately placed on the statute book, thereby copperfastening the goodwill that has been generated in Ireland towards the war effort.

Asquith is too preoccupied with war preparations to accede to Redmond's request for a meeting, but 5 August brings an encouraging letter from Churchill:

My Dear Redmond,

You may count on me to use every influence I possess to work for a *modus vivendi* on the lines you indicate.

Please see I have called the new battleship *Erin,* on account of your memorable speech, the echoes of which will long linger in British ears.

Yours very sincerely,

Winston S. Churchill

P.S. You must be no sufferer by the turn of events.

On the same day, Redmond has a meeting with Carson in the Speaker's library of the House of Commons in the hope of starting a process of co-operation between the northern and southern volunteers, but – he tells Asquith later – he finds the Ulster Unionist leader in 'the worst possible temper'. In a letter to the prime minister, Redmond says that Carson threatened that he and the Tory party would obstruct the appropriation bill – necessary for the government to be able to spend money – should the government dare to put Home Rule on the statute book. Redmond doesn't believe the unionists would do anything so extreme at a time of war, but he is worried about how Asquith might respond to the threat.

'[I]f the Government allow themselves to be bullied in this way by Sir Edward Carson a position of the most serious difficulty will arise with us,' he tells the prime minister. 'It would make it quite impossible for me to go to Ireland, as I desire to do, and to translate into action the spirit of my speech the other day ... This undoubtedly is the greatest opportunity that has ever occurred in the history of Ireland to win the Irish people to loyalty to the Empire, and I do beg of you not to allow threats of the kind used to prevent you from taking the course which will enable me to preach the doctrines of peace, goodwill, and loyalty in Ireland.'

Asquith replies the following day with an attempt to assure Redmond that there is no threat to the Home Rule Bill and that his commitment – and that of his colleagues – to seeing it on to the statute book in the current parliamentary session is 'absolutely unchanged'.

The crucial question now is how long the parliamentary session will be allowed to last. If the government prorogues parliament, thereby ending the session, the Home Rule Bill will immediately become law. If Asquith opts instead to adjourn parliament, the current session remains technically in place – allowing the government to keep the bill on ice.

Redmond is dismayed, then, to be told by Asquith that to prorogue parliament at this moment might be viewed 'as a piece of sharp practice', and he is instead considering a short adjournment. 'I trust that you will be content with my assurances, to which, in view of all that I have done during the last three years, I feel sure you will give due weight,' the prime minister writes.

Redmond is not impressed. 'I have received your letter,' he replies:

> The proposal to adjourn and not to prorogue is, in my deliberate opinion, a fatal one. In the present atmosphere the Government can quite safely proceed boldly. That atmosphere cannot survive what will be regarded in Ireland universally as an evasion and a serious menace to the fate of the Home Rule Bill.
>
> My position will be impossible. The happiest opportunity in Irish history will be lost. Not only will Ireland be divided and distracted, but the same will happen in every colony in the Empire, and throw the Irish in America into the arms of the German colonists there – and all for what? To avoid a protest from Carson, who would not have the Unionist [i.e. Conservative] Party behind him!

Birrell also gets an angry blast from Redmond, who writes to him on the same day: 'Unless I am able to announce to the party that the Prime Minister will give a definite pledge about prorogation, it will be impossible to prevent a debate which will, I fear, be very disastrous in its consequences.'

Going to bed the following night, Asquith tells his wife Margot – who records the conversation in her diary – that Redmond and Lloyd George have had a meeting that ended with them both being so furious 'that Redmond went out and banged the door, and Ll.G. went out by the window'.

Soon Redmond gets a portent of trouble on a different front, which will be another source of deep frustration. Asquith has stepped down as secretary of state for war – a post he has held, in addition to being prime minister, since the Curragh incident – and appointed the distinguished army veteran Lord Kitchener to take his place.

On Kitchener's second day in office, Redmond goes to see him about the urgent task of arming and regularising the Irish Volunteers in order to turn it into a force capable of delivering on his promise to defend the coasts of Ireland while Britain is at war.

The volunteer organisation needs government support because of a problem highlighted by its inspector general, Colonel Maurice Moore, in a letter to Redmond on 4 August. A very large number of the Volunteers – including most of its instructors – are members of the British army reserve and are likely to be called up for war duties, leaving the nascent organisation bereft of many of its best men at a time when they are most needed.

Moore was among those opposed to the Irish Party's takeover of the Volunteers in May, so the warm tone of his letter provides further evidence of how well Redmond's eve-of-war speech in the Commons has gone down. 'Your speech of last night has quite transformed the situation and left the Carsonites in gloom,' writes Moore, 'though I daresay they are glad enough to get out of their awkward fix. The mobilisation [for war] has, however, left us in a fix; it takes away in one swoop some 25,000 of our soldiers and most of our instructors, just when they are most wanted ... the loss to us if we are to defend Ireland is so great that I think you ought to approach the authorities and see if anything can be done.'

On meeting the new war secretary, however, Redmond is dismayed to learn that the Kerry-born Kitchener is incredulous at the idea of the Irish Volunteers playing any useful role; he has little hope, indeed, of Ireland being of much of assistance to him at all. 'Get me 5,000 men and I will say "thank you",' he tells Redmond. 'Get me 10,000 and I will take my hat off to you.'

Redmond finds himself writing to Asquith again.

[Kitchener's] idea, apparently, is simply to appeal for recruits in Ireland, and to take no step with regard to the Volunteers as a defence force – at any rate for the present. Of course, his appeal for recruits is certain to meet with a response in Ireland, but nothing at all like what the response would be if, at the same time, he intimated that he intended to entrust the defence of Ireland to the Volunteers, and that, for that purpose, he would supply, at any rate, some arms and some drill instructors. If this were done there would be such a wave of enthusiasm as would lead to a very large body of recruits joining the new force which is being raised. If this is not done the absence of arms and the withdrawal to the colours of the drill sergeants and the reserve men from the Volunteer ranks will have a very serious effect, and the people generally will be disheartened and hurt.

Lord Kitchener seems to have some idea of drafting some of the Territorials into Ireland. This, I am convinced, would be a serious mistake. It would be regarded as an affront by the people who have asked permission to defend the coasts for themselves. The Territorials would be absolutely wasted in Ireland, and their dispatch would certainly offend the susceptibilities of the people.

Mr Birrell informed me that there are in the depots of Ireland a large number of rifles, and some of them are of an old pattern which could not possibly be requisitioned by Lord Kitchener, but which would be invaluable for drilling purposes for the Volunteers.

I trust that you will be able to give some consideration to these matters at once. It would be lamentable if anything were done to damp the rising enthusiasm in Ireland or in any way to affront the people who are eager to be given the honour of taking the place of the troops you are withdrawing from Ireland.

This missive appears to draw a positive response, as later the same day the lord lieutenant in Dublin receives a telegram from the government expressing deep gratitude for the loyal help offered by Ireland 'in this grave hour' and confirming its hope to announce as soon as possible 'arrangements by which this offer can be made use of to the fullest possible extent'.

Nevertheless, Asquith holds to his plan not to rush the enactment of the Home Rule Bill, announcing on 10 August a two-week adjournment of the House of Commons. A disappointed Redmond goes home to Ireland, where he receives a letter from Birrell explaining that the Cabinet is split on what to do about the bill, amid fears of provoking a row with the Opposition at such a sensitive time.

This is dispiriting news for Redmond, who sincerely believes that a bold move by the government now could help to permanently unite the Irish and Ulster Volunteers and remove once and for all the threat of civil war in Ireland, and even of partition.

Presenting the colours to a parade of some three thousand members of the Irish Volunteers at the GAA grounds in Maryborough, Queen's County (the future O'Moore Park, County Laois) on Sunday, 16 August, he alludes to the many offers he has received in the past fortnight from members of the unionist community to join the Irish Volunteers and 'stand shoulder to shoulder with their Catholic nationalist fellow countrymen'. To approving cheers from the men lined up in columns before him, he continues:

> I say here, speaking to you, 'welcome these men.' They are all Irishmen as much as you are. For the first time, perhaps, a real favourable opportunity – certainly of recent times – has been afforded to them to join hands with you, and if now the ideal we all have at heart comes to be realised the result will be that out of this moment of seeming danger and difficulty we will win for our country the most inestimable treasure to be obtained in creating a free and united Ireland – united north, south, Catholic and Protestant ...
>
> You are not drilling and arming to attack any body of your fellow-countrymen. Your ideal is to work shoulder to shoulder with the Ulster Volunteers, if you are so allowed. Your ideal is to do all that men may do at any cost, and at any sacrifice, to create a united nation made up of all the various blends to be found in Ireland, but which, when so united, will, I believe, contain all the qualities necessary to make a great, prosperous, and strong nation.

Many unionists are, indeed, following Bryan Cooper's example and approaching Redmond or their local Volunteer organisations seeking to join the movement. Not all of them, however, are in tune with the objectives and aspirations of what remains, after all, a nationalist body set up for the purpose of safeguarding the campaign for Home Rule. When one peer, Lord Powerscourt, turns up at a parade of the Bray company of the Volunteers, he attempts to present them with a union flag. 'As the Volunteers declined to accept the gift his connection with the movement was brief,' Bulmer Hobson will write later.

Redmond is intensely annoyed by another approach, in this case from Lord Meath – a Unionist member of the House of Lords – who seeks a written assurance from the nationalist leader that the Volunteers acknowledge allegiance to the king and that by supporting the organisation he 'shall in no way fail in any loyal duty to His Majesty'.

'I have received your letter of the 15th inst,' Redmond replies. 'I am surprised at the request which you have made to me ... I must respectfully decline to give you any "written assurance" of any sort or kind with reference to the Volunteers. They are a body of men who are about to undertake, with the full sanction and approval of the Government, of His Majesty, of the Secretary of State for War – who are about to arm and equip them for the purpose – the duty of defending Ireland from foreign invasion. They have amongst their leaders many gentlemen of distinction and many gallant officers with honourable record of service; and you must really decide for yourself, the same as everybody else, what is your conception of your loyal duty to the King.'

Lord Meath, obviously seeing some propaganda potential for the Tories in this response, promptly sends his letter and Redmond's reply to Bonar Law.

The nationalist leader has bigger things to worry about, however. He knows that he must persuade the government to put the Home Rule Bill on the statute book as soon as the House of Commons reconvenes in the last week of August, or all the goodwill generated by his speech of 3 August will quickly disappear.

Chapter 21 ∾

'LE ROY LE VEULT!'

*I say that the manhood of Ireland will spring to your aid
in this war.*

erbert Asquith is quickly disabused of the notion that Britain's
entry into the war might have 'the good effect' of pushing the
Ulster crisis into the background.

If anything, the pressure on him to find a solution to the Irish
question intensifies, as the nationalists and unionists – both equally
fearful that the other side will gain the upper hand in the state of flux
created by the war – assail the prime minister with warnings of dire
consequences if he does not meet their particular demands.

On 6 August, the day Redmond writes to Asquith to tell him that
any delay in putting the Home Rule Bill on the statute book will be
'fatal', ministers have other things on their minds, gathering for two
Cabinet meetings about the prosecution of the war. Plans to send an
expeditionary force to the continent, as well as schemes for taking
German ports and wireless stations in Africa and on the China Seas are
among the items on the packed agenda. And ministers are digesting the
news that a British cruiser has been destroyed by a German mine with
the loss of 150 sailors' lives.

'As if we hadn't enough on hand, Redmond has started a row of
his own,' Asquith writes to Venetia Stanley. 'We are proposing a short
adjournment to-morrow or Monday, instead of proroguing: & he
is full of suspicion as to what may happen to his Bill, wh. naturally
enough he wants to see on the Statute book. Bonar Law and Carson
are equally suspicious.'

The next day, it is Bonar Law who is trying the prime minister's
patience, writing to him 'almost every two hours', Asquith tells Stanley.
Law and Lord Lansdowne are threatening to publish a manifesto
denouncing the government for proceeding with Home Rule at a time

when ninety members of the House of Commons have already signed up for military service.

Asquith buys time with his announcement on 10 August of a two-week adjournment of parliament, but the matter remains urgent, and two days later he discusses with Birrell over lunch how they might – as Asquith describes it to Stanley – 'put an effective pistol at the head of Redmond'. By now Venetia Stanley is advising Asquith on all matters of policy and on Monday, 17 August, he tells her in a letter that he has acted on her suggestion to have Redmond 'summoned' back to London for urgent talks.

Redmond evidently declines to answer the call, however, as he is still in Aughavanagh two days later when he receives a letter from Birrell: 'I am a little sorry you were not able to get over today, for in these non-parliamentary days [i.e. with the House of Commons adjourned] opinion has a tendency to *solidify*, and when once this process has taken place it is harder to deal with.'

Birrell tells Redmond that Asquith has three potential courses of action in mind. The first, which the prime minister favours, is to come to an agreement on the area of Ulster to be excluded from Home Rule, embody that in an amending bill, and put both the Home Rule and amending bills on the statute book at once. The second suggestion is that they put the Home Rule Bill on the statute book as it stands, but with a suspensory clause to delay its coming into operation until after the war. The third option is to put the bill back until the next session of parliament, preserving the status quo in the meantime.

By the end of the week, Redmond is back in London and he meets Asquith by arrangement, but their talks leave the prime minister frustrated and fearful of the Irish quarrel breaking into the open again at a most inopportune time. 'Redmond came (at last) to see me this morning with Birrell,' he writes to Stanley:

Of course he rules out my No 3, would prefer the 'moratorium' (No 2), but agreed (as I am glad to see that you do) that No 1 (agreement, with an area of exclusion) would if practicable be the best.

The old bother about Tyrone & those infernal snippets of Fermanagh Derry &c popped up again, and he doesn't see how he & Carson can be brought nearer, in regard to all this, than they were at Buckingham Palace 3 weeks ago. I have since seen Bonar Law, who won't have No 2 at any price, & says that his party would regard themselves in that case as jockeyed & cheated &c &c. He would agree to No 1, provided we could give him the 6 counties, and would then concede a 3 years time limit.

I shall try to work to some concordat on these lines, but it is difficult (if possible) to get it through in the next 2 or 3 days, and rather than have a smash next week I should be disposed to a further adjournment of the House – for a short time.

Asquith again meets Redmond, this time accompanied by John Dillon, the following day, a Saturday, but no progress is made. That evening Redmond sets out for the prime minister the nationalists' position in writing. He says of the three options put forward by the government, the second one – i.e. putting the Home Rule Bill on the statute book at the end of the current session – is 'far and away the best'.

'This action would have to be accompanied – and we would give our full assent to the proposal – by a Parliamentary pledge that no further step would be taken to bring the Bill into operation until ample time was given for the discussion, and if possible the passage by agreement, of an Amending Bill, if such an Amending Bill were still required,' he writes.

'The present condition of Ireland is peculiar and unprecedented,' he adds. 'It is difficult to exaggerate the intensity of the sympathy which is now felt for England and of enthusiastic approval of her cause in entering into war with Germany. No Irishman ever expected to see any such feeling in our generation.' He warns, however, that 'this splendid temper may be destroyed if there be any postponement of the Home Rule Bill.'

Asquith is on the point of acting, or at least thinks he may be, as he writes to Venetia Stanley: 'I am coming to think (but I want your advice about this) that in 2 or 3 days I may have to come forward myself, & risking everything, declare that they must all take (1) H[ome] R[ule] Bill on statute book (2) exclusion of 6 counties for perhaps 3 years (3) at the end of 3 years, each of the counties to opt itself in our out. A sort of ultimatum. Darling, tell me (for I rate your opinion above every other) do you counsel me to do this?'

The following Monday morning, 24 August, brings news of the unexpectedly rapid fall to the advancing German army of the Belgian city of Namur, and heavy British casualties. A now despairing Asquith, having relayed to Stanley the details of the setbacks, adds: 'Meanwhile it seems trivial & futile to be haggling about the boundaries of the 6 counties, the precise terms of a time limit, and all the other "sticking points", as you so well describe them. So I have sent Birrell to the Irish to say that these are not the urgent matters of the moment and, if the situation abroad does not mend, they must be content with further delay. Don't you think this is right?'

As the week passes, bringing more bad news from the Belgian front, the prime minister continues to dither over Ireland. On the Tuesday, he tries a new ploy to put pressure on Redmond and Dillon, sending them – through Birrell – letters from the king urging an immediate settlement. '[T]he royal handwriting & his expression of willingness to see R[edmond] again may have some effect,' Asquith writes hopefully to Stanley. But the response is disappointing, as he reports to his confidante a day later: 'Birrell tells me that Redmond & Dillon are not greatly impressed by the King's letters: they think he might very well see <u>Carson</u> & put pressure on him, but are not inclined to expose their own icy fronts to the thawing influences of Court sunshine.'

The following day, Thursday, Redmond avails of another opportunity to express Irish unity with the war effort, speaking in support of a motion in the House of Commons articulating solidarity with the King of the Belgians and his people in their 'heroic resistance' to the German invasion of their country. 'In no quarter of the world, I feel convinced, has the heroism of the Belgian people been received with more genuine enthusiasm and admiration than within the shores of Ireland,' he says, 'and there is no compliment which it would be possible for the Irish people to pay to Belgium that they would not willingly pay, and there is no sacrifice I believe which Ireland would not be willing to make to come to their assistance.'

By the end of the week, the Home Rule question remains unsettled, Birrell reporting to Redmond that Asquith has still not made up his mind on what to do about the bill. At the same time he relays the news that Carson has offered to make all the Ulster Volunteers available for army drilling, and has also advised the government that thirty-five thousand of his men are prepared to enlist and go abroad. 'I mention this for what it is worth, for Carson may and probably will make public use of it,' Birrell writes.

Asquith, who is awaiting details on the heavy casualties suffered by British forces at Le Cateau in France earlier in the week – seven hundred men were killed and up to 2,600 taken prisoner – tells Stanley on the Friday that 'the Irish are very jumpy and intractable, fearing for their Bill, & the Unionists ... equally so.'

By Monday, 31 August, he is at the end of his tether, writing again to Stanley: 'The Irish (both sets) are giving me a lot of trouble, just at a difficult moment. I sometimes wish we could submerge the whole lot of them, & their island, for say 10 years, under the waves of the Atlantic. When the tide receded & a new race had to take their place, it would not be more unmanageable, or less amenable to reason & common sense, tho' in other ways it might easily be less attractive and appealing. I have had interviews to-day – in the intervals of what are equally serious & more urgent things – with Redmond & with Bonar Law (inspired by Carson); and they almost fill one with despair.'

His immediate solution is to adjourn parliament for a further nine days. The distractions of the war, he tells the House of Commons, have prevented the government from coming up with an agreed solution to the Irish question, but it hopes it can do so after a further 'very short interval'.

Responding, a discouraged Redmond tells MPs that the delay in enacting the Home Rule Bill has produced a 'condition of uncertainty, suspicion and anxiety' which needs to be brought to an end. '[W] e must emphatically say that any proposal which would have the effect of depriving us of the enactment of the Irish measure ... an enactment to which we were entitled practically automatically when the circumstances of the war arose, would do infinite mischief, and would be warmly resented by us.'

Redmond is aware that the goodwill generated in Ireland by his eve-of-war Commons speech is dissipating. A commentary in the

Westmeath Examiner of 5 September sums up the discontent: 'The long drawn-out agony of waiting, to which the Irish people have been subjected over the enactment of the Bill, has done incalculable harm. It seems that Home Rule is to follow every other measure of justice for which Ireland has had to contend, in that its final concession will have been made in such a fashion as to rob it of all grace, and to evoke no feeling of gratitude or enthusiasm ... The Germans are in sight almost of the white cliffs of Dover. Lord Kitchener is appealing everywhere for help, and the Cabinet backs up his appeal to Ireland by a policy of procrastination, exasperating in the extreme. It is worse than maddening. It is suicidal.'

On 8 September, the day before parliament is to resume, Redmond at last receives news of a breakthrough. Birrell writes to tell him that the previous day a Cabinet committee, attended by the prime minister, concluded that the Home Rule Bill must be placed at once on the statute book, albeit with an accompanying measure to postpone its operation for a period of time. There would also have to be an assurance that an amending bill, dealing with Ulster, would be introduced in the next parliamentary session. 'The [Irish] Volunteers are in a very unsatisfactory condition,' Birrell adds, 'and I am very much afraid this tiresome delay has done an injury which cannot be repaired.'

A week later, on 15 September, Asquith is finally ready to tell the House of Commons that the government has finished its deliberations on Home Rule and has come to a decision. He rejects the opposition's demand that the bill be simply 'hung up' and the status quo maintained until after the war, insisting that effect must be given to the decision of parliament, after many contentious debates, to pass the bill into law. To further delay its enactment, he adds, would have a calamitous impact on Irish support for Britain in the war, not only in Ireland itself, but in the United States too.

The government plans to place the Home Rule Bill on the statute book, he announces, but with a suspensory bill attached preventing its coming into operation for 12 months, or until the end of the war if that is later. In the intervening period it will bring forward a new amending bill to deal with Ulster. 'Things have taken place which no one anticipated,' he adds, 'but I give the assurance that in spirit and substance the Home Rule Bill will not and cannot come into operation until parliament has had the fullest opportunity by an amending bill of altering, modifying, or qualifying its provisions in such a way as to secure, at any rate, the general consent both of Ireland and of the United Kingdom.'

In a deliberately measured and low-key speech, the prime minister tries to mollify the Conservatives and the Ulster Unionists. Addressing Carson directly, he declares:

> I say, speaking again on behalf of the Government, that in our view, under the conditions which now exist ... the employment of force, any kind of force, for what you call the coercion of Ulster, is an absolutely unthinkable thing so far as I am concerned, and so far as my colleagues are concerned – I speak for them, for I know their unanimous feeling – that is a thing which we would never countenance or consent to.

Bonar Law, however, refuses the olive branch and responds with a speech laced with bitterness. He says Asquith is guilty of a breach of a promise made to himself and Carson when, just before the war began, the two sent for the prime minister to suggest a suspension of hostilities in the interests of national unity. At that time, Law claims, Asquith pledged that no controversial legislation would be progressed until discussion on the amending bill had resumed.

> That was a definite promise of a truce, and that truce has been broken by the government. The right honourable gentleman [Asquith] also said – or I think it was I who said it, but he agreed to it – that by the adjournment no party to the controversy would be placed in a worse position. Does any honourable member opposite say that we are not placed in a worse position when we have no opportunity of discussing the amending bill?

Overcoming interruptions from the Liberal benches as he goes on to talk of government betrayal, treachery and dishonourable behaviour,

Law next directs his fire at what he calls the other party to 'this great injustice', namely John Redmond and his fellow nationalists.

> I have not at all the same feeling of indignation against the honourable gentleman [Redmond] below the gangway – not at all. The honourable member for Waterford is not the head of a government. He is not responsible for the welfare of this country. He is only doing what he has done always, putting pressure on the government to get his own way, that is all. But I do say this with all sincerity, and I believe it is true, that the honourable member for Waterford has never in his life, from his own point of view, made so great a mistake as the one he is making now. If he had allowed the government to act decently in this great crisis he would have done more to help his cause than he will do by a hundred victories such as he is going to gain in the House of Commons today.

Redmond's eve-of-war speech in the Commons, Law adds, undermined 'the strength of the unionism' of a great many Unionist members of the house. 'I was moved by it myself because I accepted it literally. I did not understand then that it was only a promise of conditional loyalty. I have no doubt the honourable member this afternoon will make a speech promising great things, now that he has got his way. We shall see.'

Determined to hold the high moral ground, the Conservative leader assures Asquith that, although the Unionists have been treated 'abominably', their loyalty may still be counted on.

Law, declaring it 'indecent' that they should be made to debate Home Rule at all under the current circumstances, then leads the Conservative and Unionist MPs, including Carson, from the chamber. Asquith is unfazed by the stunt, writing to Venetia Stanley almost immediately: 'It was not really a very impressive spectacle – a lot of prosaic and for the most part middle-aged gentlemen trying to look like the early French revolutionists in the Tennis Court.'

Redmond, speaking after Law, cannot resist opening with a humorous dig at the now absent Tory leader: 'The only controversial thing I will say about that speech is that, having told the world that the government of this empire is made up of men devoid of honour, devoid of truth, devoid of decency, he wound up his speech by saying that his one desire in life was to support the government in this crisis.'

Despite Law's determination to declare the outcome a defeat for the Unionists, Redmond is well aware that the nationalists' 'victory' is far from complete.

> Under the plan of the government, the [Home Rule] bill is immediately to pass into law, but it is not to become operative for a year or more. The idea of anyone pretending that out of a proposal of that kind we are snatching an advantage from the state of things caused by the war seems to me absolutely absurd. I certainly do not regard this settlement of the difficulty as a party triumph for my friends or myself, and I shall certainly not represent it as a party triumph either in this house or in Ireland. It is nothing of the kind. It inflicts a severe disadvantage upon us.

Redmond realises, however, that in spite of his disappointment at the way matters have turned out, the moment requires a more statesmanlike speech than that delivered by Law. 'Under all the circumstances of the case, this moratorium which the government propose is a reasonable one. Of course, when everybody is preoccupied by the war ... the idea is absurd, and cannot be entertained by any intelligent man, that under these circumstances a new government and a new parliament could be erected in Ireland.'

In fact, he adds, the delay may yet prove to be a good thing. He has still not given up hope that out of the war may come a new solidarity between nationalists and unionists that will render the partition of Ireland unnecessary. He also takes the opportunity to answer suggestions in the Tory press that Ireland is not doing its share in supporting the war effort, pointing out that there are more Irishmen than British per head of population in the regular army and many of them are already performing heroic deeds at the Front.

> I have been moved, and I dare say every man in this house has been moved, by some of the war stories that have come back from the seat of war. There is the story of the Munster Fusiliers, who stood by

their guns all day, and in the end dragged them back to their lines themselves. There was, too, the story in yesterday's papers from the lips of the wounded French soldiers, who described how the Irish Guards charged with the bayonet three regiments of German cavalry. As the wounded French soldier said, they charged singing 'a strange song that I have never heard before'. The newspaper man asked the wounded soldier what were the words, and the answer was, 'I cannot tell you what the words were, but it was something about God saving Ireland'. I saw these men marching through London on their way to the station. They marched here past this building singing 'God save Ireland'. It is unnecessary for me to tell this house of the magnificent material that the country has at its disposal in the Irish soldier, and the sneers that we have heard are a little too hard on us.

The *Times*, in an article today, says nationalist Ireland still disowns her gallant soldiers, flaunts placards against enlistment, and preaches sedition in her newspapers. That is a cruel libel on Ireland. The men who are circulating handbills against enlistment, the men who are publishing little wretched rags once a week or once a month, which none of us ever see, who are sending them by some mysterious agency through the post in this country, and day by day to members [of parliament], these are the little group of men who never belonged to the national constitutional party at all, but who have been all through, and are today, our bitterest enemies. If you take up these wretched rags you will find praises of the emperor of Germany in the same sentence as are denunciations of my colleagues and myself.

For the first time, certainly for over one hundred years, Ireland in this war feels her interests are precisely the same as yours. She feels, she will feel, that the British democracy has kept faith with her. She knows that this is a just war. She knows, she is moved in a very special way by the fact that this war is undertaken in the defence of small nations and oppressed peoples.

Redmond's claim that Ireland regards the war as 'just' is not in dispute. For several weeks the nationalist papers have been filled with stories of the atrocities committed by the advancing German army in Belgium, including mass killings of civilians and the infamous burning of the university library of Louvain as part of the sacking of that city. The feeling this has aroused in Ireland is exemplified by a telegram Redmond receives from the Christian Brothers in Cork offering to take in a hundred Belgian boys at their own expense. For Redmond it is a question of honour that Ireland play its part in the defence of a fellow small Catholic nation, and now he goes further than he did on 3 August, when he offered to have the Irish Volunteers defend the coasts of Ireland in the event of war.

> I say that the manhood of Ireland will spring to your aid in this war. Speaking personally for myself, I do not think it is an exaggeration to say that on hundreds of platforms in this country during the last few years I have publicly promised, not only for myself, but in the name of my country, that when the rights of Ireland were admitted by the democracy of England, that Ireland would become the strongest arm in the defence of the empire. The test has come sooner than I, or anyone, expected. I tell the prime minister that that test will be honourably met. I say for myself, that I would feel myself personally dishonoured if I did not say to my fellow countrymen, as I say today to them here, and as I will say from the public platform when I go back to Ireland, that it is their duty, and should be their honour, to take their place in the firing line in this contest.

This new suggestion that it is the 'duty' of Irishmen to fight in the war goes unremarked upon in the following day's national newspapers, which focus instead on the news that the Home Rule Bill is at last to become law, albeit with a delay in its implementation. Even that news is dwarfed by the extensive space given in the Irish papers to news on the progress of the war.

∽

On the morning of Friday, 18 September 1914, the House of Lords is in session, but not a single peer – Unionist or Liberal – has taken his place on the members' benches. Row upon row of seating lies empty in the almost ghostly chamber. The only people present are the five lords commissioners, dressed in ornate scarlet robes and three-cornered hats, who sit, not on the ordinary benches, but under the king's throne at the head of the chamber. And in the middle of the space sit two clerks in wig and gown.

In contrast to this peculiar scene, every available viewing space at the entrances to the chamber and the galleries overhead is crowded. John Redmond is there, alongside many fellow members of the Irish Party and its supporters. All wait patiently as the five lords give the Royal Assent – on behalf of the king – to one Act of parliament after another: the Police Constables (Naval and Military Service) Act, the National Insurance (Navy and Army) Act, the Prize Courts (Egypt, Zanzibar, and Cyprus) Act ...

After 11 Acts have been duly dealt with, the central figure among the lords commissioners, Richard Haldane, former secretary of state for war and now lord chancellor, announces an unprecedented procedure. The royal assent is now to be given, for the first time, to an Act passed under the terms of the Parliament Act of 1911, under which the House of Lords lost its veto over legislation sent from the Commons.

The clerk of the crown, standing to the side of the table in the middle of the chamber, steps to one side and reads from a printed paper, in a loud voice, 'Government of Ireland Act!' The clerk of the parliament, standing to his right, turns, bows to the lord chancellor, and pronounces the decisive words: 'Le Roy le veult!' – the king wills it. With this a tumultuous cheer rises up from all the viewing areas and rings around the building.

In the ante-room of the chamber, Redmond is mobbed by party colleagues as well as Liberal and Labour MPs who press forward to shake his hand or slap him on the back. In a moment Redmond's close friend, the Kilkenny MP Pat O'Brien, produces an Irish flag – a golden harp on a green background – and, holding it over his head, leads the way back to the House of Commons for the ceremony to be completed.

Here, in accordance with custom, the deputy speaker of the house, J.H. Whitley, announces that he has been to the House of Lords and heard the royal assent being given to the Government of Ireland Act. A round of applause ensues and as it subsides the Labour MP Will Crooks asks aloud, in his distinctive Cockney accent, if it would be in order to sing 'God Save the King'. Such a proceeding is unheard of in the House of Commons, but Crooks is off and leading before anybody has time to stop him.

All the members present, including the Irish nationalists, rise and join in, as do those watching from the press and public galleries. As the last strains of the anthem are heard, Crooks lets out a cry: 'God save Ireland!' John Redmond responds in kind: 'And God save England too!'

For Redmond, who rarely says anything without due deliberation, this is more than just a reflex reaction in the highly emotional circumstances of the moment. His remarks reflect his true feeling about Ireland's duty to stand by her neighbour in its time of great trial. With the Home Rule Bill at last on the statute book, he feels free to throw his full weight behind the British war effort.

Chapter 22 ~

IRELAND'S DUTY

*What we want, what we ask ... is a free will offering of
a free people.*

John Redmond doesn't wait for the royal assent to be given to the Home Rule Bill before fully declaring his position on Irish support for the war. Once Herbert Asquith announces on 15 September the government's intention to place the bill on the statute book, Redmond knows there is no going back; Home Rule will be law within days and there is nothing his unionist opponents can do about it.

His response to Asquith's announcement is to issue a manifesto, published in the nationalist newspapers on 17 September 1914, setting out what he sees as Ireland's duty at this moment of crisis for the British Empire, and how he expects Ireland to be treated in return for doing its part. Stating that a new era has opened in the history of the relations between Ireland and Britain, the manifesto continues:

> A test to search men's souls has arisen. The Empire is engaged in the most serious war in history. It is a just war, provoked by the intolerable military despotism of Germany. It is a war for the defence of the sacred rights and liberties of small nations, and the respect and enlargement of the great principle of nationality. Involved in it is the fate of France, our kindred country, the chief nation of that powerful Celtic race to which we belong. The fate of Belgium, to whom we are attached by the same great ties of race, and by the common desire of a small nation to assert its freedom, and the fate of Poland, whose sufferings and whose struggle bear so marked a resemblance to our own.
>
> It is a war for high ideals of human government and international relations; and Ireland would be false to her history and to every consideration of honour, good faith and self-interest did she not willingly bear her share in its burdens and its sacrifices.

We have, even when no ties of sympathy bound our country to Great Britain, always given our quota, and more than our quota, to the firing line, and we shall do so now.

We have a right honour to claim that Irish recruits for the Expeditionary Force should be kept together as a unit, officered as far as possible by Irishmen, composed, if possible, of county battalions, to form, in fact, an 'Irish Brigade', so that Ireland may gain national credit for their deeds, and feel, like other communities of the Empire, that she, too, has contributed an army bearing her name in this historic struggle.

Simultaneously with the formation of this Irish Brigade for service abroad, our Volunteers must be put in a state of efficiency as speedily as practicable for the defence of the country.

In this way, by the time the war ends Ireland will possess an army of which she may be proud.

I feel certain that the young men of our country will respond to this appeal with the gallantry of their race.

In conclusion, I would appeal to our countrymen of a different creed and of opposite political opinions to accept the friendship we have so consistently offered them; to allow this great war, as to which their opinions and ours are the same, and our action will also be the same, to swallow up all the smaller issues in the domestic government of Ireland which now divide us; that as our soldiers are going to fight, to shed their blood and to die at each other's side in the same Army against the same enemy and for the same high purpose, their union in the field may lead to a union in their home, and that their blood may be the seal that will bring all Ireland together in one nation, and in liberties equal and common to all.

Redmond's call for all-out Irish support for the war, following his earlier statement in the House of Commons that it was the 'duty' of Irishmen to take part in it, is again not what catches the attention of the headline writers in the next day's national newspapers. Rather, it is his suggestion than an Irish brigade be formed to give the country its own distinctive place on the battlefield.

One man unlikely to be paying attention to Redmond's manifesto is Edward Carson. On the day it is published the Ulster Unionist leader, now aged 60, marries 29-year-old Ruby Frewen, a colonel's daughter, in a quiet ceremony at Charlton Musgrave parish church in London. The couple met in Hamburg two years previously after Carson watched his future bride playing tennis. His approach to winning her affections over the following months was somewhat unconventional, as one of his letters to her attests: 'Here I am stuck in bed for another day with that horrid pain in my side ... I am becoming a chronic invalid.'

They will have one son, who Carson no doubt hopes will please him more than his four children with his late wife, Annette, most of whom disappoint him in one way or another: 'My children are a rum lot,' he tells his friend Lady Londonderry in a letter.

In the political arena, however, he continues to get his way in most things, and even before Redmond's manifesto is published Carson has secured a commitment that the Ulster Volunteers will be allowed to form their own division, with officers from within the UVF ranks. Redmond is confident that the southern Volunteers will be given equal recognition.

Also on the day his manifesto is published, Redmond writes to Michael Ryan, the state solicitor in Philadelphia and national president of the United Irish League of America, an important fundraising and networking vehicle for the Irish Party. Redmond knows that many Irish people in the United States, including Ryan, whose wife is German, will instinctively side with Germany in the war and he is keen to ensure that his position is clearly understood there.

'The general sentiment of our people is unquestionably on the side of England in this war,' he tells Ryan. 'I have made a claim that Irish recruits should be put into an Irish unit and should form an Irish brigade with Irish officers, and my hope and belief is that when the War is over we will then ourselves have a large Irish Army, consisting of those who have joined the Expeditionary Force and those who have defended the country in the ranks of the Volunteers in Ireland. I need not point out to you what a source of enormous strength this will be to us if any attempt be made by any party – which personally I think most unlikely – to tamper with the Home Rule Act.'

Betraying an anxiety that his argument may not be persuasive enough to convince the influential Ryan, Redmond adds a postscript: 'The truth is that the only way we can make sure of arming and drilling a properly efficient force to make it sure that at the end of the War we will have a real Irish Army is through the War Office and the British Army. You will easily understand what the position will be if, at the end of the War, Carson has even 10,000 or 12,000 thoroughly trained men who have seen war and we have nothing on our side except a lot of half-armed and half-disciplined Volunteers who have never seen any service.'

Ryan's reply gives Redmond an early indication of the difficulties he faces in keeping Irish American support on board. 'I have not expressed myself publicly in any way regarding the War, excepting that, through my wife, I have given one hundred dollars to the German fund; but I feel very keenly the position in which we are placed,' he writes. 'It seems to me to be at entire variance with all the traditions of our people. I have no doubt that you have acted, from your point of view, with the hope of advancing Ireland's interests, and that you are convinced you are so doing, but all my sympathies are with Germany, and I believe that nine-tenths of the Americans of Irish blood think as do I.'

Former US president Theodore Roosevelt takes a different stance, writing to Redmond to tell him: 'I unreservedly admire the way you have stood by the cause of democracy as against the sheer brutal militarism of the German Empire, under its Prussian leadership, in this crisis.'

In spite of Ryan's reservations, Redmond gets on with his mission of drumming up Irish support for Britain in the war. Returning home from London to Aughavanagh on Sunday, 20 September, after the Home Rule Bill has been given the royal assent, he learns that a parade of Irish Volunteers is taking place at Woodenbridge, County Wicklow. Many of the men are known to him personally, and Redmond stops off to offer some encouragement. 'The duty of the manhood of Ireland is twofold,' he tells them. 'Its duty is, at all costs, to defend the shores of Ireland against foreign invasion. It is a duty more than that, of taking care that Irish valour proves itself; on the field of war it has always proved itself in the past.' He then makes clear exactly what Ireland's duty, as he sees it, entails:

The interests of Ireland – of the whole of Ireland – are at stake in this war. The war is undertaken in defence of the highest principles of religion and morality and right, and it would be a disgrace for ever to our country, and a reproach to her manhood, and a denial of the lessons of her history, if young Ireland confined their efforts to remaining at home to defend the shores of Ireland from an unlikely invasion, and shrunk from the duty of proving on the field of battle that gallantry and courage which has distinguished her race through all its history.

I say to you, therefore, your duty is twofold. I am glad to see such magnificent material for soldiers around me, and I say to you, 'Go on drilling and make yourselves efficient for the work, and then account yourselves as men, not only in Ireland itself, but wherever the firing line extends, in defence of right, of freedom, and of religion in this war.'

The men's cheers in response suggest Redmond has hit the right note and that, despite the frustration caused by the delay in getting the Home Rule Bill enacted, enthusiasm in Ireland for the war effort remains high. Everything is now in place for a full-scale recruitment drive and on 25 September Herbert Asquith returns to Dublin to appeal for maximum Irish support for the Allies. It is the prime minister's third stop-off in a recruiting campaign that has already taken in London and Edinburgh.

'I have come to ask you in Ireland, though you don't need my asking, to take your part,' he tells a crowd of three thousand that greets him with loud and prolonged cheers, in the Round Room in the Mansion House. 'There is no question of compulsion or bribery. What we want, what we ask, what we believe you are ready and eager to give, is a free will offering of a free people.'

Most pleasing to Redmond's ears are the warm words Asquith has for the Irish Volunteers and his declared support for the proposal that they be kept together to fight as an Irish unit.

We have of late been witnessing here in Ireland the spontaneous enrolment and organisation in all parts of the country of bodies of volunteers [cheers]. I say nothing – for I wish to avoid trespassing even a square inch on controversial topics – I say nothing of the causes or motives that brought them originally into existence [laughter], and fostered their growth and strength. I would only say, and this is my nearest approach to politics tonight, that there are two things which to my mind have become unthinkable. The first is that one section of Irishmen is going to fight another, and the second is that Great Britain is going to fight either.

I may, perhaps, for a moment address myself to the National Volunteers. I am going to ask them all over Ireland, not only them, but I make an appeal to them particularly, to contribute with promptitude and enthusiasm a large contingent of recruits to the second new army of half a million which is now growing up, as it were, out of the ground.

I should like to see, and we all want to see, an Irish brigade, or better still, an Irish army corps [cheers].

Don't let them be afraid that by joining the colours they will lose their identity and become absorbed in some invertebrate mass, or, what is perhaps equally repugnant, be artificially distributed into units which have no national cohesion or character.

We wish to the utmost limit that military exigencies will allow men who have been already associated in this or that district in training and in common exercises to be kept together and to continue to recognise the corporate bond which now unites them ... no Irishman in responding need be afraid he is prejudicing the future of the volunteers [cheers].

Redmond, who is also greeted with loud and sustained cheering as well as a rendition of 'For He's a Jolly Good Fellow', says that the heart of Ireland has been profoundly moved by the heroism and sufferings of Belgium. 'Ah yes, Belgium, Poland, Alsace and Lorraine, France – these are words to conjure with the Irish people ["hear, hear!"]. I believe it is the universal sentiment of the Irish people that there never was a juster war, or one in which higher or nobler issues or principles were at stake [cheers].'

He is aware that there are some in Ireland, though not many, who say this is an English war and not an Irish one, but this is 'absolutely and fundamentally' untrue. Hard as it is to realise in the spell of 'splendid autumn weather' now being enjoyed, and in the midst of apparent peace, but Ireland is already at war, he tells his audience, which is composed of representatives of both the nationalist and southern unionist communities.

> It is true our cities have not been sacked; it is true our cathedrals and our universities have not been burned to the ground; it is true our peaceful and happy villages have not been burned to the ground; it is true our women and children have not been slaughtered before our eyes. Why is that so? Under God, there is only one reason, and that is the army and the navy [loud cheers], and the brave men – thank God, many of them gallant Irishmen – who are day and night risking and giving their lives to defend our property, our liberty and our honour. Remove that barrier tomorrow, and in 48 hours the liberties of Ireland would be gone, our country would be devastated, our cities would be sacked and our women and children would be slaughtered [cheers]. Under these circumstances, is not this an Irish war? ['Hear, hear!'] And what is Ireland's duty in this war? ['Fight! Fight!']

Redmond also moves to underscore Asquith's promise of an Irish army corps, poking fun at himself in the process over his 'lamentable ignorance of military affairs' that led to his asking for the lesser unit of a brigade. 'I meant a corps,' he says, to laughter. He has seen, he says, that in Wales a committee has been formed for the purpose of bringing an army corps into existence. Could the prime minister or Lord Kitchener not see to it that the same procedure be applied in Ireland? he asks. 'I say to the prime minister, and through him to the people of Great Britain,' Redmond concludes to further loud cheers, 'you have kept faith with Ireland, and Ireland will keep faith with you.'

The uniformly positive coverage of the event in the next day's national newspapers – including the *Irish Independent* – indicate that while Redmond is keeping faith with Britain, Ireland is keeping faith with him. The headlines and sub-headings in the *Cork Examiner* are typical: 'IRELAND & THE WAR – MR ASQUITH IN DUBLIN – MAGNIFICENT MEETING – SPLENDID RECEPTION'.

An editorial in the *Independent* provides unqualified backing for Redmond's stance. 'The Prime Minister had a reception in Dublin last night which was in perfect accord with the sympathy which Ireland as a whole has with the mission on which he came,' it begins, before stating later: 'Mr Redmond made last night the point upon which we have ourselves laid stress, that Ireland's material interests are at stake in this war. Whatever she has gained by years of agitation would be lost were it not for the protection given by the British fleet.'

The papers carry reports of minor protests during the Mansion House meeting, but only by the same few 'malcontents' – as the *Independent* calls them – who have always been opposed to Redmond and his party. These include the labour leaders Jim Larkin and James Connolly, who organise an anti-enlistment demonstration that threatens to get out of hand when members of the Irish Citizen Army fire shots outside the recruiting office of the Royal Dublin Fusiliers on College Green.

In an unrelated incident, two leading suffragettes, Hannah Sheehy Skeffington and Margaret Connery, and Sheehy Skeffington's husband, Francis, a supporter of the movement, are taken into custody for a short period to ensure that they don't disrupt the Mansion House meeting.

Another challenge to Redmond's authority comes in the form of a statement released the night before the Mansion House meeting by the original provisional committee of the Irish Volunteers, repudiating the sentiments expressed by Redmond at Woodenbridge and, in effect, announcing the expulsion of his representatives from the movement. Written by Eoin MacNeill and signed by 20 members of the provisional committee, including P.H. Pearse, Joseph Plunkett, Thomas MacDonagh, Éamonn Ceannt and Seán Mac Diarmada, the statement says that Redmond has announced a policy and programme fundamentally at variance with the Volunteers' aims and pledges.

> He has declared it to be the duty of the Irish Volunteers to take foreign service under a Government which is not Irish. He has made the announcement without consulting the Provisional Committee, the Volunteers themselves, or the People of Ireland to whose service alone they are devoted. Having disregarded the

Irish Volunteers and their solemn engagements, Mr Redmond is no longer entitled through his nominees to any place in the administration and guidance of the Irish Volunteers organisation.

The establishment view of this development is encapsulated in the *Cork Examiner*'s dismissive sub-headline over its short, single-column report on the statement: 'DUBLIN SOREHEADS'.

In the ensuing split the vast majority of the organisation's members follow Redmond into the newly constituted National Volunteers, which is later estimated to have a membership of 160,000 compared to 12,000 in the original body, which remains known as the Irish Volunteers.

With Home Rule now on the statute book and majority support in Ireland for his policy on the war secured, John Redmond's next objective is to ensure that the British government delivers on the promise to allow nationalist Irishmen to fight in the war as a distinct unit. Five days after the Mansion House rally he receives a welcome letter from the prime minister, confirming the pledge in writing. 'I have spoken to Lord Kitchener,' Asquith writes, '... and he will have the announcement made that the War Office has sanctioned the formation of an Irish Army Corps.'

Redmond is now fully engaged in supporting the British war effort and he spells out his reasons to a large crowd of supporters at a rally in Wexford, conducted amid huge fanfare, on Sunday, 4 October. On arrival by motor car from Aughavanagh, Redmond is led in a parade through streets lined with well-wishers shouting support. The procession begins on Redmond Square at the monument to Redmond's grand uncle, also John Redmond MP, underlining the extent to which – though he may live in County Wicklow and represent Waterford in the House of Commons – this is still a homecoming for the nationalist leader.

Numerous local bands and more than five thousand armed and uniformed members of the National Volunteers give the occasion an air of pageantry, and before his main speech Redmond tells the men that it is the government's intention not only to form an Irish army corps for the duration of the war, but – as Asquith also promised in his

Mansion House speech – to maintain the volunteers after the war 'as a recognised permanent force for the defence of the country'.

He asks the volunteers present to 'mark what this means'. There is no provision in the Government of Ireland Act for the establishment of an Irish army, he points out. But now they have a pledge that when the war is over, Ireland will have its own permanent defence force. This does not place the men under any obligation to fight in the war, he adds, dismissing as 'a lie' the 'absurd and malicious rumour' that he has entered into a bargain with the government to compel the volunteers to go to France to fight. 'This matter of recruiting is a matter for the conscience of every individual Irishman whether he is a volunteer or not [cheers].'

A short time later, before a crowd of thousands in a packed Bull Ring – the Wexford square that has seen similar rallies addressed by O'Connell, Parnell and other political leaders, and which was also the location of a pike-making factory during the 1798 rebellion – Redmond makes the case anew for Ireland's participation in the war.

> I have heard words, not many, and not in many places, I have heard words which have convinced me that in some quarters there is some misapprehension as to the meaning of this war. We hear men talking about fighting England's battle, as if Irishmen and Ireland were not concerned! This is not a question of England's battle. It is a question of the maintenance of the independence and the liberty of all the smaller nations of the world, Ireland included [cheers]. Poland, Belgium, Holland, Servia [Serbia] – every one of these small nations has its independence at stake.

Redmond cites one further reason for nationalist Ireland to join the war in its own interests. His overtures to the Ulster Unionists on the potential for co-operation between the northern and southern Volunteers have so far failed to bear fruit. Edward Carson, indeed, has stepped up his anti-nationalist rhetoric since the beginning of the war, telling an Ulster Day commemoration event in Belfast that Home Rule has been made law 'by treachery' and that unionists will continue to resist it 'to the last'.

Nevertheless, Redmond clings to the hope that the war can bring the two communities on the island together, and could yet be the means by which partition is avoided, telling his Wexford audience:

> I pray with all my heart and soul that out of this terrible war, with all its suffering, with all its bloodshed ... one blessed result may come to Ireland, and that is that the blood shed side by side on the field of battle, by Catholics and Protestants, by north and south of Ireland Irishmen, may prove to be the seal of the future unity of our Irish nation [cheers].

The enthusiastic reception for Redmond is indicative of widespread support for his policy on the war, but a vocal minority – including the radical if small Sinn Féin group and followers of the socialist leaders James Connolly and Jim Larkin – undertake energetic anti-recruitment campaigns.

A foretaste of things to come is witnessed in Dublin city centre on Sunday, 11 October, when the National Volunteers, marching to commemorate the death of Charles Stewart Parnell 24 years earlier, encounter a party of the rival Irish Volunteers who have been called out by Eoin MacNeill. Members of the Irish Citizen Army are also marching, with Jim Larkin at their head, and a skirmish between the rival groups results in shots being fired and bayonets drawn. Nobody is injured, however, and the incident receives only minor attention in the following day's newspapers, in contrast to the blanket coverage – as is the case every day – of developments in the war.

A week later, at a ceremony in Kilkenny to present him with the freedom of the city, Redmond provides further justification for his stance and hits back at those agitating against him. Every leader of the constitutional nationalist movement – including O'Connell, Butt and Parnell – made it clear that if Ireland was allowed to take its place as an autonomous nation with the British Empire, it would take its share of the burdens as well as the advantages that flowed from that, he says.

He and his colleagues have been telling the truth over the past four years, he adds, when on hundreds of English platforms they have said: 'Give us Home Rule and we will be a strength, not a weakness, to your empire.' They now accepted the responsibility that the concession of Home Rule cast upon them, he continues before castigating his opponents:

> A little body of men who, if you look back on the past 20 or 30 years, have done absolutely nothing to gain our free constitution ['hear, hear'], whose names you won't find in the nationalist movement of the last 20 years – hunt in the history of that movement how you will – a little body of men who have never been known there, who have been working the movement as cranks and mischief-makers, lurking in dark corners, to endeavour to stab us and trip us up in our work, a small body of these men are saying to the Irish people, 'Oh! It is true England has passed Home Rule and given it to you, but you have got a chance now of doing her an ill turn, and of having it out with her for some of the wrongs committed on your fathers two or three hundred years ago. Never mind your promises, never mind your treaty, tear up the pledges and refuse to stand by the words of your leaders and their colleagues.'
>
> Well, of course, the Irish people will do nothing of the kind [applause]. The Irish people are too politically intelligent ... they are too politically educated to adopt a suicidal policy of that kind, a policy which everyone who is not a fool, a madman or a knave must know would end in untold suffering and misery for this country in the future.

He also again emphasises that recruitment for the war is voluntary, dismissing as a 'ridiculous falsehood' a report in the *Irish Independent* that suggests that the government is planning to make it compulsory for some classes of Irishmen.

All the same, Redmond sees it as a matter of national honour that Ireland provide a proportionate share of soldiers for the Front, and over the previous fortnight his priority has been to ensure that the government delivers on its promise to establish an Irish army corps. He is convinced that nothing would do more to boost recruitment in Ireland, but he finds the War Office inexplicably reluctant to move on the matter. On 14 October – almost three weeks after he promised the formation of such a corps in his Mansion House speech – Asquith writes to Redmond to say that he has again spoken to Kitchener on the matter, 'and I hope that a satisfactory official announcement will now be made without delay'.

No such announcement is ever made, but two days later an apparent breakthrough comes in the form of a friendly letter from Lieutenant General Sir Lawrence Parsons, who tells Redmond that he has been appointed by Kitchener to command the 16th Division of his new army, 'because I am an Irishman and understand my fellow countrymen'. Parsons writes:

Now I have been reading your recent admirable speeches stimulating recruiting, and your references to an 'Irish Brigade' induce me to think that you have not been informed that three essentially Irish Brigades form the 16th Division, and that, therefore, it has every claim to be called an Irish Division, a much finer and larger unit than a Brigade.

I have had a considerable share of selecting the officers of the Division, who are almost all Irishmen, of every political religious creed except Jews.

I trust, therefore, that you will deem us worthy of acknowledgment as the 'Irish Division', and that in the future you will assist us by your eloquence.

It would give me and my command very real pleasure if you would come and speak at any or all of the places where we have Brigades – i.e. Fermoy, Buttevant and Tipperary.

I am one of the Birr, King's County family of Parsons, was born there, and, I think, may call myself an Irishman and a descendant of one of the strongest opponents of the Union, and an equally strong supporter of Catholic emancipation and endowment of the Catholic Church.

Redmond is encouraged by this development, but it proves to be the beginning of a deeply frustrating and at times absurd series of exchanges between the two men. Parsons' views, it transpires, oppose Redmond's on almost every matter the nationalist leader raises with him. He consistently rejects candidates recommended by Redmond for an officer's commission, and when it is suggested to him by a third party that thousands of Irishmen in Britain are anxious to join the division, Parsons replies that he does not want to fill his ranks 'with Liverpool, and Glasgow, and Cardiff Irish, who are slum-birds that we don't want'.

'I want to see the clean, fine, strong, temperate, hurley-playing country fellows such as we used to get in the Munsters, Royal Irish, Connaught Rangers. I was on service with all these regiments, and they could march round most English regiments and stand heat, cold, and wet like salamanders,' he writes.

While this correspondence is taking place, Redmond feels compelled to defend Ireland's contribution to the war effort against 'shameful and dishonest' criticism in the Tory press, telling supporters at a rally in Tuam, County Galway, on 6 December that according to official figures there are 130,000 Irishmen in the British army. Since the war broke out, he adds, 53,498 Irishmen have signed up, of whom 27,828 are Catholics. More than sixteen thousand members of the National Volunteers have joined as recruits or reservists in the same period. 'These taunts about Ireland shirking are infamously untrue,' he states.

Yet even those figures indicate that only about one in ten of the National Volunteers is signing up for military service, and that the rate of recruitment among Catholic Irishmen is much lower than among Protestants. They also mask the fact that while northern nationalists are enlisting at the same rate as their unionist counterparts, recruitment in the south and west of Ireland remains much slower than throughout the rest of the United Kingdom.

Redmond believes that critics of the rate of recruitment in Ireland are overlooking factors such as the high rate of emigration, which has left the country with proportionately fewer men of fighting age, and the fact that a predominantly rural, agriculture-based society is less able to spare its young male workers than one in which most people live in large cities.

He is convinced, however, that enthusiasm would be greater if the War Office acted on his advice to allow a distinctive Irish division to have its own colours and badge. Some progress has been made. In response to a memorandum submitted by Redmond to the Cabinet in November, the War Office has agreed to increase the number of Catholic chaplains and to provide the men of Parsons's 16th Division with a distinctively Irish badge to wear on their caps; Redmond's suggestion is a harp. It is has also been agreed to consider his proposal to allow Irishmen enlisting in Britain to be transferred to an Irish division.

Yet again he finds that promises made in London do not translate into action. His correspondence with Parsons on the badge issue alone epitomises his difficulties. After Redmond advises the general of the War Office's approval of an Irish badge, Parsons replies that he is opposed to any special badge for the regiments of his division. 'That the Ulster Division has a special badge is no reason that we should have one, as I think it was wrong to give them one, as it was wrong to form that division at all,' he writes, with typical candour. And if the division must have a badge, he adds, 'I would not recommend a harp ... I would prefer a plain sprig of shamrock on an Irish cross'.

The correspondence between the two men on the badge continues into the new year. Parsons holds to his position but reluctantly agrees to allow a committee to draw up a design for the badge for consideration by the War Office. The committee's suggestion of an emblem incorporating the four Irish provinces is rejected by Kitchener, who considers it too complicated, and sends word back to Redmond that he would prefer something simple, such as a shamrock – or a harp!

Most exasperating of all for Redmond is a comment in a letter by Parsons in a letter that he does not mind seeing Irish soldiers dispersed to regiments in England, Scotland and Wales. 'They act as leaven on dough,' he writes. 'In my thirty years' regimental service I always had the leavened dough in my battery and it was very good.' This more than any other comment demonstrates to Redmond the extent to which the two men have been at cross purposes from the beginning.

Despite the obstacles being placed in his way, he and party colleagues continue to support the recruitment campaign on platforms throughout the country. Speaking to members of the Cork battalion of the National Volunteers, Redmond's brother Willie, the MP for East Clare – after affirming his nationalist credentials by reminding his audience that he once served time in Kilmainham Gaol with Charles

Stewart Parnell – urges his audience: 'Don't go, but come with me.' Willie is as good as his word, going off in 1915 with the 16th Division to fight on the Western Front at the age of 54. John's son William (Billie) also joins up.

John Redmond continues to push for the National Volunteers remaining at home to be reconstituted as a home defence force. But on this issue too, he finds Kitchener and the War Office wholly uninterested in progressing matters.

Redmond has been scrupulous in avoiding any note of public controversy since the war began, but addressing 12,000 members of the Volunteers in Limerick on 20 December his frustration gets the better of him. 'I cannot for the life of me understand', he says, 'why it is that the government and the war office are so chary about giving assistance and instruction to help turn these volunteers into an efficient home defence.'

As 1915 arrives and Redmond's persistent representations to the Cabinet and the War Office continue to bear little fruit, the government's recalcitrance places a strain on his relationship with his deputy leader, John Dillon.

At the outset of the war Dillon supported the recruitment campaign, telling an audience in Ballaghaderreen, County Roscommon, on 4 October – the same day Redmond spoke in Wexford – that Ireland cannot be neutral in the war. 'For 40 years successive Irish leaders, with the full assent of the Irish people, have told England that if she granted Home Rule to Ireland the Irish people would be her loyal friends. The Irish race have never in the past broken their faith, and I do not believe they will break it now.'

Within weeks, however, Dillon is pushing Redmond – unsuccessfully – to demand a debate in the House of Commons on the government's failure to deliver on its promises to establish an Irish army corps and to train and equip the Volunteers. By the turn of the year, he has withdrawn from the recruitment campaign in disillusionment and has taken to referring to Redmond, in correspondence with colleagues, as 'the chairman'. He has always considered General Parsons to be an 'Orange ass', he tells T.P. O'Connor, 'but the chairman would hear nothing against him'.

In February, Kitchener explicitly rejects Redmond's demand that the Volunteers be trained as a home defence force, conveying the message that such a move would not 'fall in with the military requirements of the moment'. The problem, T.P. O'Connor tells Redmond, is that in Kitchener they are dealing with 'an Irish Orangeman who takes the Irish Orange view'.

Redmond's big problem is that while Asquith remains sympathetic to his concerns, he has higher priorities in leading the prosecution of a war that is killing more than 3,000 British soldiers a week. When Augustine Birrell tries to draw the prime minister into the row between Redmond and Parsons over the Irish badge question, Asquith writes despairingly to Venetia Stanley: 'I suppose that as usual I shall have to try to compose the controversy – a storm in a slop-basin, if ever there was one.'

The prestige of the National Volunteers receives a boost on Easter Sunday 1915, when more than 25,000 members stage what the *Irish Independent* describes as a 'magnificent display' in the Phoenix Park in Dublin. An estimated 250,000 people turn out to witness the Volunteers march in a parade reviewed by Redmond and Colonel Maurice Moore. Even the reporter from the London *Times* is moved to describe the event as 'spectacular' and an 'undoubted success'.

If anything, though, the demonstration serves to mask the state of decline into which the Volunteers have fallen. The force lost many of its drill instructors, who were members of the British army reserve, at the outset of the war. The refusal of the War Office to replace them or assist in turning the organisation into one fit to replace the army as a coastal defence unit has resulted in a sharp fall in enthusiasm around the country and a decline in volunteer activity.

There are no speeches at the Easter Sunday demonstration, but in an interview with the press afterwards Redmond expresses public frustration at the government's failure to capitalise on the offer made by him at the start of the war to provide the Volunteers for the defence of Ireland's coasts.

'I am informed,' he says, 'that 20,000 regular troops are today engaged in the work of home defence, which most undoubtedly could be quite efficiently carried out by the quite magnificent body of volunteers who visited Dublin today in conjunction with their brethren in the north of Ireland, and it seems inconceivable to me that after the spectacle in the streets of Dublin today, and the Phoenix Park, that the government will any longer refrain from utilising in this way for the defence of Ireland these splendid fellows.'

Redmond's despair at the government's ineptitude in dealing with the Volunteers is palpable. An unexpected opportunity to directly influence British policy on the war and Ireland, however, is about to come his way.

Chapter 23 ～

O'DONOVAN ROSSA COMES HOME

There is a limit to our patience. We cannot, and will not, agree to this.

I n the early hours of 19 May 1915, John Redmond receives a telegram from the British prime minister. The nationalist leader has been difficult to find, because the messenger from Dublin Castle initially went to Redmond's home in Aughavanagh, only to be told he has been staying elsewhere that night, at the south Dublin address of his daughter, Johanna, and her family.

It is 3 a.m. when Redmond is presented with an invitation from Herbert Asquith to join the British Cabinet. The prime minister, facing a crisis over press revelations of a shortage of shells for soldiers fighting in France, as well as the disastrous prosecution of the Gallipoli campaign, has decided to bring all of the main parties – including the Irish nationalists – into the government.

Roused from sleep, Redmond reads Asquith's unexpected note: 'The Ministry is about to be reconstructed on a broad national basis, and certain Opposition and Labour Ministers will be asked to join. I am most anxious you should join. The administration will be a war administration, and will cease when the War is ended. I cannot mention names as nothing is settled. The Opposition are anxious that Carson, whose administrative gifts they value, should be included. Present [Irish] Chief Secretary [Birrell] will remain in his office and in the Cabinet. Would like to hear from you or to see you at your earliest convenience.'

The offer to join the Cabinet and take a direct role in the prosecution of the war comes at a time when anti-German sentiment has reached new heights, in Ireland and throughout the world. Just 12 days earlier, the sinking by a German u-boat of the *Lusitania* passenger ship off the Old Head of Kinsale, with the loss of almost two thousand lives, has provoked unprecedented anger.

'Whatever sympathy may have been hitherto exhibited in neutral countries with Germany must have been cancelled by this foul and ghoulish crime,' the *Irish Independent* said in an editorial on 10 May. 'So far as the Allies are concerned, the moral of the horrid massacre is plain. Our military efforts must be augmented in every possible way ... Beyond all doubt, the outrage will give an immense fillip to recruiting.'

Redmond, long frustrated by the British government's inept recruitment policies in Ireland, now has an opportunity to join that very government and put things right. He can also ensure that he is on hand to thwart any efforts by Edward Carson, should he too join the Cabinet to obstruct the introduction of Home Rule. Carson and his supporters have already made several threats that, as soon as the war is over, the Ulster Volunteers will again take up the anti-Home Rule fight. Asquith's invitation is, in addition, an opportunity for him to gain Cabinet experience while he waits for the day, not far off, when he assumes the leadership of the government of his own country.

Redmond gives his answer there and then to the young Englishman who has delivered the message, to be conveyed back to the prime minister. It's a no.

Later that morning, following a meeting with John Dillon, he writes to Asquith setting out his reasons:

> While thanking you, I feel sure you will understand when I say the principles and history of the party I represent make the acceptance of your offer impossible.
>
> From the commencement of the War the Irish Party and myself have been anxious to do, and have done, all in our power to aid your Government in the successful prosecution of the War, and in the future you can fully rely on us for all the help in our power to give; but, even if I were free to accept your offer, I am convinced my doing so would not increase my power to be of service.

Later the same day Redmond sends the prime minister a second message: 'In view of the fact that it is impossible for me to join I think most strongly Carson should not be included. From Irish point of view inclusion would do infinite harm, and make our efforts to help far more difficult.'

The following day, Redmond receives a further communication, this time from Augustine Birrell:

> Prime Minister directs me to send you another message expressing his urgent desire that you should reconsider decision and come in. Labour has joined, and without Ireland broad national basis and the consequent appeal for confidence will be endangered. If personal objections prevail, can you name anyone else, anyone except T.P., to represent Ireland within the Cabinet?
>
> Carson is put as leading member of the Opposition. Do not know his own wishes. Nothing decided yet, but he might have to come in.

Redmond is taken aback by the suggestion that his refusal to accept Asquith's offer might have been seen as personal rather than political, and writes back:

> My objections are not in the least personal, and apply with full force to anyone representing the Irish National Party. By adhering to principles on which our party was founded our power to help any Government which may be formed will be much greater than it would be if we joined.

Asquith refuses to give up, writing again to Redmond on 24 May, 'I am sorry to appear to be importunate, but I attach more value than I can describe to your active participations in the new National Government.' He urges Redmond to bring the matter before the Irish Party and impress upon his colleagues the importance that he – Asquith – attaches to it.

Redmond is unmoved, writing again to Asquith to tell him that the party unanimously takes the same view as himself on it, adding:

> I would like to say I feel more sorry than words can express at having to refuse any request coming from you, or at having the appearance of refusing any small assistance to you in the extraordinary difficulties of the position in which you stand, which difficulties, I fully realise, are not at all of your making.

He insists on his opposition to Carson's inclusion in the new Cabinet:

> For the Irish people, it will mean installed in power the leader of the Ulster revolters who, the other day, was threatening hostilities to the forces of the Crown and the decision of Parliament. It will arouse grave suspicion and will certainly enormously increase the difficulties of my friends and myself.

The sudden collapse of the Liberal government and its replacement by a coalition, albeit under the continued leadership of Asquith, has left Redmond in an extremely vulnerable position. His acceptance of a place in the Cabinet would have gone down poorly with many of his supporters in Ireland, but by remaining outside it he has no means of counteracting the influence of the Tories, who are now back in a position to impose their views on policy on Ireland.

Redmond soon fires off another letter to Asquith urging that no Unionists in the new government be given a role in the administration of Ireland. He is dismayed, then, to learn from Birrell that the position of lord chancellor of Ireland is to be offered to James Campbell, Carson's fellow Unionist MP for Trinity College, who only months previously was urging on northern unionists the idea that it was their 'duty' to fight a civil war against their nationalist fellow countrymen.

For days, rumours of Campbell's imminent appointment circulate in the nationalist press, though the *Cork Examiner* says they are 'almost impossible to believe', arguing, in a leader article on 2 June, 'Irish public opinion can scarcely be expected to stand such a proposal, and if an attempt be made to put it into practice there will be an end to the political truce as far as Ireland is concerned.'

Echoing the *Examiner*'s words, Redmond telegraphs Asquith on 5 June: '… proposal to appoint Campbell has created intense feeling in Ireland, and would inevitably mean end of political truce in Ireland and necessitate immediate discussion of question in the House of Commons.'

Asquith attempts to head off any potential controversy with an emollient letter to Redmond explaining that the Tories insisted on having a say in the administration of Ireland and Scotland, and proposed the Campbell appointment. Both he and David Lloyd George – they were admittedly too preoccupied with other things to give the matter much attention – accepted the idea, given that the lord chancellor does not appoint judges and has an increasingly limited role in administration generally. As a result the position has been offered to Campbell and he has accepted it.

When they realised how much difficulty the appointment was causing the Irish Party, Asquith adds, they asked Bonar Law to be released from it, but the Tory leader replied that they were honour bound to stand by the offer to Campbell, and that if his name had to be withdrawn they would insist on another role in the Irish administration. They had particularly suggested the lord chancellorship on the basis that it should not cause the nationalists any difficulties, Law said.

'I need not say,' Asquith concludes, 'that I should regard a declaration of hostility from you and your friends, to whom I am bound by so many ties of gratitude, and I hope I may say of service, as all but fatal to the prospects of the new Government. A situation of the gravest kind would then be created.

'I know you will handle this matter with your wonted tact and consideration, and, for the moment, as quietly as may be.'

Redmond refuses to be placated. Holding nothing back in his response, he reminds Asquith of the litany of broken promises made to his party over the previous months and points out that, notwithstanding, between sixty thousand and seventy thousand new recruits from Ireland have enlisted. There has been nothing in the history of Ireland like the transformation in public opinion towards Britain, he says.

Then, suddenly, without a moment's notice, this Coalition has been launched. We have been the allies of the Liberal Party and the Liberal Government for several years; but this step was taken without any consultation whatever with, or notice given to, your Irish allies; and the first intimation received by me included the statement that Sir Edward Carson, the leader of the small Unionist Party in Ireland, who had constituted himself the apostle of physical force against law, was to be included in the new Cabinet. I was offered, with great kindness, by you a place in the Cabinet – some unknown and unnamed English office. I was not offered a place in the government of my own country.

You tell me that the Unionist leaders have insisted on the application of the principle of coalition to the government of Ireland. *We* cannot, however, ignore the fact that the Home Rule Act is on the Statute Book. We were called upon to make a great sacrifice, and we did make a great sacrifice, for the sake of the Empire, in agreeing, in the face of the War, that the Act should not come into operation until the War was over. Is the return to us to be, for all this, that we are to be asked to agree to Mr Campbell being made Lord Chancellor of our country, an office which is not merely a judicial one, but has been, for one hundred years or more, a thoroughly political office, held by one of the most powerful members of the Irish Executive Government? ...

I protest most vigorously ... that one of the most powerful positions in the Executive Government of Ireland should be handed over, not merely to a Unionist, but to a Unionist with Mr Campbell's record.

There is a limit to our patience. We in Ireland have kept the truce faithfully. Since the War broke out I have not made one single political speech in Ireland. I am sorry to say the Unionist Party in Ireland have not adopted the same attitude. The Tory Press, especially in the North of Ireland, has teemed, day after day, with the bitterest controversial political articles; while some Irish Unionist members have delivered the bitterest political harangues.

We cannot, and we will not, agree to this. A truce by all means; but, if this appointment is made, it means the deliberate breach of the truce.

I know what a serious situation has arisen. We fully recognise it; but we will face it and its consequences.

The feeling in Ireland is of the most intense character.

To emphasise the point, Redmond encloses a letter he has received from Bishop Michael Fogarty of Killaloe, complaining bitterly that 'Home Rule is dead and buried and Ireland is without a national party or a national Press. What the future has in store for us God knows. I suppose conscription, with a bloody feud between people and soldiers. I never thought that Asquith would consent to this humiliation and ruin of Irish feeling.'

The protest has its intended effect and the offer of the lord chancellorship to Campbell is withdrawn. It's a victory for Redmond, but as the year progresses his problems mount. He continues without success to lobby the War Office to train and fully equip the National Volunteers, which is still seeing a fall-off in activity as members become disillusioned by the government's failure to recognise the organisation or provide any practical support in turning it into a home defence unit.

∼

Redmond retains broad popular support, but the critics of constitutional nationalism who have always been there, though in a small minority, become louder and bolder as impatience grows over both the delay in implementing Home Rule and the perceived failure to match Redmond's gestures of goodwill towards the government.

On 1 August, opponents of Redmond's Home Rule policy score a propaganda coup when thousands line the streets for the funeral procession of Jeremiah O'Donovan Rossa, the veteran Fenian leader who died in early July in the United States. All of nationalist Ireland is represented at the funeral in Glasnevin Cemetery, including members of the Irish Party, who pay tribute to him on platforms throughout the country. But supporters of the physical force tradition take ownership of the event, and police decline to intervene when armed members of the Irish Volunteers – the original organisation from which Redmond's followers have broken away – fire a volley over the grave.

The oration is delivered by Patrick Pearse, whose concluding words, reported in the following day's *Freeman's Journal*, provide a signpost to the turbulent times ahead:

> They think that they have pacified Ireland. They think that they have purchased half of us and intimidated the other half. They think that they have foreseen everything, think that they have provided against everything; but the fools, the fools, the fools! They have left us our Fenian dead, and while Ireland holds these graves, Ireland unfree shall never be at peace.

The increasingly self-confident hardliners are boosted in their efforts to undermine Redmond by an unlikely ally: William Martin Murphy's *Irish Independent*. Unlike the *Freeman's Journal*, regarded as the Irish Party's official organ, the *Independent* – which by now has a daily circulation of 100,000 compared to the *Freeman's* twenty thousand – has never been reluctant to criticise Redmond and his colleagues.

It now takes its onslaught to a new level, frequently attacking the Irish Party and its leader for a variety of perceived failures. 'We should have expected at least as vehement a protest against the proposal for the partition of Ireland as was made against the proposed appointment of Mr Campbell as Lord Chancellor,' it states in an editorial on 28 June. In a further leader article on 15 July, it laments that a 'bad' Government of Ireland Act will be 'mutilated' by the promised amending bill to deal with Ulster. 'Through Liberal weakness and Irish supineness we may be given only a parody of a Constitution.' There are other attacks in a similar vein.

Redmond shrugs off the denunciations. 'I really do believe criticism is good for every man and makes him, or should make him, better and better,' he tells guests at a banquet for Australian priests in the Gresham Hotel in Dublin on 1 July, reported in the *Freeman's Journal*. 'In that case, I really ought to be at this moment a perfect saint [laughter]. I do not object ['hear, hear!']. I have simply gone on throughout my public life on the principle of doing what I thought right and of not appealing to the gallery [applause].'

He knows, all the same, that further criticism is inevitable as the first anniversary of the Suspensory Act – under which the implementation of Home Rule was delayed by a year or until the end of the war – approaches. In mid-July the members of Dublin Corporation debate a motion calling for Home Rule to be put into effect for the whole of Ireland immediately from when the Suspensory Act expires on 17 September. The motion is defeated after an amendment, expressing confidence in the ability of Redmond and his party to adopt the best and speediest means of bringing Home Rule into operation, is passed by 30 votes to 22. But the debate is a heated one and the narrowness of the margin is evidence of the extent to which increasing numbers of nationalists are prepared to openly question Redmond's judgement.

Redmond attempts to calm nerves at a nationalist convention in Waterford just over a month later, on 23 August, telling his audience that 'the position of Irish national self government is impregnable' and that under the Suspensory Act Home Rule, if it does not come into effect during the war, must do so the moment the war is over. He draws laughter from his audience by dismissing his opponents as 'the Mrs Gummidges of politics, who will always be with us', in reference to the permanently grumpy character in Dickens's *David Copperfield*.

The following day's *Freeman's Journal* praises Redmond for his deft putting down of the 'panic mongers' and 'chronic counsellors of despair', and the *Cork Examiner* hails his 'stirring' speech, but the more influential *Independent* renews its attack, criticising the Irish Party's tactics of the previous several years before concluding with a lament about the advent of an amending bill that will inevitably bring about the partition of Ireland: 'It cannot be said that the position of Ireland is strong when her representatives, without consulting the people as a whole, have already agreed to accept a proposal mutilating the [Home Rule] Act; a proposal regarded by them three years ago as unthinkable, and still regarded by all Home Rulers with abhorrence.'

Those opposed to Redmond's policy on the war are boosted by increasingly loud calls from Tory politicians and press for the introduction – in Britain and Ireland – of conscription as a means of filling the ranks left depleted by the horrifically high death toll in the war. Redmond is opposed to such a measure being applied to Ireland, knowing that nothing could be more counterproductive to the cause of recruitment.

At the end of September he makes yet another attempt to persuade Kitchener to adopt the measures needed to copperfasten Irish support for the war, and at last he makes some progress. 'Lord Kitchener admitted that the appeal for recruits in Ireland from this day on should be based upon the necessity of the Irish people standing by the Irish divisions that Ireland has already sent to the Front,' Redmond notes following a meeting with the war secretary. Kitchener also agrees with Redmond that it is wrong that the three brigadier generals of the 16th (Irish) Division should be Englishmen and Protestants, and that more Catholic Irish officers must be appointed.

Days later, Redmond breaks with decades of tradition by attending a conference on recruitment at the Viceregal Lodge in the Phoenix Park in Dublin. It is the first time since the Irish Party was formed under the leadership of Charles Stewart Parnell that a leader of the party has set foot in the residence of the lord lieutenant – the British government's representative in Ireland. The conference brings together senior figures from the nationalist and Ulster unionist communities on a national level for the first time since the outbreak of the war, and it is agreed to establish a department of recruiting in Ireland.

Redmond is pleased with this development, not least because he believes an improvement in the recruiting rate in Ireland will lessen the threat of conscription, the introduction of which would be 'a folly and a crime', he tells the House of Commons on 2 November.

On the same occasion, he finally unburdens himself of the frustrations of the previous year, telling his fellow MPs: 'I can speak with knowledge of what has happened in Ireland, and there, until the other day, the voluntary system [of recruiting] has never had fair play.'

Redmond raises another issue that has caused increasing discontent in nationalist Ireland: the perceived lack of acknowledgment by the authorities of the heroic deeds of Irish soldiers at the Front. 'The total absence of the official recognition of the gallantry of Irish regiments does more harm to recruiting in Ireland than anything you can conceive,' he says. 'In the end we get to know from letters and the statements of wounded officers and men who come home what our troops have been doing, but in no official statements are they mentioned.'

> The latest case in point is Admiral [John] de Robeck's dispatch relating to the landing at Seddul Bahr [in Gallipoli] in April. He mentions the work of the Australian forces and several Scotch, Welsh and English regiments in glowing terms, but not more glowing than they deserved. And yet when he comes to the landing on V Beach, which he says was the most difficult to capture, he makes no mention of the troops engaged. We know that the troops who landed on that beach were the Dublin Fusiliers and the Munster Fusiliers. The few surviving officers have given us the fullest particulars. The officer in charge of the Australians sent a message to the Dublin Fusiliers thanking them for their action. And yet in this official dispatch, while other regiments are picked out for special praise, there is not a word about the Munsters or the Dublins ['hear, hear']. That kind of thing is doing us untold mischief in Ireland [cheers].
>
> One of the battalions of the Dublin Fusiliers was known as the 'Pals'. It was made up of well-educated young men from the universities, public schools and the professions. They were all practically annihilated. I know scores of families in Dublin who are in terrible anguish over the deaths of their children. I have seen numbers of letters from survivors who speak in the highest terms of the gallantry of those lads. The feeling that prevails is expressed by the answer returned by young Dublin men when they are asked to enlist: 'yes, send us out to be killed, and when we have done our duty to our country and our regiment not one word is allowed to be said publicly in appreciation of our achievements.'

For the previous three months the Irish newspapers have carried extensive accounts of the incredibly brave exploits of the Dublin Fusiliers in horrific conditions at Suvla Bay in August, and Redmond next complains that the truth about this disaster has not yet been told. He has received communications from some of the Irish officers involved, he says, which he dare not read to the house. '[S]ome day these things will have to be inquired into, and when they are known I think it will be found that never in your military history have troops been subjected to such horrible sufferings or shown such gallantry as the 10th (Irish) Division commanded by Sir Bryan Mahon.'

Nevertheless, he concludes with a rousing assurance of continued Irish support for the war effort:

> There is only one condition in the minds of the [Irish] people. There must be no talk of a premature peace [cheers]. Any peace that does not bring condign punishment on the authors of cruelties far worse than those which earned for the Sultan of Turkey the title of 'The Grand Assassin'; that does not restore the independence of Belgium; that leaves any German troops on French soil; which does not give freedom to Alsace and Lorraine; which does not secure the independence of all smaller nations, and especially Serbia; and which does not provide some reasonable guarantee for the future peace of the world, would be regarded in Ireland as a betrayal of the living and the dead [loud cheers]. As long as that is the object we have in view – to bring the war to a glorious conclusion on those lines – no matter how long the war lasts, and no matter what sacrifices it may entail, you may rely on Ireland [cheers].

While Redmond undoubtedly retains majority support for his views, those at home who think Ireland should not be sacrificing its young men in the cause of the British Empire are growing in number. A column by 'City Man' in the *Skibbereen Eagle* of 16 October about a church gate collection by the 'Sinn Feiners' – a catch-all term for Redmond's nationalist opponents, whether or not they are members of the still tiny Sinn Féin party – gives an indication of the changing mood. The columnist writes:

> I was curious enough to watch how they were faring. I must say I was surprised at the support they were getting from those passing in and out of the Churches, from people one would think would

not countenance such a body. I expected that they would be hunted from the Church doors, but the reception they got must have the effect of making these hot-headed youths more sure of themselves than ever. ... [I]t is evident that the general public have a sneaking regard for the Sinn Feiners, and the claim the latter makes of being for Ireland only. Only this week a brother of an ex-National Volunteer, who was killed in the recent great advance, answered my sympathy with the remark: 'If he had only died for Ireland.' I expressed surprise and said he had died fighting for Ireland, and keeping the German out, but he said, 'He joined when Redmond said so, because he thought they would come home trained soldiers to fight for Home Rule, but now Home Rule will not trouble him any more.' I could not argue with the poor fellow suffering as he was from his great loss, but the old feelings will rise up in such circumstances, and the fact that such sacrifices demonstrated Ireland's loyalty to the Empire [will] be forgotten.

Redmond follows up his Commons address of 2 November with a further warning to Asquith, by letter, against the introduction of conscription to Ireland.

In your Dublin speech, you asked the Irish people for 'a free will offering of a free people', and the response has been, taking everything into account, in the words of Lord Kitchener, 'magnificent'.

Recruiting is now going on at a greater rate than ever in Ireland, and it would be a terrible misfortune if we were driven into a position on the question of conscription which would alienate that public opinion which we have now got upon our side in Ireland.

The position would, indeed, be a cruel one, if conscription were enacted for England, and Ireland excluded.

On the other hand, I must tell you that the enforcement of conscription in Ireland is an impossibility.

Faced with this dilemma, if a Conscription Bill be introduced, the Irish Party will be forced to oppose it as vigorously as possible at every stage.

On 19 December, Redmond receives a disturbing assessment from Birrell of the growing strength of the Irish Volunteers and other dissident elements. Whereas the Redmond-supporting National Volunteers are doing 'next to nothing', Birrell writes, the rival Irish Volunteers are increasing in number month by month. 'Wherever there is a plucky priest and two or three men with a little courage the *movement* is *stamped out*, but unluckily such priests and laymen are not always to be found. I am afraid it is no exaggeration to say that there are now nearer 14,000 than 13,000 of these Volunteers, and though many of them are men of *straw* and *wind*, still wherever there is an organisation it is a centre of sedition, both to Dublin Castle and the Government, and the *revolutionary* propaganda grows in strength and, I think in sincerity of purpose.'

For some time now, Redmond has been pushing the idea that the Royal Irish Constabulary (RIC) is an untapped resource of potential recruits for the Front, but Birrell disagrees: 'I don't think ... this is the time to underrate the services of the *police*, or to draw a rosy, *however truthful* picture of the crimelessness of Ireland.'

Redmond is clearly less attuned than Birrell to the real strength of the rebels, because days later he writes to Lord Wimborne, the lord lieutenant and now director of recruiting in Ireland, arguing that the RIC's numbers are 'ridiculously excessive' when related to the needs of the country. 'It is not an edifying sight, when one is appealing to young men to enlist, to see, in little country villages, four or five Royal Irish Constabulary hanging around, doing nothing, when we know that not only are they invaluable material, but that they would be only too glad to enlist if it were made possible for them to do so.'

At this point Redmond is back from a visit to the Front and on 21 December he again raises in the Commons the continuing absence of an official dispatch about the Suvla Bay massacre: 'I think it is unworthy of the government that the men who faced the untold sufferings which these men faced in that land and showed unparalleled heroism in their conduct should be left today without any official dispatch recording what they had done. What is the meaning of it?'

He finds an unlikely ally in Edward Carson, who has resigned from the Cabinet following a dispute with Asquith. Carson tells the house: 'I think it is a great public scandal that three months have elapsed since the landing at Suvla Bay, and that, except a telegram or two, we have never heard one word of those operations. The honourable member for Waterford and myself are deeply interested in those operations because there was a brave division, of which I am as proud as he is, who were fighting there.'

The two men are back on familiar ground in early January, however, arguing across the floor of the house over the government's Military Service Bill, introducing conscription for unmarried men and widowers aged between 19 and 41. Asquith has excluded Ireland from the bill. Nevertheless, the Irish Party initially opposes the measure, knowing that its introduction in Britain would inevitably lead to pressure for its extension to Ireland, before deciding to abstain when it becomes clear that it has majority support among British MPs.

Redmond defends Ireland's contribution to the war, saying that the 91,000 Irishmen – from north and south – who have signed up have exceeded the number sought by the War Office. Carson, however, responds that he is 'profoundly disappointed' at the exclusion of Ireland from the bill, asking government ministers on what basis Ireland is being treated differently from the rest of the United Kingdom. 'Is she less concerned with the result? If the Germans win, will she be less affected by the victory? Is she less bound, and, if so, on what principle, to make sacrifices to bring about a victory that is as important to her as it is to Great Britain?'

He challenges Redmond's statements that Ireland has contributed its share of recruits, saying the figures show that 92,000 Irishmen have enlisted – a slight variation on Redmond's figure – out of a total of 562,000 men of military age. An amendment by the Irish Unionists to have Ireland included in the bill is defeated, and Redmond receives congratulations from his supporters for seeing off the conscription threat.

The nationalist leader is more determined than ever to ensure that the voluntary recruitment system is seen to work in Ireland and that it provides the 1,000–1,100 recruits per week promised since the conference at the Viceregal Lodge in October. He throws himself into a new round of recruiting meetings, including one in Galway town hall on 2 February. The venue is decorated for the occasion with a banner declaring: 'God Save Ireland from the Huns'.

Sharing a platform with Wimborne and Birrell, Redmond delivers an uncompromising speech, describing as 'contemptible' the position of a tenant farmer who is not prepared to fight 'for the land of his children who are coming after him'. And he also returns to a favourite theme: the enormous potential, as he sees it, for recruitment from within the RIC. Out of 10,000 RIC members in the country, only 31 officers and 536 men have enlisted, he says, adding that a force half the size would be sufficient to carry out police duties in Ireland, thereby freeing up many more for military service.

But there is a lot more work in Ireland for the police than Redmond realises. Easter 1916 is approaching, bringing violence to the streets of Dublin and a radical change in the political landscape.

Chapter 24 ~

INSURRECTION IN DUBLIN

You are washing out our whole life work in a sea of blood.

The note from Augustine Birrell to John Redmond, sent to his flat in Kensington, London, on the evening of Easter Monday, 1916, could not be more alarming: 'I have been trying to reach you through the telephone, but you seem out. There is bad news from Dublin – a serious *insurrection*, and lives of soldiers already taken. Shall have a fuller account *very shortly*. It looks bad, though, as the troops are coming in from the Curragh. It can have, I suppose, but one ending.'

For the past three days, the security forces in Ireland have been in a state of alert following the news on Saturday morning of the arrest of Sir Roger Casement and the interception off the Kerry coast of a German ship with a cargo of arms. The following day, Easter Sunday, John Dillon writes to Redmond from Dublin to tell him the capital is 'full of most extraordinary rumours' and he has no doubt 'the Clan men' – a reference to the republican revolutionary organisation Clan na Gael – are planning 'some devilish business'.

'What it is I cannot make out,' Dillon adds. 'It may not come off. But you must not be surprised if something very unpleasant and mischievous happens this week.'

By the Monday morning, however, the Dublin Castle authorities – encouraged by the publication of an order by the leader of the Irish Volunteers, Eoin MacNeill, countermanding plans for a parade that day – are relaxed enough to allow troops stationed in the city out on leave. Many of them go to the Fairyhouse races, as does Redmond's son, William, who is at home on a break from the Front and due to return that night to France, with a stop-off in London to see his father.

On his way to Kingstown harbour after the races to catch the boat to Holyhead, William meets a barricade set up by the Irish Volunteers.

Wearing his army uniform, he puts the boot down and drives on, just making it in time for his ferry's departure. The city he leaves behind will soon be in flames; the Easter Rising has begun.

There is not much the young army captain can relay about the events in Dublin to the senior Redmond, who is desperate for news. The rebels have seized the General Post Office, cutting off telegraphic communication, and only the government wire to the Viceregal Lodge in the Phoenix Park is operating. On the Tuesday, John Redmond receives a telegram from Dillon advising that it is 'vitally important' that he remain in London for the present, adding that it is 'impossible to communicate further at present'.

Stranded in London with no means of accessing information about developments at home, Redmond can only wait and hope for the opportunity to have a proper consultation with Dillon about how best to respond to the insurrection. But his deputy leader is hampered on two fronts: the lack of a communication line to London, and the fact that he is housebound with his family in their home on North Great George's Street, which is at the centre of the fighting now raging between the army and the rebels.

A letter written by Dillon to Redmond on the Wednesday takes several days to reach him because it is impossible for the office secretary of the United Irish League, a Miss O'Brien, who is to take it to London, to get past the many barricades in the city, many of which are under sniper fire. 'The situation here is terrible,' Dillon writes. 'We are in almost absolute ignorance of what is going on, beyond the fact that fierce fighting has been in progress in many parts of the city. This morning the firing has been very heavy all round this house and in O'Connell Street. The troops appear to be at last closing in on the Sinn Feiners. I have been *completely isolated* since Monday morning, and this part of the city has been practically in possession of the Sinn Feiners up to this morning, when the troops appeared at Findlater's Church and at the top of George's Street.'

The following day, Thursday, Herbert Asquith tells the House of Commons that the Cabinet has decided on the immediate introduction of martial law in Ireland and that General Sir John Maxwell is being sent there at once 'with plenary powers ... over the whole country'.

Edward Carson declares himself 'quite satisfied' with this and says he will gladly join with Redmond 'in everything that can be done to denounce and put down these rebels now and for ever more'.

Redmond – not yet in receipt of Dillon's letter – makes his first public comment on the revolt, but keeps it short, telling the house: 'I think it is scarcely necessary for my part, but perhaps I ought to give expression on behalf of all of my colleagues of the nationalist party here, and, as I believe, the overwhelming majority of the people of Ireland, to the feeling of detestation and horror with which we have regarded these proceedings.'

He holds back from saying more until further information becomes available, but he is to endure several more days of silence before a communication from Dillon finally reaches him on Monday, a week after the rebellion broke out. 'The heart of the city on this side is burnt out, including the *Freeman* office,' Dillon writes.

> Devlin I have heard nothing of.
>
> This part of the city is quiet today. Several hundreds surrendered last night. But up to now we are told that the Four Courts and several places on the South Side are still holding out. The fighting has been terrific, and the whole business was evidently superbly organised.
>
> I am determined not to make any public statement of any kind until I have had time to consider the position with full knowledge. Probably not for several days.
>
> You should urge strongly on the Government the *extreme* unwisdom of any wholesale shooting of prisoners. The wisest course is to execute *no one* for the present. This is the *most urgent* matter for the moment. If there were shootings of prisoners on a large scale the effect on public opinion might be disastrous in the extreme.
>
> *So far* feeling of the population in Dublin is *against* the Sinn Feiners. But a reaction might very easily be created. [Redmond's private secretary T.J.] Hanna was here yesterday and proposed to call again to-day. He had absolutely failed to reach me the three previous days. Even now *no one* is allowed to go into O'Connell Street or to cross town.

I shall write more fully in a day or two.

Do not fail to urge the Government not to *execute any* of the prisoners.

I have no doubt if any of the well-known leaders are taken alive they will be shot. But, except the leaders, there should be no court martial executions.

Redmond replies at once, in a letter sent under seal in the 'government bag', to inform Dillon that he has had a long conversation with Asquith that day.

He entirely agrees with the view which I proposed to him that, while the recognised ringleaders who may be captured alive must be dealt with with adequate severity, the greatest possible leniency should be shown to the rank and file.

With regard to Casement and the other real ringleaders, they will have to be dealt with in the most severe manner possible. I have been assured by the Prime Minister and also by Lord [John] French [commander in chief of the British army home forces] that there has been no military execution whatever amongst prisoners up to the present, and that the casualties to the civilians have been very few indeed, and happily not a single woman or child was injured.

This last comment underlines how out of touch Redmond is with events on the ground in Dublin, and causes exasperation to Dillon, who replies: 'The PM and Lord French are rather reckless in their statements. There is a list in today's *Irish Times* of the dead women and children lying in hospitals, and all day yesterday and to-day, the searches and arrests are going on.'

Redmond, meanwhile, has also sent Dillon news of the first political casualty of the rising: Irish Chief Secretary Birrell has offered his resignation and it is likely that it will be accepted.

As Redmond and Dillon continue their correspondence across the Irish Sea, General Maxwell quickly sets about his work, and on Wednesday, 3 May, Thomas Clarke, Patrick Pearse and Thomas MacDonagh – three of the signatories of the proclamation of an Irish

Republic, with which the rising was announced at the GPO nine days earlier – are the first of the leaders of the revolt to face the firing squad.

Their executions are announced in the House of Commons on the same day by Asquith, who tells MPs the three men were 'tried by court martial, found guilty and sentenced to death by being shot', adding: 'The sentence was duly carried out this morning.' This is immediately followed by the announcement of Birrell's resignation, the now former chief secretary admitting that he underestimated the possibility of the rebellion.

A sorrowful Redmond responds with a warm tribute to Birrell's record in Ireland and an admission of his own part in his downfall, 'because I entirely agreed with his view that the danger of an outbreak of this kind was not a real one'. He then appeals to the government to show leniency in its dealings with the rebels.

> This outbreak, happily, seems to be over. It has been dealt with with firmness, which was not only right, but it was the duty of the government to so deal with it. As the rebellion, or the outbreak, call it what you like, has been put down with firmness, I do beg the government, and I speak from the very bottom of my heart and with all my earnestness, not to show undue hardship or severity to the great masses of those who are implicated, on whose shoulders there lies a guilt far different from that which lies upon the instigators and promoters of the outbreak. Let them, in the name of God, not add this to the miserable, wretched memories of the Irish people, to be stored up perhaps for generations ... I beg of the government, having put down this outbreak with firmness, to take only such action as will leave the least rankling bitterness in the minds of the Irish people, both in Ireland and elsewhere throughout the world.

He is supported in this by Edward Carson, who says that 'this conspiracy of the Sinn Féiners' should be put down with courage and determination, 'yet it would be a mistake to suppose that any true Irishman calls for vengeance. It will be a matter requiring the greatest wisdom and the greatest coolness, may I say, in dealing with these men, and all that I say to the executive is, whatever is done, let it not be done in a moment of temporary excitement, but with due deliberation in regard both to the past and to the future'.

Back in Dublin, however, Dillon – justifiably fearful that Redmond's and Carson's advice will go unheeded – goes to see Maxwell to appeal for restraint. 'Sir J. [Maxwell] denied that any persons had been shot without trial,' Dillon writes to Redmond. 'I made a very strong protest against the continuation of the execution of unknown men. Sir J. did not admit all my contention. And I gathered that he contemplated considerable further executions. But after a considerable discussion, in the course of which [Under Secretary for Ireland Sir Matthew] Nathan supported my view, Sir J. said that, having heard all I had to say, he could only assure me that my views would have his careful consideration.'

Redmond continues to make his own representations to Asquith, meeting the prime minister again on 3 May, the same day Birrell's resignation is announced in the Commons. He writes to Dillon immediately: 'Asquith tells me that he had given orders to the War Office to go slowly, and said he was shocked when he read the news of three men being shot. I begged him to promise me that no one else would be executed, but he said he could not give an absolute promise to that effect, but that, except in some very special case, that was his desire and intention. As for the rank and file, nothing will be done to them at all.'

He follows this the same day with an urgent handwritten message to Asquith: 'I see by the evening papers that courts martial are being held in Dublin. I would most earnestly beg of you to prevent any wholesale trials of this kind – wholesale executions would destroy our last hopes.'

Nevertheless, his fury with those responsible for the rising is unabated, and on the same day – 3 May – he issues his first full public statement on the outbreak, decrying it as a German plot.

> My first feeling, of course, on hearing of this insane movement was one of horror, disappointment, almost despair. I asked myself whether Ireland, as so often before in her tragic history, was to dash the cup of liberty from her lips. Was the insanity of a small section of her people once again to turn all her marvellous victories of the last few years into irreparable defeat, and to send her back, on

the very eve of her final recognition as a free nation, into another long night of slavery, incalculable suffering, weary and uncertain struggle? ...

Surely I need not argue the principle, especially with anybody who professes himself to be a Home Ruler, that the policy of Ireland must be decided by Ireland herself. That doctrine has been contested only by the very same men who to-day have tried to make Ireland the cat's paw of Germany.

In all our long and successful struggle to obtain Home Rule we have been thwarted and opposed by that same section. We have won Home Rule not through them, but in spite of them. This wicked move of theirs was their last blow at Home Rule. It was not half as much treason to the cause of the Allies as treason to the cause of Home Rule.

This attempted deadly blow at Home Rule carried on through this section is made the more wicked and the more insolent by this fact – that Germany plotted it, Germany organised it, Germany paid for it. So far as Germany's share in it is concerned, it is a German invasion of Ireland, as brutal, as selfish, as cynical as Germany's invasion of Belgium ...

Is it not an additional horror that on the very day when we hear that men of the Dublin Fusiliers have been killed by Irishmen in the streets of Dublin we received the news of how the men of the 16th Division – our own Irish Brigade and of the same Dublin Fusiliers – had dashed forward, and by their unconquerable bravery retaken the trenches that the Germans had won at Hulluch [in France]?

As to the final result, I do not believe that this wicked and insane movement will achieve its ends. The German plot has failed. The majority of the people of Ireland retain their calmness, fortitude and unity. They abhor this attack on their interests, their rights, their hopes, their principles. Home Rule has not been destroyed; it remains indestructible.

The following day, Thursday, 4 May, the *Irish Independent* is published for the first time in over a week, its city centre premises having been put out of commission by the fighting. The executions have already begun, then, when the country's most popular newspaper, in recent times vehemently anti-Redmondite, pronounces its verdict on the rebellion.

In a leader article headlined 'Criminal Madness', it says no terms of denunciation would be too strong to apply to those responsible for the 'insane and criminal rising of last week'.

> Around us, in the centre of Ireland's capital, is a scene of ruin which it is heartrending to behold. Some of the proudest structures in what was one of the finest streets in Europe are now reduced to shapeless heaps of smouldering ashes. It is as if foreign invaders, as ruthless as those who have devastated Belgium and Poland, had wrought their evil will on the erstwhile peaceful city of Dublin. In one sense, indeed, it is too true that the ruin around us is the work of the common enemy, but Irishmen have been the agents for the commission of the crime, from the consequences of which it will take us many years to recover. The events of last week in Dublin and in certain other parts of the country have quenched our hopes for at least a quarter of a century to come, were it not for the splendid part which Ireland has played since the beginning of the war. On the battlefields of France and Flanders, on the blood-stained heights of the Gallipoli Peninsula, and in the more distant lands, wherever the fight raged hottest, the outpouring of Irish blood is as an expiation for the acts of unfilial ingrates who have besmirched the honour of their native land. Were it not for the glory which has irradiated the Irish arms in the fields where the battle for human freedom is being fought, our heads might now hang low in shame for the misdeeds of those who have been the willing dupes of Prussian intrigue.
>
> When we come to think of what the incendiaries have accomplished, the result is pitifully meagre. They set out to establish an Irish Republic. They held a few strong positions in certain parts of the metropolis for about 28 hours. From that time onwards they were surrounded, many of them surrendering, others escaping, and many of them being shot. A good many of the military fell beneath the insurgent fire, and so did large numbers of civilians, including women and children. The net result of the outbreak is, in brief, the loss of many valuable lives and a large toll of wounded, extending

to many hundreds, perhaps thousands; the wholesale surrender of the Sinn Feiners; the monetary loss to Dublin and to Ireland of many millions of pounds, the ruin of some of the finest business districts, and the destruction of many buildings, the beauty of whose architecture was a legitimate source of pride to the citizens of the capital. The men who fomented the outbreak, and all who were responsible for the devastation surrounding us, have to bear a heavy moral and legal responsibility from which they cannot hope to escape. They were out, not to free Ireland, but to help Germany. Doing the enemy's work, they looked for succour and support from that quarter and, doubtless, they received subsidies in money and kind. ...

The men who took the initiative in disturbing the peace of the country had not, and have not, a shred of public sympathy. Whilst they held certain strongholds the military were being called for and longed for by the citizens. These men are now held prisoners in England, and the leaders who organised [it] and the prominently active spirits in this rising, deserve little consideration or compassion. So far as we are concerned, when we think of the many valuable lives lost; the hundreds of innocent victims – many of them buried in unknown graves because their friends could not be discovered; when we think of the enormous material damage which has already been done and the huge loss of trade and employment which must be the consequence, we confess that we care little what is to become of the leaders who are morally responsible for this terrible mischief. ...

Many widows and orphans and many innocent victims represent the toll of a week of anarchy in Dublin. Circumstances favoured the incendiaries, inasmuch as they were fairly well armed and supplied with ammunition, and England's military resources were taxed to the uttermost by the demands of a war of unprecedented magnitude. Yet the 'rising' was a mere matter of hours, a miserable fiasco, leaving behind its trail of woe and horror. Let the moral not be lost upon us or upon our rulers. Let us, in God's name, be done with revolution, or thought of revolution, in Ireland, whatever be its guise or pretext.

Alongside the editorial the paper carries a short report of 'sad scenes' at Glasnevin cemetery, where, it says, scores of bodies – most of them unidentified – are arriving for burial each day. Many of them have no coffins, and the bodies include those of women and children.

The same day, 4 May, brings news of four further executions – those of Joseph Plunkett, Willie Pearse, Edward Daly and Michael O'Hanrahan. This prompts Redmond to make yet another appeal to the prime minister, this time accompanied by a threat of resignation: 'Saw Asquith again and told him if any more executions took place I would feel bound to denounce them and probably retire,' he records in a memo of the meeting. 'I specially mentioned John [Eoin] MacNeill. He said he had written and wired to Sir John Maxwell to stop executions and that he was writing especially to save MacNeill.'

But Maxwell doesn't stop the executions; yet another prisoner, John MacBride, is shot the following day, Friday, 5 May. Redmond doesn't resign, continuing instead to lobby Asquith, urging him to halt this 'insane policy', which he says will make things 'impossible for any constitutional party or leader'.

At the weekend Dillon is at last able to leave for London, but while Redmond is waiting for his arrival, on the Sunday, he receives an urgent message from his deputy: 'Rumour just reached me through reliable channel further executions intended to-morrow morning. Any more executions would be desperate evil and do immense harm. Communicate P.M. any cost, and get him suspend execution sentences. Wire reply through Castle.'

By now, however, it is clear that Asquith has entrusted all responsibility for the handling of matters in Dublin to Maxwell. A despairing Redmond replies to Dillon that he has already communicated with the prime minister and can do nothing more, but he sends a further letter to Asquith to his place in the country. It has no effect, and on Monday, 8 May, four more prisoners – Eamonn Ceannt, Michael Mallin, Seán Heuston and Conn Colbert – are taken from their cells in Kilmainham Gaol and shot.

In the Commons that day Redmond asks the prime minister if he is aware that the continuance of military executions has caused 'rapidly increasing bitterness of exasperation amongst large sections of the population who have not the slightest sympathy with the insurrection'. Asquith replies that nobody is more anxious than the government and Sir John Maxwell that the executions should be 'confined to the narrowest limits, and cease at the earliest possible moment'.

The following day, Thomas Kent is executed by firing squad in Cork for his part in a shoot-out with RIC members in which an officer was killed. No further executions take place over the next couple of days, but Dillon, in a debate on the issue on Thursday, 11 May, lets Asquith know – in an angry and uncompromising speech – just how much damage has been done to the constitutional nationalists' cause.

> It is the first rebellion that ever took place in Ireland where you had a majority on your side. It is the fruit of our life work. We have risked our lives a hundred times to bring about this result. We are held up to odium as traitors by those men who made this rebellion, and our lives have been in danger a hundred times during the last 30 years ... and now you are washing out our whole life work in a sea of blood.

Dillon emphasises that the executions are not the only problem; the application of martial law to the whole of Ireland – even to areas that had no part in the rising – is a cause of deep resentment, he warns. But it is the next part of his speech that shocks many of his listeners. Dublin is 'seething with rumours', Dillon says, of wholesale shootings after secret trials, or, in some cases, no trial at all. There are some things, however, that he says he knows to be true:

> One of the practices going on in the barracks is that these unhappy persons, and they have taken numbers of them, are threatened with instant death in order to force them to become informers. They are given half-an-hour of life, and then put up against a wall, and several of them have given evidence against their comrades. Is that approved of by the House of Commons without any trial? Do they approve of that form of torture, because it really is torture? I believe a number have given evidence, but not many considering the great number of prisoners. For my part I think it is a scandal,

and it is exasperating the people of Dublin. Was that reported to
the prime minister, and does he approve of it? Let me give the
right honourable gentleman another case. A boy of 15 years of
age was ordered to give evidence against his commanding officer,
and the boy said 'I won't.' 'Then,' said the officer, 'you will be shot
in half-an-hour,' and the boy said, 'shoot away'. They blindfolded
that boy and put him with his back to the wall, and made him
hear the click of the rifle, and finally he was asked before he died
would he answer the question, and he said 'no'. Then they told
him to go home to his mother. Is that British justice? I call it
damnable, and the British House of Commons ought to be
ashamed of it. Is it not intolerable that such things should go on,
and the prime minister know nothing about them, and yet he says
that he has the most absolute confidence in the administration
of military law. Another boy of 14 – this is a different case, and I
make no complaint of it at all – was called up. The officer looked
at him, and, being a kind-hearted man, he said, 'what on earth
am I to do with you?' The boy said to him, 'shoot me, for I have
killed three of your soldiers'. That may horrify you, but I declare
most solemnly, and I am not ashamed to say it in the House of
Commons, that I am proud of these men. They were foolish, they
were misled ...

Interrupted by cries of 'Shame!' and a shout of 'Now you have shown
your hand', Dillon continues:

Did I ever fail to show my hand in the House of Commons, or
conceal anything? I say I am proud of their courage, and, if you
were not so dense and so stupid, as some of you English people
are, you could have had these men fighting for you, and they are
men worth having [MPs: 'You stopped them!']. That is an infamous
falsehood. I and the men who sit around me have been doing our
best to bring these men into the ranks of the army [an MP: 'Ask the
honourable member for Cork!']. I say that we have been doing our
best to bring these men into the ranks of the army, and it is the
blundering manner in which our country has been ruled which has

deprived you of their services. These men require no compulsory service bill to make them fight. Ours is a fighting race.

Dillon also asks for a public inquiry – which is immediately granted by Asquith – into one of the most notorious episodes of the past ten days, the shooting dead at Portobello barracks of the political activist and pacifist Francis Sheehy Skeffington, who had taken no part in the rising – before concluding with further praise for the rebels.

[I]t is not murderers who are being executed; it is insurgents who have fought a clean fight, a brave fight, however misguided, and it would be a damned good thing for you if your soldiers were able to put up as good a fight as did these men in Dublin – 3,000 men against 20,000 with machine-guns and artillery. [An MP: 'Evidently you wish they had succeeded.'] That is an infamous falsehood. Who is it said that? It is an abominable falsehood. I say that these men, misguided as they were, have been our bitterest enemies. They have held us up to public odium as traitors to our country because we have supported you at this moment and stood by you in this great war, and the least we are entitled to is this, that in this great effort which we have made at considerable risk – an effort such as the honourable member who interrupted me could never have attempted – to bring the masses of the Irish people into harmony with you. In this great effort at reconciliation, I say, we were entitled to every assistance from the members of this house and from the government.

Responding, Asquith says he will try not to cause any further embitterment of feeling. The executions are a 'horrible business', he says, but there are two other men who have been sentenced to death and, as they were signatories to the proclamation of a republic, the government sees no grounds for interfering in Sir John Maxwell's decision to apply the 'extreme penalty' in their case. After all, he explains, the other five signatories of the proclamation have already been shot, justifiably in the government's view, so it would hardly be fair or just to spare these men's lives because they were tried at a later date.

The following day James Connolly – strapped to a chair because he is unable to stand as a result of injuries suffered in the fighting – and Seán Mac Diarmada are the last two prisoners to go before the firing squad in the yard of Kilmainham Gaol.

A few days later Redmond receives a cablegram from Michael Ryan in Philadelphia telling him something he already knows: the executions have done incalculable political damage to the nationalist leader and his party.

> IRISH EXECUTION [sic] HAVE ALIENATED EVERY AMERICAN FRIEND AND CAUSED RESURGENCE OF ANCIENT ENMITIES YOUR LIFE WORK DESTROYED BY ENGLISH BRUTALITY OPINION WIDESPREAD THAT PROMISE OR [sic] HOME RULE WAS MOCKERY
>
> MICHAEL RYAN

His policy on Ireland in disarray, Asquith decides to travel to the country himself to assess conditions at first hand. Returning after a five-day visit, during which he meets representatives of the nationalist and unionist communities and speaks with prisoners detained after the rising, he tells the House of Commons that his trip left him with two dominant impressions. The first is that the existing machinery of Irish government at Dublin Castle has broken down; the second is the strong feeling on both sides of the community that a unique opportunity has arisen 'for a new departure, for the settlement of outstanding problems'.

He has already found the man who will try to make this settlement a reality. Among his first actions on his return from Ireland was to send a handwritten note to David Lloyd George, now minister of munitions in the coalition government, asking him to 'take up Ireland', if only for a short time. 'It is a unique opportunity,' Asquith writes, 'and there is no one else who could do so much to bring about a permanent solution.'

Lloyd George accepts the poisoned chalice and sets about trying to solve the Irish question once and for all.

Chapter 25 ∿

WALTER LONG GETS TO WORK

Some tragic fatality seems to dog the footsteps of this government in all their dealings with Ireland.

David Lloyd George wastes no time in 'taking up Ireland' and by the time Herbert Asquith tells the House of Commons, on 25 May 1916, of this latest effort to solve the Irish question, his minister of munitions has already opened discussions with John Redmond and Edward Carson.

He will soon find, however, that the biggest obstacle to a deal will come not from the nationalist and unionist leaders in Ireland, but rather from ministerial colleagues in the coalition government. Two men in particular, one of them Anglo-Irish and the other English but with strong Irish connections, will combine to do all in their power to defeat Lloyd George's best efforts to secure a permanent settlement in Ireland.

The first of these, Lord Lansdowne, is leader of the Conservative and Unionist Party in the House of Lords and owner of more than 120,000 acres in Ireland, including a large holding in south Kerry, where he spends his summers. The second is Walter Long, a Tory former chief secretary for Ireland who once served as an MP for Dublin South and, though now representing a constituency in his native England, has maintained close links with the Irish unionists.

Long's attitude towards the majority Catholic population in Ireland can be gleaned from his view, expressed in late 1914, that a 'strong unflinching' approach towards those who are 'openly disloyal' is what is needed most. 'It is the only form of Government which the Irish understand,' he wrote to the under secretary for Ireland, Sir Matthew Nathan. 'They are very quick, and when they see that disloyalty not only goes unpunished but is sometimes even rewarded they naturally do not hesitate to indulge in their own tastes. It is not because they want to do mischief as much as, like naughty children, they think it is amusing to give way to their inclinations.'

Long initially welcomes Lloyd George's appointment to the Irish assignment, describing it as 'a most happy inspiration' and wishing his colleague well. But an extraordinary battle soon unfolds between Long and Lansdowne on one side and Lloyd George on the other, the outcome of which will shape Ireland's long-term political future.

Central to the dispute is the precise nature of Lloyd George's role; as far as Long and Lansdowne are concerned, the former chancellor is mandated to do no more than hold confidential discussions with the nationalist and unionist leaders and report back to the Cabinet on what he sees as the potential for a deal. This may well be Lloyd George's understanding too, but once left to his own devices he ignores the limitations placed on him and sets about trying to negotiate a lasting deal.

In the process he employs large measures of what will in the future be known as 'constructive ambiguity': he misrepresents to Redmond and Carson the extent of his mandate; he leads Redmond to understand that the exclusion of Ulster from Home Rule will be temporary and Carson to comprehend that it will be permanent; he deliberately overstates the importance of the 'American factor' in the need to do a deal; and all the while he keeps his Cabinet colleagues in the dark – insofar as he can – as to what he is doing.

By such tactics, he brings about what had seemed impossible: an agreement between John Redmond and Edward Carson on the future governance of Ireland.

A key demand from Redmond at the outset is that Home Rule be introduced immediately. He knows that, in the changed circumstances in Ireland, the nationalist population is no longer prepared to wait patiently for the war to end before getting its own parliament; the constitutional party needs to deliver results right away if confidence in its methods is to be restored.

Lloyd George's response is to tell Carson, despite its not being true, that the Cabinet has accepted the need for immediate Home Rule with the exclusion of six counties of Ulster. He agrees to put it in writing that such exclusion will be permanent, despite having told Redmond it will be reviewed after the war.

While these negotiations are taking place he receives a delegation from the Irish Unionist Alliance, representing the southern unionists, urging him to ensure they are included in any proposed deal. Lloyd George tells them – according to a memo of the meeting by their leader, Lord Midleton – that a settlement is essential 'owing to the conditions in America'. He cites figures, but not their source, illustrating that prior to the Easter rebellion 75 per cent of Irish-Americans supported the Allies in the war, but now the whole of Irish America is pro-German. This has obvious implications for American support for Britain in the war and even threatens the supply of munitions, he states.

At this stage Walter Long begins to take a direct interest in the negotiations and Lloyd George invites him to a meeting at the Ministry of Munitions on the morning of Tuesday, 30 May. There he hands Long a memorandum which he says has already been seen by Redmond, Carson and their senior colleagues, as well as by the southern Irish unionists.

Two things strike Long immediately as a problem: for the first time he learns that Lloyd George is proposing the immediate establishment of a parliament in Ireland, in spite of this not having been discussed by the Cabinet; and he notes a suggestion that the exclusion of Ulster is to be reviewed at the end of the war. Lloyd George tells Long that the scheme outlined has met with a favourable response from all parties – in spite of the fact that the southern unionists have not indicated any approval for it. Before Long can say much, however, the discussion is cut short by the arrival of Redmond.

Alarmed by what he has seen, Long contacts Lansdowne, who meets Lloyd George and tells him that the Unionists could not accept a scheme along the lines being drawn up. This view is reinforced at a Cabinet committee meeting on 1 June attended by Asquith, Lloyd George and Long, and from this day on Long and Lansdowne work together to undermine their Cabinet colleague's efforts to secure an agreement.

In a lengthy memo to Asquith, Lansdowne says this is not the time 'for imposing upon the country, in the guise of an interim arrangement, a bold and startling scheme which at once concedes in principle all that the most extreme Nationalists have been demanding, viz the disappearance of Castle government and the establishment of an Irish Parliament with an Irish Executive responsible to it. The triumph of lawlessness and disloyalty would be complete.'

Undaunted, however, Lloyd George continues his work and in early June he circulates a draft scheme to Redmond and Carson. It proposes:

1. To bring the Home Rule Act into immediate operation.
2. To introduce at once an Amending Bill as a strictly War Emergency Act, to cover only the period of the War and a short specified interval after it.
3. During that period the Irish Members to remain at Westminster in their full numbers.
4. During this war emergency period six Ulster counties to be left as at present under the Imperial Government.
5. Immediately after the War an Imperial Conference of representatives of all the Dominions of the Empire to be held to consider the future government of the Empire, including the question of the government of Ireland.
6. Immediately after this Conference, and during the interval provided for by the War Emergency Act, the permanent settlement of all the great outstanding problems, such as the permanent position of the six exempted counties, the question of finance, and other problems which cannot be dealt with during the War, would be proceeded with.

For Redmond, the exclusion of six counties is a big concession and a significant retreat from the nationalists' position when the parties last negotiated, at the Buckingham Palace conference just before the war, when neither side would give up its claim to Fermanagh and Tyrone. Crucially, however, the draft scheme is clear in stating that exclusion is to be for the duration of the war only, pending further discussions on a permanent arrangement.

Carson, however, has in his pocket his earlier written commitment from Lloyd George that the proposed settlement would be permanent, and he and his followers insist on interpreting the scheme to mean exactly that – permanent exclusion of the six counties. He is also under the false impression that the proposals have been approved by the Cabinet, including its Unionist members.

Before taking the scheme back to Ireland for approval, Redmond, John Dillon and Joe Devlin have one final meeting with Lloyd George to ensure that there are no misunderstandings. They ask for a guarantee that no further concessions will be 'sprung' on them. 'He gave us the most emphatic assurance', notes Redmond, 'saying he had "placed his life upon the table and would stand or fall by the agreement come to". He assured us also that this was the attitude of the Prime Minister. We said on that assurance we could go to Ireland and ask the consent of our people, but not otherwise.'

It falls again to Devlin and his fellow MP Jeremiah MacVeagh to undertake the thankless job of 'selling' this unpalatable deal to the nationalists of Ulster. They did so successfully in 1914, but in that case the temporary exclusion of most likely four counties was envisaged. Now Tyrone and Fermanagh, with their nationalist majorities, are also to be asked to accept exclusion from Home Rule, while doubts persist over whether this is to be temporary or permanent. They receive a hostile response before it is decided to call an Ulster nationalist conference for 23 June.

In the meantime, Carson presents the proposals to the Ulster Unionist Council on 6 June. In a two-hour speech, he underlines the merits of the deal, offering as it does a 'clean cut' of six counties and emphasising – incorrectly, as he will later learn – that it has the backing of their 'hitherto most trusted leaders' in the government. He suggests, however, that the scheme should not be adopted without the approval of loyalist representatives in the three Ulster counties that would be placed under the Dublin parliament – Donegal, Cavan and Monaghan.

Six days later some members of the council shed tears at a reconvened meeting as Lord Farnham from Cavan, called back from the Front for consultation on the deal, gives his blessing to the proposals – while decrying the 'deplorable situation' in which they now find themselves – on behalf of the three omitted counties. Lloyd George now has Ulster Unionist support for his settlement.

Redmond and his party, however, will have to overcome an angry response to the threat of partition from across nationalist Ireland if they are to get the deal approved. Making his first public statement on the matter, at a meeting of the Irish Party in the Mansion House in Dublin on 10 June, the party leader explains the terms of the proposals but says he is not seeking a decision until there is time for 'full and careful consideration'.

The *Irish Independent* has renewed its attacks on him, with even more vigour than previously, pointedly inserting a box into its report of the Mansion House meeting quoting Redmond's words at a rally in Limerick on 13 October 1913: 'I have to say here to-day that that suggestion (the possible exclusion of a portion of Ulster) is a totally impracticable and unworkable one ... A unit Ireland is, and must remain, and we can never assent to any proposal which would create a sharp eternal dividing line between Irish Catholics and Irish Protestants ... The two-nations theory is to us an abomination and a blasphemy.'

The same edition of the paper publishes a sample of the 'chorus of condemnation' from leader writers in the provincial press, including the *Westmeath Independent* ('The repugnant past or the military administration of the hour would be preferable to a bit of Home Rule for a bit of Ireland'); the *Roscommon Herald* ('The idea of "Ireland a Nation Once Again" as a three-quarters nation with the fairest province left out would expire of ridicule if nothing else'); the *Leinster Leader* ('The country is certainly hostile to the dismemberment of Ireland, and any proposal of a permanent dismemberment would, we believe, be met by very stern and uncompromising opposition'); the *Leitrim Observer* ('We know this, that the Nationalists of Ireland will never agree to such a fatal and fanatical suggestion as the exclusion of Ulster'); and the *Midland Tribune* ('In union with Nationalists all over Ireland, we enter our emphatic protest against any separation of Ulster or any portion of it from the rest of the country').

The day after the Mansion House meeting, Walter Long makes what he hopes will be a decisive move in wrecking the deal, writing to Lloyd George to tell him he will not support it in Cabinet. He has received the 'gravest accounts' of conditions in Ireland, he says, and therefore this is 'not the moment to embark on any political experiment'.

Lloyd George's response comes to Long as a bombshell:

It would have been fairer to a colleague who was undertaking a risky and a thankless task had you expressed the views now embodied in your Memo at the time I was chosen to negotiate. Had you done so even when I consulted you some days ago it was not too late to avert irretrievable committal.

Now things have gone so far they cannot be put right except by my resignation and in face of your letter I have written to the P.M. withdrawing from the negotiations and from the Government. The task is a difficult one – without loyal support it is impossible.

He adds a handwritten postscript: 'I was sorry to hear you had been unwell, but hope you are now all right.'

Long is presented with the prospect of being held responsible for the loss to the government of its most senior Cabinet member after the prime minister, and the one who holds the key role of minister of munitions, at a critical time in the war. But he doesn't blink, feistily firing back a letter to Lloyd George expressing amazement at his 'most unreasonable' attack, and adding: 'No charge of unfairness or loyalty lies at my door & I cannot believe that you seriously intend to base your resignation upon this excuse.'

Lloyd George duly writes his letter of resignation to Asquith, telling him: 'Without a united Government settlement is impossible, and as I am so committed to both Irish sections I could not assent to the withdrawal of the proferred terms.' In offering his resignation, he is delivering on the commitment he gave to Redmond, Dillon and Devlin at their meeting days earlier, when he said he would 'stand or fall by the agreement come to'.

But the minister of munitions doesn't fall; his resignation letter to Asquith will remain in his files, marked 'not sent'.

Next to play the threat-of-resignation card is Redmond, when the Ulster nationalist conference convenes, amid scenes of great tension, behind closed doors at St Mary's Hall in Belfast at midday on Friday, 23 June. All the usual organisations at an Irish Party gathering – including the United Irish League, the Ancient Order of Hibernians and the

Irish National Foresters, as well as many members of the clergy – are represented. But gone are the days when John Redmond will be greeted by such an audience with uniform cheers.

Overcoming some interruptions from his largely muted listeners, he asks them to support the Lloyd George proposals, but insists that a united Ireland is still at the top of his party's agenda.

> The practical question is how we are to get a united Ireland. Every man of you knows that at the present time you cannot compel your opponents in Ulster by force of arms. There is no such power in existence. Suppose you had the power to compel Ulster by force of arms, would that get you a united Ireland?
>
> I say it is not possible to inaugurate an Irish Government by bringing fire and sword and bloodshed into Ulster. There is only one way you can get a united Ireland, and that is to show your opponents that their fears are unreasonable and unfounded, and that it is safe for them to join hands with the rest of their fellow-countrymen, and the only way you can to do that is by giving them [a voice: 'Everything they want!'] an exhibition of good government.

Redmond also insists that the exclusion of the Ulster counties is to be temporary, until the matter is dealt with after the war, and he dismisses as 'an absolute lie' a claim by Edward Carson reported in that day's *Irish Times* that the arrangement is to be permanent. The proposals are temporary and provisional, he reiterates. 'If they were not, I would oppose them.'

Redmond concludes by reminding his audience of his long service to the Irish cause. To a mixture of cheers and hostile interruptions, he says it is the duty of a leader to lead; should his people decline to follow him, however, he will not accept responsibility for a course of action that is against his conscience. 'If then this is the last time that I ever can appeal to the people of Ireland I will have done so in obedience to the dictates of my heart and conscience,' he says, this time to roars of approval.

While the reception for Redmond has been largely respectful, John Dillon faces a barrage of interruptions when he speaks later. After shouts of 'You betrayed Derry!', 'Derry walls!', 'No surrender!' and – to much laughter – 'You're only a lot of jellyfishes!', proceedings momentarily break down in disorder. Speakers opposed to the party leadership include a parish priest from the Waterside in Derry, W.B. MacFeely, and an Omagh solicitor, F.J. O'Connor, who says that the Lloyd George proposals are more destructive of the spirit of nationality than any scheme proposed to the people of Ireland since the Act of Union.

Redmond, Dillon and Devlin – who also speaks – win the day, however, and the proposals pass by 475 votes to 265.

∼

David Lloyd George has made a historic breakthrough, securing the support of the constitutional nationalists and Ulster unionists for a settlement on how Ireland is to be governed. But Walter Long and Lord Lansdowne are not done yet.

In their attempts to destroy the deal, they find themselves in dispute not only with Lloyd George, but also with Edward Carson, and the row with the Ulster Unionist leader soon threatens to bring down the government and tear the Conservative Party asunder.

Carson is dismayed to learn that Lloyd George was acting on his own initiative and without the backing of the Cabinet when he put forward the settlement proposals now adopted by the Ulster Unionist Council. He directs his ire, however, not at the munitions minister, but at his fellow unionists in the Cabinet for failing to keep him informed. He writes angrily to Long on 16 June that he feels he has been 'disgracefully treated'.

The Conservative Party leader, Bonar Law, is in France at the start of the controversy and returns to find his fellow Unionist ministers divided over whether to support the Lloyd George scheme. With Carson standing by the deal he has made, matters come to a head at a Cabinet meeting on 27 June. Lansdowne and Long both prepare memos in advance defending their stance; they are opposed, however, by the influential former Tory leader and prime minister Arthur Balfour.

Best remembered in Ireland for the polices of coercion he oversaw when chief secretary there in the late 1880s, Balfour says – also in a memo for the Cabinet meeting – that he is more concerned with the future than what may or may not have happened in the past. He argues that a unique opportunity has been presented for settling 'peaceably and permanently' the problem of Ulster, while giving the south and west of Ireland its own parliament.

This prompts Lloyd George to report to T.P. O'Connor, who in turn relays the news to Redmond in Aughavanagh, that Balfour fought for the settlement 'as if he had been a Home Ruler all his life'.

The Cabinet meeting splits the Conservative ranks, pitting Bonar Law and Balfour on one side against Lansdowne and Long on the other. Another Tory member, Lord Selborne, has already resigned in protest at the Lloyd George proposals. If Lansdowne, Long and any others follow, the government is unlikely to survive.

Lloyd George, seeing an opportunity in the Unionist rift to keep his scheme alive, proposes the establishment of a sub-committee to see if any further safeguards can be introduced to ease unionist fears. There is nothing in the measures it proposes – such as renewed emphasis on the paramount position of the Westminster parliament – that Redmond finds unduly disturbing, so on 10 July Asquith is at last able to outline details of the proposed Irish settlement in the House of Commons.

Lansdowne and Long, however, are unhappy to hear the prime minister describe the terms as 'provisional', in spite of Asquith immediately following his use of the word with this clarification: 'I see all sorts of possibilities of misapprehension in the use of the term [provisional]. To relieve any possible doubt on that point, let me say, speaking for those who, like myself, look forward to and are anxious for a united Ireland, we recognise and agree in the fullest and sincerest sense that such union can only be brought about with, and can never be brought about without, the free will and assent of the excluded area.'

Carson, picking Asquith up on his use of the word 'provisional', asks a question. 'I ... understand, from what [the prime minister] said, that the six counties will be definitely struck out of the [Government of Ireland] Act of 1914. Of course, at any time afterwards they could be included by a bill?'

Asquith's succinct response – 'They could not be included without a bill' – is clearly enough to satisfy Carson's legally precise mind, because he pursues the matter no further. But it proves an insufficient guarantee for Lansdowne, who tells the House of Lords next day that the amending bill providing for the exclusion of the six counties will make 'permanent and enduring' changes to the Government of Ireland Act. This prompts Redmond to swiftly issue a statement condemning Lansdowne's speech as a 'gross insult to Ireland' and amounting to 'a declaration of war on the Irish people'.

'If this speech were taken as representing the attitude and the spirit of the government towards Ireland there would be an end to all hope of settlement,' he adds. 'The speech seems to me to have been made with the deliberate object of wrecking the negotiations for a settlement.'

His assessment is correct. This was indeed Lansdowne's aim and, worse for Redmond and his party, the Unionist peer succeeds. Over the next eight days Lansdowne and Long rally support for their position, securing Cabinet backing on 19 July for making permanent the exclusion of the six counties from Home Rule. For good measure, they also succeed in having Irish representation in the House of Commons reduced.

On Saturday, 22 July, Redmond is asked to meet Lloyd George and Home Secretary Herbert Samuel at the War Office, where he is told of these unilateral decisions to change the terms of the deal, upon which Lloyd George was once prepared to 'stand or fall'. A bitterly disappointed Redmond writes to Asquith: 'I wish to take the earliest opportunity to inform you that any bill framed upon these lines [i.e. with permanent exclusion of six counties] will meet with the vehement opposition at all its stages of the Irish Party.'

The curtain on what proves the final realistic attempt for a generation to find an agreed settlement between Ireland's nationalists and unionists is brought down on a sombre House of Commons on the night of 24 July. In a special debate on the issue demanded by Redmond, he outlines the story of the failed negotiations of the previous month and concludes in a sorrowful tone:

> Some tragic fatality seems to dog the footsteps of this government in all their dealings with Ireland. Every step taken by them since the coalition was formed, and especially since the unfortunate outbreak in Dublin, has been lamentable. They have disregarded

every advice we tendered to them, and now in the end, having got us to induce our people to make a tremendous sacrifice and to agree to the temporary exclusion of six Ulster counties, they throw this agreement to the winds and they have taken the surest means to accentuate every possible danger and difficulty in the Irish situation.

Carson, in a more conciliatory mood towards the nationalists than at any time since the Home Rule crisis began, expresses the hope that an agreement can yet be salvaged. He pays tribute to Joe Devlin, the MP for West Belfast, whom he says he does not know and to whom he has never spoken. 'I know well what he has had to do there to get his part of this matter through. Yes, sir, he played a whole man's part in the matter, and I gladly recognise it. Let us not lose it all now.'

It would be a calamity, Carson adds, if the parties broke the settlement they have just made. He looks with horror to the idea that the two communities in Ireland might resume their quarrel when the war is over, and urges that nationalists accept the exclusion of Ulster from Home Rule 'and then go on to win her if you can' with good government in the south and west of Ireland.

He embarrasses Redmond, however, by suggesting that the two men shake hands 'on the floor of the house', just as they did after the failed Buckingham Palace conference. Redmond sits in his seat and stares straight ahead, ignoring the offer.

A few days later he receives a letter from Herbert Asquith, who says he is 'more afflicted than I can say' about the breakdown in the deal and urges Redmond to 'keep the "negotiating" spirit alive'. But the nationalist leader has no stomach for further negotiations with the British government.

Lord Lansdowne and Walter Long have won their fight to prevent the introduction of Home Rule. In doing so they have helped change the course of Irish history, accelerating the demise of Redmond and his party and strengthening the hands of those with more extreme views on how Ireland should pursue the fight for independence.

Chapter 26

DE VALERA'S RISE

In the name of God we here who are about to die ...

John Redmond's initial response to the shattering collapse of the settlement reached with Edward Carson in July 1916 is to shut himself away in Aughavanagh for a couple of months of recuperation. He spends the time – as he puts it later – 'lying in the purple heather and trying to entice the wily trout out of the water, and trying to circumvent the still more wily grouse'.

He reads few newspapers during his self-imposed isolation, which is probably just as well. The *Irish Independent* gleefully regurgitates condemnatory reports from the provincial press, such as this from the *Midland Reporter*, carried in the *Independent* on 14 September: 'The foulest plot in Irish history was the attempt made by our Imperial leaders, Mr Redmond, Mr Dillon, Mr Devlin and Mr TP O'Connor to sell Ulster to Sir E Carson. By consenting to that sale and degradation, whether it was to be for a week or for eternity, was [sic] an act of treachery that can never be forgotten to these men.'

Nationalist Ireland has by no means uniformly turned against Redmond, however, and in an almost daily joust with the *Independent*, the *Freeman's Journal* carries report after report of expressions of support for the nationalist leader from public bodies around the country. A County Cork tailor skilfully exploits the division with an eye-catching advertisement in the *Southern Star* newspaper on 12 August under a heading in large type: 'Redmond is Deceiving Ireland'. The text continues, in a smaller type size:

According to some; others say he is doing the best possible in the present trying circumstances. It is not my business to decide; my business is to supply the

Very Best Value in Suitings and General Drapery,
At Lowest Possible Prices.
J. Collins
50, North Street, Skibbereen

Redmond has other than political worries on his mind. His brother, Willie, and son William – known in the family as Billie – are both away at war, and Billie's letters home have not spared details about just how precarious life is at the Front. On 14 July he writes:

> My dear Father,
> I am actually writing this from my dug-out – or rather what was once a dug-out – in the firing line. I have been here now for eight days in command of my company ... Our first and second battalions were in the very front, as usual, and both suffered, as was inevitable, exceedingly heavily. We lost over 50 per cent of our officers and men ... I am the only captain left in the battalion ...
> Don't worry about me. I have had several lucky escapes so far, and will come out all right. I had not left my dug-out two minutes the other day when it was blown to smithereens by a Jack Johnson! I was only about 30 yards away, and fell flat on my face – not a scratch. My poor servant was killed ...
> Best of love to you and Amy,
> Your,
> Billie

While Redmond is taking time out he receives news of the death in the Battle of the Somme of Tom Kettle, the 36-year-old former Irish Party MP who, as writer, barrister and social campaigner has been one of the brightest figures in Irish political life. He will be best remembered for the concluding lines in a poem written for his daughter four days before he is killed:

> Know that we fools, now with the foolish dead
> Died not for flag, nor King, nor Emperor
> But for a dream, born in a herdsman's shed
> And for the secret Scripture of the poor.

His death is announced in the *Freeman's Journal* of 19 September, adjacent to a report disclosing the death in action of another barrister, Herbert Asquith's son, Raymond, at the age of 37.

It is against this bleak background at home and abroad that Redmond eventually makes his first public appearance since the summer, delivering a speech in Waterford town hall on Friday, 6 October. Speaking in the constituency he has represented for a quarter of a century, he is given an enthusiastic reception, but only after a fist fight in the gallery of the hall between supporters and opponents. With order restored, Redmond tells his audience that except in the case of the war, the Irish Party will from now on maintain a stance of 'vigorous opposition' to the government.

He dismisses as a 'fantastic lie' the suggestion he has heard that the Irish Party is in favour of army conscription; the party will resist any attempt to introduce such a measure, which is the way to 'madness, ruin and disorder'. Another fashionable lie is the claim that he and his colleagues were in favour of the partition of Ireland. 'Nothing in this world,' he says to loud cheers, 'would ever induce me to accept as a settlement of the Home Rule question any scheme providing for a permanent division of our ancient nation.'

'A Long Silence Broken', the *Irish Independent* will headline its report of the event next day, over the sub-heading: 'Mr Redmond's New Policy – Belated Firmness.'

With his party now, in effect, in opposition for the first time since the election of January 1910, he follows up his Waterford speech with a motion of censure against the government in the House of Commons on 18 October, stating that 'the system of government at present maintained in Ireland is inconsistent with the principles for which the Allies are fighting in Europe, and has been mainly responsible for the recent unhappy events and for the present state of feeling in that country.'

Nearly six months after the Easter rebellion, Ireland remains under martial law and discontent among nationalists has not been abated by the appointment of a Unionist MP, Henry Duke, as chief secretary in succession to the popular Augustine Birrell.

Reviewing the 'slow and gradual' slippage into the present crisis, Redmond points out that since the start of the war, when Irish people showed 'genuine enthusiasm' for the allied cause, the government has ignored every piece of advice offered to it by the Irish Party. 'I am sorry to say that from the very first hour our efforts were thwarted, ignored, and snubbed. Our suggestions were derided. Everything, almost, that we asked for was refused, and everything, almost, that we protested against was done.'

He sets out a litany of errors, including the refusal to adopt any of the suggestions made by him to aid army recruitment, the appointment of Edward Carson to the coalition government and the violent suppression of the Easter rising. 'Executions, spread out day after day, and week after week – some of them young boys of whom none of us had never even heard, and who turned out to have been young dreamers and idealists – shocked and revolted the public mind of Ireland.'

He concludes with a call for an immediate lifting of martial law and the release of all prisoners being held without trial since the rising. Those convicted should be given political status, he argues.

> So long as the Irish people feel that England, fighting for the small nationalities of Europe, is maintaining by martial law a state unionist government against the will of the people in Ireland, so long no real improvement can be hoped for. Let the government withdraw martial law, let them put in command of the forces in Ireland some man who has not been connected with the unhappy actions of the past ... Let the 500 untried prisoners be released, let the penal servitude prisoners be treated as political prisoners, and, above all, and incomparably more important than all, let the government take their courage in both hands and trust the Irish people once and for all, by putting the Home Rule Act into operation and resolutely, on their own responsibility, facing any problems that that may entail.

Duke responds with a defence of the government's actions and an assertion that it is ready to concede any measure of Home Rule that Irishmen can agree on, overlooking the fact that the two key Irishmen involved – Redmond and Carson – did agree on a scheme before Lansdowne and Long succeeded in bringing it down.

Through November, Redmond and Dillon continue to press the prime minister to lift martial law and introduce an amnesty for the prisoners, arguing that keeping them in jail is helping nobody but the 'extremists'. In a letter to Asquith on 30 November, Redmond insists that the rebels 'can do much more harm as prisoners in Frongoch than at liberty in Ireland'. Unknown to both men, however, Asquith is in his last days in office and is about to be ousted by Lloyd George, who succeeds him on 7 December. Among the new prime minister's first acts is to bring Carson back into the government – as first lord of the Admiralty – and appoint other Unionists to key posts; Bonar Law becomes chancellor of the exchequer and Arthur Balfour foreign secretary.

On 9 December Lloyd George meets Redmond – at the new prime minister's request – and tells him he is 'determined' to release the untried prisoners held since the rising, though he must first discuss the matter with Bonar Law and Henry Duke. He also tells Redmond that if any proposal is made to impose conscription in Ireland, he will propose immediate Home Rule for all of Ireland as a condition. 'On this matter I told him,' notes Redmond in a memo of the meeting, '[that] we could never agree to conscription as a condition of Home Rule and that under any circumstances conscription was impossible in Ireland.'

Redmond's influence with the government is now greatly diminished, however, as demonstrated by his bitter exchanges with Lloyd George when the new prime minister makes his first statement to the House of Commons as head of government on 19 December. Disappointed that Ireland gets no more than a passing mention in Lloyd George's speech of just over two hours, Redmond says he listened 'with the greatest pain' and asks: 'In the general programme of energy, promptness, quick decision [promised by Lloyd George], is the Irish question to be the only one to be allowed to drift?'

The effect of government policy, he argues, is plain to see: the 'absolute disappearance' of enthusiasm for the war in Ireland; the strengthening of anti-British forces in the country; a slump in recruiting; and profound resentment and disappointment in every overseas British dominion.

Then you are holding in English prisons – it is an extraordinary thing to think of – between 500 and 600 untried prisoners. Let the house understand what that means. Those men are imprisoned under a certain provision or proclamation under the Defence of the Realm Act which gives power to keep interned men who are proved to be of enemy association. If they are not men of enemy association they are illegally detained. Now I venture to say that, in the majority of those cases, it would be impossible to prove that these young men are of enemy association. ... You may say they are dangerous men and you do not want to let them loose because they have extreme opinions. Surely that is going back to the old evil English rule in Ireland. These men are dangerous so long as they are where they are. They cease to be dangerous – they become far less dangerous – the moment they are released, and if the right honourable gentleman wants to create a better atmosphere in Ireland and a better feeling, let him instantly release these men. Let him do it tomorrow. Let him do it as a Christmas gift to the Irish people, and let him withdraw the proclamation of martial law.

Twice Lloyd George interrupts Redmond to remind him that he has been ill and has not had time to deal with the prisoners issue, but to no avail, as the nationalist leader keeps up his attack. Afterwards a furious prime minister tells T.P. O'Connor that Redmond's speech 'bewildered' him and was 'one of the most ill-considered utterances' he has ever listened to in the Commons. Any release of prisoners has now, he claims, been 'robbed of all good grace' by Redmond's behaviour.

Nevertheless, two days later, Duke, the Irish secretary, announces the immediate release of the interned prisoners. All of them, including the future Free State leaders Michael Collins and Arthur Griffith, are home in time for Christmas. Redmond's assurance to the government, however, that the interned men become 'far less dangerous' the moment they are released is very soon open to question. The freed prisoners, many of them now more radicalised than when initially detained, immediately resume revolutionary activities.

They are set to make 1917 a testing year for Redmond politically. It begins, however, with a personal tragedy, when he is cabled from the United States with news of the sudden death of his elder daughter, Esther, at the age of 32. A mother of four small children, she had emigrated eight years earlier following her marriage to a New York doctor, William Power. She lived to be just four years older than her mother, Johanna – Redmond's first wife – was when she died in childbirth, leaving behind a five-year-old Esther and two younger children.

Just days after his daughter's death Redmond receives a confidential memo from T.P. O'Connor outlining details of a conversation he has had with Lloyd George. The prime minister says he is still anxious to find a settlement in Ireland and one that does not involve partition would be far and away the best, but he fears Protestant feeling in the north of Ireland remains irreconcilable to the idea of a united Ireland.

Lloyd George also warns O'Connor that pressure for conscription to be extended to Ireland is growing. Recruitment in Ireland, which has fallen sharply since the rising, is now down to eighty per week, the Cabinet has been told – a fraction of the one thousand-plus per week needed to keep the Irish divisions up to strength. 'I pointed out to him the impossibility of enforcing conscription in Ireland,' writes O'Connor, 'but he said that in the present temper of the English people, with so many of them sending their sons to the War and losing them, these perils must be faced; and he even expressed the opinion that on the issue of conscription he could be beaten in the House of Commons, and a purely Tory Government take his place.'

A longstanding problem for Redmond and his colleagues is that such behind-the-scenes lobbying of the government, of its nature, wins no public credit for the Irish Party. And the first measurable test of its standing in the country in the light of the Easter rebellion and its aftermath is about to be delivered: a by-election has been called in North Roscommon to fill the seat vacated by the death in December of the Irish Party MP, J.J. O'Kelly.

O'Kelly was a Fenian of old with a colourful past as either a participant in or reporter on wars in Mexico, Cuba, the USA, Algeria and Sudan. On his death he was described in his obituary in the *Freeman's Journal* as the last member of parliament to have challenged a fellow MP to a duel. He had represented North Roscommon for twenty unbroken years but was not well known by sight in the constituency, having rarely set foot in it in his later years. To replace him, the United Irish League – the Irish Party's grassroots organisation – nominates Thomas Devine, a local merchant who has a rather less exciting cv than O'Kelly's, but is a locally well-known county councillor.

As yet the anti-Redmondite movement has not formed itself into a coherent political party, but the various groups on the scene – including Sinn Féin and the recently established Irish Nation League, coalesce around a candidate to oppose Devine: a 65-year-old papal count, George Noble Plunkett. A more unlikely revolutionary it would, in many ways, be hard to find. To the embarrassment of some of his supporters, it is revealed during the election campaign that Plunkett, a former director of the National Museum of Science and Art and member of the Royal Dublin Society (RDS), has twice in recent years applied for the position of under secretary at Dublin Castle. In 1911 he flew a papal flag from his house in Kimmage for the visit to Dublin of King George V.

But Plunkett has a trump card that is hard to match: he is the father of Joseph Plunkett, one of the executed signatories of the Easter proclamation. Two of his other sons remain in prison as a result of their participation in the rebellion. He has also acquired martyr status of a sort in his own right, having been dismissed from his museum post following the rising – for no other reason than that his sons were involved – and expelled by the RDS after declaring his candidature in the election.

Plunkett, however, has an even more important card than these. He is backed by energetic and enthusiastic canvassers – many of them released internees, including Collins and Griffith – who overcome the worst winter snows in living memory to take their campaign to the people of the constituency. The Irish Party – unused to having to fight elections in many parts of the country, where seats have gone uncontested for long periods – is no match on the ground for this concerted opposition.

A third candidate, former Irish Party MP and local newspaper owner Jasper Tully, enters the race to campaign on an anti-partition platform while also attacking Plunkett as a 'place hunter'. The charge may have some merit. Plunkett was once an active supporter of the Irish Party and in 1906 wrote to John Redmond asking him, unsuccessfully, for a nomination for the party's North Kilkenny seat, arguing that after all he had done for the party 'a seat is now due to me'.

The result is a stunning reverse for the Irish Party, with Plunkett winning by 3,022 votes to Devine's 1,708 and Tully's 687. In spite of their opponents' more vigorous campaign, the party did not expect to lose the seat, and certainly not by so wide a margin. Among Plunkett's first acts on election is to announce he will not take his seat at Westminster, a move that disappoints some of his supporters.

Redmond is tempted to respond to the result by issuing a manifesto to the Irish people urging them not to abandon the path of constitutional nationalism, but is dissuaded from doing so by Dillon, Devlin and O'Connor.

The nationalist MPs, in particular Dillon, continue to press the government to release the prisoners still held since the rising and to lift martial law in Ireland. They at least get the government's attention when time is set aside on 7 March for a major debate on a motion moved by T.P. O'Connor: 'That, with a view to strengthening the hands of the Allies in achieving the recognition of the equal rights of small nations and the principle of nationality against the opposite German principle of military domination and government without the consent of the governed, it is essential without further delay to confer upon Ireland the free institutions long promised to her.'

Seconding the motion, Willie Redmond, now a major in the army and on leave from the Western Front, delivers the speech of a lifetime. Standing in his army uniform, he tells first hand of the impact on Irish soldiers of hearing rumours that suggest the 'new and better chapter' in relations between their country and Britain, which encouraged them to join the war in the first place, may not be a reality after all. He speaks of calls from other countries in the empire, including Canada and Australia, for Britain to settle the Irish question once and for all, and asks: 'In God's name, why cannot you do it?'

He then urges Edward Carson, in the name of Irishmen who have died and will die on the battlefield and may be dying as they speak, to 'rise to the demands of the situation' and lead his followers in shaking hands with their fellow countrymen.

What stands in the way? We read in our history books of the Battle of the Boyne. The friends of the right honourable gentleman espoused the cause of William hundreds of years ago. Our people passionately adhere to the cause of the fallen Stuarts. Is the sentiment engendered at that time to go on for ever? In the face of a war which is threatening civilisation, which is destroying all that mankind has built up in the Christian era, in the face of all that are we still to continue in Ireland our conflicts and our arguments and disputes about the merits of the Stuarts, about the Battle of the Boyne and the rest? Why does the right honourable gentleman opposite not meet us half way? I want to know what is the reason?

He feels strongly on the matter, Willie Redmond adds, because he wants to represent the wishes, as strongly as he can, of the tens of thousands of Irishmen who went with him and their colleagues to France, many of whom will never return.

I want to speak for these men, and if they could all speak with one voice and with one accord they would say to this house, to men in every part of it, to Conservatives, Liberals and Labour men, to their nationalist countrymen and to their countrymen from the north of Ireland, in the name of God we here who are about to die, perhaps, ask you to do that which largely induced us to leave our homes, to do that which our fathers and mothers taught us to long for, to do that which is all we desire, make our country happy and contented, and enable us when we meet the Canadians and the Australians and the New Zealanders, side by side in the common cause and the common field, to say to them, 'Our country, just as yours, has self-government within the empire.'

Despite the profound effect of this speech on the house, the debate descends into acrimonious exchanges between Lloyd George and the nationalist MPs. When the prime minister insists that the government cannot coerce Ulster into accepting Home Rule, but is prepared to grant it to the part of Ireland that demands it, Joe Devlin interjects:

'Does that include west Belfast?', followed by Willie Redmond: 'What about Tyrone and Fermanagh?'

Things degenerate when John Redmond, his voice trembling with anger, tells Lloyd George he will take part in no more negotiations with the government, before warning: '[I]f the constitutional movement disappears, I beg the prime minister to take note that he will find himself face to face with a revolutionary movement ... He will have to govern Ireland by the naked sword.' He invites his colleagues, 'instead of remaining here to continue a useless, futile, and humiliating debate, to withdraw with me and to take counsel with me as to our next step'.

In a manifesto issued the day after its walkout, the Irish Party emphasises that it never signed up to permanent partition. It initially agreed, it says, on the strict understanding that it would never be asked for a further concession, to the exclusion from Home Rule of certain counties for a limited period only. Then, in the negotiations of the previous July, the exclusion of the six counties was agreed as a 'strictly temporary war arrangement'.

A test of the party's attempt to re-establish its anti-partition credentials quickly comes with another by-election, this time for the South Longford seat vacated as a result of the death of another veteran Fenian, John Phillips. Redmond selects county councillor Patrick McKenna as the party candidate. A committee including Count Plunkett, Arthur Griffith and Michael Collins puts forward Joseph McGuinness, a participant in the rising serving three years' penal servitude in an English prison, to run for the Sinn Féiners. They adopt the slogan: 'Put him in to get him out.'

This time the Irish Party is up for the fight. Redmond, who has been hit by a succession of illnesses since the beginning of the year, is confined to his sick bed for much of the campaign, but other senior figures including John Dillon and Joe Devlin play an active part. On 5 May, the Saturday before polling day, the two arrive by train to address a rally outside the Longford Arms Hotel in the centre of town. While Devlin, on stage, condemns the 'incongruous collection of cranks and frauds' who are attempting to divide the Irish people, three motor cars with Sinn Féin supporters shouting derisive comments pass by.

The Irish Party supporters seize from them what the *Freeman's Journal* describes in its report as a republican flag – a green, white and orange tricolour – which is subsequently burned. Waving the recognised Irish national flag of a gold harp on a green background, Dillon concludes the rally with a rhetorical flurry: 'There it is! There is no yellow discolouration. Under this flag we have stood in hours of trial and difficulty. Under this flag we stand today. Under this flag we will stand tomorrow, and with this flag Mr McKenna will go to victory!' Cheers ring out, followed by a shout of 'Up McKenna!'

Throughout this and other by-election campaigns Redmond's supporters continually deny an allegation, repeatedly made by their opponents, that in the House of Commons the Irish Party MPs cheered the executions of the 1916 leaders. The claim is untrue, but it gains currency over time.

McKenna's chances are also damaged by an extraordinary eleventh-hour intervention by the Archbishop of Dublin, William Walsh, declaring that 'anyone who thinks that partition, whether in its naked deformity, or under the transparent mask of "county option", does not hold a leading place in the practical politics of today is simply living in a fool's paradise ... the mischief has already been done, and the country is practically sold.'

When the votes are counted at Longford courthouse on 9 May, McKenna is initially deemed the winner by a margin of 15, but a supporter of McGuinness's points out that the combined vote of the two candidates is 50 short of the total valid poll. On a recount, McGuinness is declared the winner by 1,498 votes to 1,461, a margin of 37. An exultant Griffith knows who to thank for the victory; the result will be nowhere more welcome than 'in the palace of the archbishop of Dublin', he tells supporters, to cheers.

The result is a devastating blow for the Irish Party, but an even harder one awaits its leader. On 7 June, on the first day of an offensive against German forces on the Messines ridge in West Flanders, the 56-year-old Willie Redmond – disobeying orders to wait until the third wave of the attack by joining his men in the first line – suffers shrapnel wounds to the wrist and leg. Stretcher-bearers from the 36th (Ulster) Division carry him to an advance aid post. Expecting to die, he asks the

Anglican chaplain to send a message to his wife: 'Please thank her for all she has done for me and tell her that if we do not meet again in this world I hope we shall meet in the next.'

John Redmond receives a letter, written the same day, from a field ambulance officer, Captain J.L. Dunlop, who tells him that his brother was brought in early in the morning. 'Although [his] wounds were not of themselves very serious, and probably in a younger man would not have mattered, at his age the shock was too much for him, and he never rallied but died about 6.30 this evening. Everyone here is unanimous in their opinion of his plucky and gallant conduct in persisting in going over with his men. The 16th [Irish] and 36th [Ulster] Divisions had a glorious victory today and they advanced side by side carrying all before them, and it seems very hard lines that Major Redmond did not live to see it.'

Lloyd George, Asquith and Carson are among those who pay tribute to the late MP in the House of Commons, and among the hundreds of personal expressions of sympathy received by John is one from Bonar Law explaining his absence from the Requiem Mass at Westminster Cathedral: 'I was very sorry not to be at the service to your brother, for whom I had not only the greatest respect and even admiration, but a personal liking. On the morning of the service, however, I received a Press indication that my boy whom I had regarded as dead was still alive, and I was in such a state of nervous excitement that I could not face anyone.'

Although outwardly John Redmond and his younger brother had very different personalities – the one reflective and serious, the other outgoing and gregarious – they were very close personally and politically. Willie's death is not just a personal tragedy for John, but it robs him at a critical moment of his most trusted supporter and adviser.

It also throws the Irish Party into another by-election, this time for the East Clare seat. The local branches of the United Irish League select barrister Patrick Lynch to represent the nationalist party; his opponent is another prisoner, Éamon de Valera, sentenced to penal servitude for life for his role in the Easter rebellion as commander of the rebel forces at Boland's Mill. His candidacy is endorsed at a meeting of Sinn Féin activists, including a number of priests, in the Old Ground Hotel in Ennis. A feature of the North Roscommon and South Longford by-elections was the support for the anti-Redmondite candidates by younger members of the clergy.

With electioneering just beginning, de Valera is released under a general amnesty, enabling him to campaign. Extra police are drafted into the county to keep order amid fears of clashes between rival supporters and also in light of sporadic acts of violence through the country since the passing of the first anniversary of the rising. In the worst incident, in Dublin on 11 June, an unarmed policeman involved in arresting Count Plunkett and Cathal Brugha on their way to a banned public meeting was struck in the head with a hurley and killed.

The authorities' fears are confirmed when the election campaign begins in earnest on Sunday, 24 June and, the *Irish Independent* reports next day, is marked by episodes of stone-throwing by both sides. Days later Lynch condemns a reported gun attack on a carload of de Valera supporters, who escape uninjured.

Lynch campaigns vigorously, employing the slogan 'Clare for a Clareman', but his is no match for the furiously energetic campaign conducted by de Valera and his team, which includes Plunkett, Griffith, Collins, Eoin MacNeill, Countess Markievicz and other prominent members of the Sinn Féin movement. Hotels in the county are booked out by canvassers, many sleeping six or eight to a room. Lynch is further hampered by a lack of support from the Irish Party leadership; seeing the writing on the wall from the outset, they keep their distance from their candidate's campaign in the hope of minimising damage to the party.

At a rally in Scariff chaired by the parish priest, Fr Scanlan, de Valera says his policy is for 'a free and independent Irish republic', which would be unattainable if they followed the attitude of John Redmond. At another event in Killaloe, also chaired by the local priest, he says that Sinn Féin's policy is to 'stand up to John Bull' and not to beg from him, and if the Ulster Unionists are not prepared to come in to a united Ireland they will have to 'go under'.

Polling day, 10 July, passes without major incident, but there are scuffles between rival groups of supporters and some claims of personation. De Valera emerges a clear winner, by 5,010 votes to Lynch's 2,035. After the result is declared he steps outside the courthouse to be greeted by a large crowd, many of them women – who press forward to get his autograph – and members of the clergy. 'I call for three cheers for the Irish republic!' he shouts, and 'Three cheers for Clare!' Tricolours are waved and 'The Soldiers' Song', which is becoming the anthem of the new movement, is sung as the triumphant candidate returns to his headquarters in the Old Ground Hotel, followed by his exultant supporters.

Having taken Willie Redmond's old seat, de Valera will go on to represent County Clare for the remainder of his long parliamentary career.

The day after the result is announced John Redmond learns of the death, following a stroke days earlier, of his closest friend in the Irish Party, the Kilkenny MP Pat O'Brien – the third personal tragedy to strike this year following the deaths of his daughter and younger brother. At O'Brien's funeral he breaks down in public and has to be led away from the grave.

Faced with the annihilation of his party at the polls, his health deteriorating and beset by personal tragedies, Redmond must be tempted to leave the political stage. He is not ready to give up yet, however, and has already begun one more attempt at achieving his lifelong political goal: an independent parliament for a united Ireland.

Chapter 27

A LIFE UNDONE

*He was a broken man, and death was already written
on his face.*

Of all the lavishly decorated rooms in the Palace of Westminster, the Royal Gallery of the House of Lords is probably the most sumptuous. Among its striking features are the vast wall paintings on each side of the room, depicting scenes from the Napoleonic Wars, by the nineteenth-century Irish painter Daniel Maclise. This is where members of the highest echelons of government and parliament – from both lower and upper houses – gather for state dinners and official receptions.

On the night of 17 May 1917, the guest of honour is South African Lieutenant General Jan Smuts, a Boer War veteran who has recently accepted a position in David Lloyd George's imperial war cabinet. Proposing the toast, Field Marshal Lord John French – his military career intact in spite of his resignation over the Curragh affair and his subsequent disastrous leadership of the British Expeditionary Force in the war – recalls what a wonderful time he and Smuts had opposing each on the battlefield 16 years earlier.

It was 'an honour', indeed, to have faced as an enemy such a great strategist and tactician, French effuses. 'Our guest tonight will go down in history with these other great names as living illustrations of what we mean when we talk of born leaders of men. Personally, I do not know which I am proudest of, having crossed swords with him, or fought by his side.'

Replying to the toast, Smuts continues the repartee, regaling his hosts with his recollections of a seemingly hilarious escapade when he found himself surrounded in a 'nasty block of mountains' by French. This draws laughter from his audience, reports *The Times*, as does the next part of the general's routine: 'I was face to face practically with disaster. Nothing was left me but the most diligent scouting to find a way out. I did some of the scouting myself, with a small party. I ventured into a place which looked promising, and which bore the appropriate name "Murderer's Gap" [laughter]. I am sorry to say I was the only man who came out alive from that gap. In an account which I saw subsequently of this incident I saw the remark made that one Boer escaped [laughter and cheers], but he probably had so many bullets in him that he would be no further danger [laughter].'

Among the guests listening to the two military chiefs swap amusing stories is another leader who finds himself in a tight corner, John Redmond. Four days earlier, the Irish Party lost the closely fought South Longford by-election and its future looks bleak. But the man sitting next to Redmond, the Liberal peer Lord Crewe, has surprising news.

David Lloyd George, he tells Redmond, has written to him offering to establish an Irish parliament immediately for all but the six north-eastern counties of Ulster. Redmond, knowing the partition ship has sailed and there is now no chance of having such a proposal approved in nationalist Ireland, tells Crewe the offer is impossible to accept. Asked for an alternative, he suggests the only hope is the establishment of an Irish conference, representing all interests, to draw up a constitution for Ireland.

Crewe undertakes to relay the suggestion immediately to the prime minister, who in turn includes the idea in a formal proposal sent to Redmond the next day. The new plan provides for the exclusion of the six Ulster counties to be reviewed by parliament after five years unless they have joined the Irish parliament in the meantime. And a Council of Ireland would be established – made up of members from north and south – with the power to pass legislation for the whole island. It also suggests the establishment of a conference of representative persons to work through any remaining difficulties after the proposed new legislation has had its second reading in the House of Commons. A revision of the much-criticised financial provisions of the existing Government of Ireland Act, to alleviate the potential burden on the Irish taxpayer, is also promised.

These proposals are 'earnestly recommended' by the government, Lloyd George writes, and it is planned to proceed at once to give them effect. If the proposals prove unacceptable, however, there is the alternative of 'a Convention of Irishmen of all parties for the purpose of producing a scheme of Irish self-government'.

Redmond's response is unequivocal. He writes to the prime minister to tell him he has laid the two proposals before his colleagues. 'The first proposal [for 26-county Home Rule] would, in their opinion, find no support in Ireland, and they desire me to inform you that they are irreconcilably opposed to this scheme, and that any measure based on it will meet with their vigorous opposition.' The convention proposal, however, they are prepared to support, provided it is representative 'of Irishmen of all creeds, interests, and parties' and is summoned without delay.

On Monday, 21 May, Lloyd George announces to the House of Commons that the government has decided to establish immediately a convention of representative Irishmen to submit to the British government and parliament a constitution for the future government of Ireland within the empire. He expresses the hope that Sinn Féin will participate in the convention, along with representatives of all interests in Irish life, including local government, churches, trade unions, and commercial and educational bodies. To have a reasonable chance of success, it should be held behind closed doors, he adds.

Redmond, unsurprisingly, given that it was his suggestion in the first place, welcomes the announcement, saying that it is the first time in its history that Ireland has been asked to settle its own problems. He allows himself a moment to express his deep regret at the accumulation of setbacks that has left him and his party where they stand today, reciting as he does so some lines by the poet James Clarence Mangan.

The recent developments have been for me and for my friends naturally in the nature of bitter disappointment. The life of a politician, especially of an Irish politician, is one long series of postponements and compromises and disappointments and disillusions. As we grow old, and this of course bears in upon me, we feel our ideals grow dimmer and more blurred, and perhaps many of them disappearing one by one. One of the greatest of our poets said: –

'Gone, gone forever is the fond belief,
The all-too-generous trust in the ideal.
All my divinities have died of grief
And left me wedded to the rude and real.'

And many many of our cherished ideals, our ideals of a complete, speedy and almost immediate triumph of our policy and of our cause have faded, some of them almost disappeared. And we know that it is a serious consideration for those of us who have spent 40 years at this work, and now are growing old, if we have to face further postponements. For my part I feel we must not shrink from compromise if by this convention which is now proposed, we can secure substantial agreement amongst our people in Ireland; it will be worth all the heart burnings and the postponements and disappointments and disillusions of the last 30 or 40 years ['hear, hear'].

Two months later, on 25 July, the convention holds its first meeting, at Regent House in Trinity College, Dublin. A range of interests from both sides of the nationalist/unionist divide is represented. Lords Midleton, Mayo and Oranmore are among the southern unionist representatives. The Ulster Unionists have also sent a delegation – including Lord Londonderry – but notably it does not include Edward Carson or any of their senior MPs. The four delegates of the Catholic hierarchy include Bishop O'Donnell of Raphoe, a steadfast supporter of the Irish Party. The Church of Ireland primate, Archbishop John Crozier, is one of several representatives of the minority churches.

Redmond and his fellow MPs Joe Devlin, J.J. Clancy and Stephen Gwynn are among the Irish Party contingent, though to Redmond's disappointment John Dillon declines to take part, insisting that he can be of more use to the convention outside it than in it. The nationalist representation is boosted by the presence of 31 county council chairmen, while government nominees include the provost of Trinity College, John Mahaffy, the writer George Russell (Æ), Sir Horace Plunkett, who is elected chairman, and Redmond's long-time adversary, the *Irish Independent* owner and business magnate William Martin Murphy. There are seven labour representatives but the organised workers' movement has rejected an invitation to participate. Even more conspicuously absent is Sinn Féin, which turns down the five seats allocated to it.

The absence of the party that is rapidly becoming the dominant force in Irish nationalism does not augur well for the convention's prospects, but Redmond is determined to make the initiative work. Operating, for the first time, in an all-Ireland forum representative of both traditions on the island, he is infused with a new spirit and energy.

'Never in my life did I find so much cause for admiration of Redmond as in the early stages – which were in many ways the most important – of our meetings,' Stephen Gwynn will write later. 'Never at any time did I know him to exert so successfully his charm of public manner ... His mastery both of the form and substance of procedure was conspicuous. One of the ablest among the Southern Unionists said to me in these days: "He is superb: he does not seem able to put a word wrong".'

Redmond is still coming to terms with Willie's death six weeks earlier, but Gwynn's conclusion is that in the convention, he is happier than he has been for a long time. 'There was a note in it that I never felt in the House of Commons, even when he was at his best. There he always spoke as if almost a foreigner, no matter among how many familiar faces. Here he was among his own countrymen, and for the first time in his life in an assembly in no way sectional.'

Outside the convention doors, however, it is a different story. As Redmond leaves Trinity College after the opening session, he is set upon by a crowd that follows him down the street, booing and heckling him. One of those involved, a 15-year-old Todd Andrews, who is in town to do a message for his mother when he happens on the scene, will boast about the incident in a memoir more than 50 years later:

> The booing was taken up by the rest of us and as the crowd grew larger and larger the boos grew louder and louder while Redmond walked along Westmoreland Street. By the time he reached *The Irish Times* office, the crowd was transformed into a threatening

mob. Some passers-by with a sense of responsibility threw a cocoon around Redmond, taking him into the office of *The Irish Times*; the crowd then dispersed. One of the passers-by who stepped in to rescue Redmond was, I learned afterwards, RC Barton, who was to be a signatory of the Treaty in 1921. I am quite sure that if any of the mob had offered physical violence to Redmond I would have joined in.

The episode constitutes a shocking fall from grace for a man who, not long before, was addressing a rally in O'Connell Street that filled the capital's main thoroughfare with admirers from one end of it to the other. It does not prevent him, however, from carrying on his work at the convention with enthusiasm.

He is not alone in this, and the convention has the almost immediate good effect of eliminating suspicion and mistrust between its nationalist and unionist members. Gwynn will recall an Ulster delegate telling him they expected the county council chairmen to be 'noisy demagogues', but were surprised to encounter instead 'solid, substantial business men ... all of them most good-humoured in their tolerance of dissent'.

A successful visit is made to Belfast at the invitation of the Lord Mayor, Sir Crawford McCullagh, during which the attitude of the Ulster members, notes Gwynn, 'which had till then been somewhat guarded and aloof, changed into that of the traditional Irish hospitality'. The delegates are given a tour of the shipyards and great linen mills, and workers who line up to observe them are all heard asking one question, according to Gwynn: 'Which one is Redmond?'

In Belfast, Redmond makes a speech to the convention in which he compliments the Ulster Unionists for their 'true patriotism' in taking part and offering to accept 'the most stringent safeguards' to ensure that their rights are protected in an Irish parliament. A return visit to Cork builds further on the goodwill being created, though the main excitement is caused by a group of Sinn Féin supporters who – shouting 'Up Dublin!', 'Up de Valera!' and 'Who cheered the executions?' – attack Joe Devlin at the harbour and attempt to throw him into the water. Devlin shows 'a bold front' to his assailants, reports the *Irish*

Independent, before, 'excited and warlike', he is induced to leave in a waiting car.

While the convention proceeds with its bridge building, events outside it underline the continuing change of mood in nationalist Ireland. On 11 August, W.T. Cosgrave, a Sinn Féin member of Dublin Corporation who fought in the rising, is declared the winner – by a two-to-one majority over the Irish Party candidate – of the Kilkenny city by-election, giving him the seat previously held by Redmond's close friend Pat O'Brien. Cosgrave's campaign is helped by a counter-productive decision by the authorities to suppress the *Kilkenny People* newspaper, previously a supporter of the Irish Party but now backing Sinn Féin.

The re-arrests of a number of Sinn Féin activists for continuing to foment revolution serves only to further boost the anti-Redmonites' cause. They receive another propaganda boost with the death on 25 September of Thomas Ashe while on hunger strike in Mountjoy prison in pursuit of a demand – supported by Redmond – for political status by about thirty Sinn Féin prisoners. The 32-year-old Ashe was being force fed by the prison authorities when he became ill and died of heart failure. His death provokes a new wave of anti-British sentiment in the country and his funeral, reminiscent in scale of that of O'Donovan Rossa just over two years earlier, takes on all the trappings of a state event, culminating in the firing of a volley of shots over the grave and an oration by – as he is described in the *Independent* – Vice Commandant Michael Collins.

Moving a motion of censure against the government in the House of Commons, Redmond says its repressive measures threaten to wreck any chance of a successful outcome to the convention. 'They [the authorities in Ireland] have been arresting men up and down the country,' he says, 'mostly unknown and insignificant men, and trying them on trivial charges before military tribunals, mostly for silly speeches made here and there at public meetings in the country, thereby turning these men into martyrs ... They issued a proclamation forbidding men to carry hurling sticks on their shoulders, sticks something similar to your hockey sticks in this country. They have made that an offence and they have actually sent men to prison for doing it.'

Henry Duke, the Irish chief secretary, insists in response that only those who have incited violence or taken part in 'deliberate or determined infringement of regulations intended for the public safety' have been arrested. He cites at length statements made by 'the member for East Clare' – Éamon de Valera – urging that the time for speechmaking is past and the time for action has begun, and advising his followers to get hold of guns and other weapons. But Duke declines to answer directly when challenged by a Conservative MP as to why de Valera remains 'at large'.

A day after the Commons debate, Sinn Féin activists gather for a convention at which de Valera is elected president of the organisation, finally establishing it as a united, republican party. A split is averted when the hitherto monarchist Griffith agrees to support the new direction of the party he founded, and remains on as vice-president.

The Irish Convention, having discussed various schemes including different types of dominion Home Rule – involving autonomy within the empire – is now getting down to the serious business of trying to reach a consensus. It is hampered by the fact that the Ulster unionist delegates do not have the authority to strike a deal without reference to their political masters and are in effect there on a watching brief.

They make it clear, however, that they are not prepared to countenance a scheme involving fiscal autonomy for Ireland, which emerges as the key sticking point in the negotiations. Although the existing Government of Ireland Act does not provide for full fiscal independence, changing circumstances – which have seen Ireland's contribution to the imperial exchequer increase since the start of the war – have made this a priority demand for the nationalists. For the unionists, fiscal autonomy is tantamount to complete separation from Westminster. They also fear that, granted this power, an Irish parliament could impose trade barriers between Ireland and Britain that would be detrimental to industry in Ulster.

Redmond, fearful that the convention is about to collapse, urges Lloyd George to intercede, writing to the prime minister to suggest that he and Edward Carson 'speak plainly' to the Ulster unionists about what is at stake. 'Unless some power outside now intervenes, the convention will prove abortive, and no one knows better than yourself what that will mean,' he writes. 'It will mean governing Ireland at the point of the bayonet. Do not imagine that anything else will be possible. Sinn Féin will be omnipotent, and you will be forced to appoint a military governor. The nationalist party will be helpless, and will inevitably disappear, and you will have a scandal in Ireland which will echo right round the world, and the effect of which will most undoubtedly be very serious, in America especially.'

Lloyd George responds with an assurance that he fully realises the importance of getting an agreement if possible. 'I know too well what the consequences of a failure of the convention would mean to Ireland. The alternative to that failure is one which I, with my record of opposition to anything in the nature of coercion in Ireland would regard with perfect horror.'

There is renewed hope of an agreement, however, when the southern unionists, led by Lord Midleton, propose a compromise: they will support an all-Ireland parliament as long as Britain retains control over customs. This would involve a major concession on the part of the nationalists, but for the first time Redmond has an offer from Irish unionists to place themselves, subject to certain conditions, under the jurisdiction of an all-Ireland parliament. He writes again to Lloyd George seeking a commitment that, should the nationalists come to an agreement with the southern unionists, the prime minister would put their scheme before parliament and fight the Ulster unionists on it.

Lloyd George replies that he would put such a scheme before Cabinet, but there would need to be reasonable provisions for the 'difficulties of Ulster'. This is nowhere near a strong enough commitment for Redmond, who continues in vain to press Lloyd George for a commitment that the government will enforce an agreement reached by the nationalists with the southern unionists – whether their Ulster brethren are on board or not. Ironically, having persuaded Lloyd George that the best hope for Ireland lay in allowing its own people to come together to work out arrangements for the governance of their country, Redmond is now harrying the prime minister to step in and impose a settlement.

In spite of Lloyd George's refusal to engage, on 4 January 1918 Redmond makes an impassioned speech to the convention in support of the Midleton scheme. Underlining the degree to which he prizes the maintenance of a united Ireland over almost all other considerations, he declares that his 'modest ambition would be to serve in some quite humble capacity under the first unionist prime minister of Ireland'.

An 11-day break in discussion on the issue follows, during which Redmond is confined to bed in Aughavanagh with a chill. He is confident that when he returns to the convention on Tuesday, 15 January, a motion he will move in favour of the Midleton proposals will have the backing of at least 75 per cent of the convention delegates.

He returns to Dublin on the Monday, however, to devastating news. Bishop O'Donnell, a consistent ally up to now, tells him he cannot support the Midleton compromise because, without the backing of the Ulster unionists, he believes it is destined to fail. And, in a fatal blow, Joe Devlin informs his party leader that he too is withdrawing his support.

Arriving at Regent House for the Tuesday session, Redmond is greeted by Stephen Gwynn, who informs him that he has a seconder for the motion. Redmond tells him not to bother, as 'Devlin and the bishops are voting against me.'

Standing up in the convention moments later, Redmond explains that he has been ill and therefore unable to consult anybody about the motion in his name. He believes it would be carried by the convention but only at the cost of dividing the nationalists, so he will not now move his proposal, but simply leave it to stand on the notice paper. He feels, he adds, that he can be 'of no further service to the convention'.

A moment of silence follows, while all those present absorb the fact that they have just witnessed – as the Unionist MP Ronald McNeill will describe it – 'the fall of a notable leader'.

Redmond still does not give up, writing yet again to Lloyd George – to no avail – urging him to personally intervene with the convention leaders to secure a settlement. By now, the Irish Party is fighting yet another by-election against Sinn Féin, this time for the seat in South Armagh. At a rally in Bessbrook on 26 January, de Valera describes the Ulster unionists as a rock on the road that must be blasted out of the way. But, as the *Freeman's Journal* reports, he faces a barrage of interruptions such as: 'What is your nationality?!', 'Spanish!', and 'Go back to Spain!'

After its facile victories over the Irish Party in southern constituencies, Sinn Féin finds that it is facing a more organised and determined opponent in the north. This is partly due to Joe Devlin's personal popularity and his superb abilities as a political organiser. Another factor is that the parliamentary party is more used to fighting elections in the north, where it routinely comes up against unionist candidates, than in the south, where many constituencies have gone uncontested for successive elections.

The result in South Armagh is a resounding victory for the Irish Party, its candidate Patrick Donnelly defeating his Sinn Féin rival by 2,324 votes to 1,305.

The outcome should be a major fillip for Redmond, but, dogged by continuing bouts of ill-health and disillusioned over the inevitable failure of the convention, he is beginning his withdrawal from public life. Conscious that his life's work has unravelled, he is overtaken by a sense of doom about the future of his country, telling Gwynn that he sees nothing ahead 'but ruin and chaos', and advising an acquaintance, Elizabeth Burke-Plunkett, the Countess of Fingall, in a letter: 'Do not give your heart to Ireland, for if you do, you will die of a broken heart.'

Writing to another friend, Michael Governey, on 14 February, he laments: 'People talk about taking a strong course. They remind me of the man in Shakespeare who was described as "ever strong upon the stronger side". The strong man today, I am sorry to say, in Ireland is the man who shouts with the biggest crowd.'

He continues his political work, writing once more to Lloyd George on 16 February, from his flat in Kensington, to appeal to the prime minister to reverse a decision to close the Arklow explosives factory. 'I need not point out to you the alarming effects which are bound to be produced by the dismissal of three thousand men and the complete destruction of the little town of Arklow, with its six thousand inhabitants,' he writes.

Ten days later, his health continuing to deteriorate, he writes to Dillon to inform him that he is to have an operation for suspected gallstones and, given that he will be out of action for some time, the party ought to select a new leader. 'It would be absurd for me to remain Chairman, when I am constantly absent and unable to do anything, and, of course, in a position where I could have no share in guiding the party.'

A few days later he is operated on in a London nursing home for an intestinal blockage. He initially seems to recover well and on the afternoon of 5 March his private secretary, T.J. Hanna, issues a statement to the press: 'Mr Redmond had a good night, and his progress is maintained.' A further bulletin at 9 p.m. states: 'Mr Redmond has had a fair day, and his progress is maintained.' In fact, his heart has weakened and his family have been called to his bedside, where they find him in great pain.

He dies, aged 61, at 7.45 a.m. on 6 March, in the company of his wife Amy, son William and daughter Johanna, as well as Willie's widow, Eleanor.

Speaking in the House of Commons later that day, just half an hour after hearing the news of his death, Lloyd George says there was no position which Redmond could not have attained.

> He gave all his great gifts, not merely of parliamentary oratory – which were almost unrivalled – but his gifts of real statesmanship, he gave them all, his time, his opportunity, his strength, his health, and even his life, he gave them all to the service of Ireland. And it is one of the tragedies of a land of many tragedies that he was not afforded the opportunity to use to the full those great powers of leadership and wise and sagacious statesmanship for the benefit of his native land.

He adds that he last saw Redmond just a few days earlier.

> He was a broken man, and death was already written on his face. But his last word to me was a plea for concord – concord between the two races that providence has decided shall work together for the common ends of humanity as neighbours. He has passed away. We can only here in this house extend sympathy to his sorrowing family and his friends – yea, and to the sorrowing country which is bereft of his wise leadership at the greatest crisis of its fate.

Asquith describes Redmond's death as an 'indescribable shock', and Carson pays tribute to his long-time adversary, recalling that during the failed negotiations of July 1916 Redmond had said to him: 'Unless we can settle this interminable business, you and I will be dead before anything has happened to pacify Ireland.'

> That is a very tragic recollection. After all, this is not the occasion on which we can fully appreciate his work. As far as I am concerned, it is enough for me that he was a great Irishman and a most honourable opponent, and as such we mourn his loss.

The following day's *Freeman's Journal* devotes four pages to the news and obituary, its main headline running across a page: DEATH OF THE IRISH NATIONAL LEADER.

The *Irish Independent* pays tribute to an 'honourable, upright and chivalrous' politician, but suggests his ultimate failure to achieve his goals was down to his own weakness.

> Rightly or wrongly, a great proportion of Nationalists had grown cold in their attachment to him. His last days resembled very closely those of O'Connell, Butt and Parnell. Such has been the tragic fate of Irish leaders. Had the reasonable aspirations of the Irish people been realised, his career, otherwise so brilliant, would have ended in triumph. Unfortunately, the hopes of the country were disappointed; and while the Government have been blamed, the feeling has been widely entertained that, had Mr Redmond been more robust as leader and enforced Ireland's demand with more vigour, they might have been compelled to satisfy our claim.

After Requiem Mass at Westminster Cathedral, attended by Lloyd George, Bonar Law, Carson and other leading figures of the British establishment, Redmond's body is taken home for interment in the family vault in Wexford town. The coffin is conveyed by steamer from Holyhead and, on arrival at Kingstown pier, is carried by members of the National Volunteers to the special train taking it to Wexford.

A large crowd of mourners gather outside the pier gates to pay their respects and, the *Independent* reports, workmen and women in the fields bow their heads as the train passes, while at every train station en route people kneel and pray. 'Passing the grounds of the Convent of the Benedictine Nuns of Ypres near Macmine Junction,' the paper adds, 'the Sisters knelt in the fields beside the line and recited the Rosary, the scene being a particularly touching one. It was, it will be remembered, Mr Redmond who helped to find a home for the refugee nuns, one of whom is a niece of the deceased.'

The coffin is carried through streets thronged with people and, in a graveside oration, John Dillon says Redmond was a great statesman, a great patriot and a great orator, in addition to being a great leader, who had the art of making himself not only respected but also beloved by all who followed his lead.

The greatness of the work which he accomplished for Ireland and the immensity of the obstacles which he, during the last 17 years, has removed, and finally removed, from the path of Ireland's freedom it would be idle today to attempt to describe. Time will do justice to his work and to his statesmanship ['hear, hear'], and all the people of Ireland – even those who today misunderstand him – will in time to come understand the greatness of his life and of his work and of the unselfishness of his career.

EPILOGUE

On Sunday, 30 September 1956, Wexford honoured the memory of John Redmond by hosting a number of events to mark the centenary of his birth.

Members of the inter-party government present for the unveiling of a plaque to the late nationalist leader in Redmond Square – so named after John Redmond's grand uncle and namesake – included James Dillon, the minister for agriculture. He recalled the day when, as a boy, he stood beside his father John while he delivered the graveside oration at Redmond's funeral. James Dillon said he remained, as he had been that day nearly forty years before, 'a proud and unrepentant Redmondite'.

That evening academics gathered in the town's Theatre Royal for a symposium on Redmond chaired by the chancellor of the National University, Éamon de Valera.

Bringing the proceedings to a close, de Valera – also leader of the opposition Fianna Fáil party – said that one reason he had accepted the invitation to preside over the conference was because he wanted to acknowledge that it was through the efforts of the Irish Party that the University Act of 1908 had been enacted. It was his duty, then, as chancellor, to be there when honour was being paid to the man most responsible for securing the establishment of the National University.

He had not changed his views on his differences with Redmond, he said, but 'I am happy to play my part in doing honour to a great Wexford man to whom we are quite ready to give credit for having worked unselfishly according to his views for the welfare of this country.'

By this time the Irish Parliamentary Party name had long been erased from the political scene. However, in the weeks following Redmond's death the party, under John Dillon's leadership, had enjoyed a brief renaissance.

Redmond's son William, campaigning in his Irish Guards uniform, retained for the party his father's old Waterford seat in a by-election marked by outbursts of violence on both sides. Voters meeting the younger Redmond were greeted by a stocky man sporting a moustache, looking every inch a younger version of his father, with the diminutive Joe Devlin at his shoulder.

The party also retained the seat for East Tyrone relinquished by William to enable him to contest the Waterford vacancy, giving it three by-election victories in succession over Sinn Féin.

For a moment, it appeared that the Irish Party was regaining the initiative from its upstart rival, but the British government – ever helpful to the hardliners – stepped in to give them a new gift, deciding to extend conscription to Ireland. The surrender of the Bolsheviks at Brest-Litovsk, enabling a million German soldiers to move to the Western Front, combined with other developments on the battlefield, had left the British forces desperately in need of recruits.

One report suggested that it could boost its ranks by 200,000 Irishmen through the introduction of conscription in the country. Lloyd George, disregarding the protests of the Irish Party MPs in the House of Commons, found this too tempting a prize. But nationalist Ireland – including Sinn Féin, the Irish Parliamentary Party, the labour movement and the Catholic Church – combined forces to make implementation of the measure impossible, forcing the government to back down.

Although the Irish Party had played a prominent part in defeating conscription, Sinn Féin was the main beneficiary of the new wave of indignation provoked by the attempt to introduce it. In the December 1918 general election, the new movement's supremacy was confirmed, as Sinn Féin took 73 seats to the Irish Party's six. It was helped by the British parliament's first-past-the-post system, which gave it far more seats than its 48 per cent vote – compared to 23 per cent for the Irish Party – would have secured under proportional representation.

On the other hand, the Sinn Féin percentage vote would undoubtedly have been higher had the Irish Party not left uncontested 25 constituencies that it knew it had no chance of winning. In 37 straight fights between the two parties, Sinn Féin won 35 – the exceptions being victories for William Redmond in Waterford and the ever-popular Devlin in West Belfast.

Although a successor party initially led by Devlin continued to operate in the north for many more decades, it was the end of the Irish Parliamentary Party as it was known.

John Redmond's family, too, continued to suffer more than its share of misfortune. On 3 March 1922, Max Green, chairman of the Irish Prisons Board and husband of Redmond's daughter, Johanna, was leaving St Stephen's Green by a gate opposite the Shelbourne Hotel when he came face to face with an escaping armed robber. Responding to a shout of 'Stop that man!', he attempted to apprehend the criminal, who drew a revolver and shot him dead. Johanna, already unwell, died nine months later aged 35 at her home on Appian Way in Dublin, leaving behind the couple's nine-year-old twin boys, Max and Redmond.

William Redmond remained in politics, winning a Dáil seat in Waterford as an independent nationalist in 1923. He later joined Cumann na nGaedheal, but his life too was cut short when, in 1932, aged 45, he suffered a heart attack and died while attending the funeral of a friend. His wife, Bridget – with whom he had no children – went on to hold a Waterford seat for Fine Gael until her death, aged 47, in 1952 brought to an end a long unbroken sequence of parliamentary politics featuring the Redmond name.

A NOTE ON SOURCES

Rather than use footnotes throughout the text, I have attempted to make sources clear within the narrative.

Specific newspaper reports are credited in most instances, though in some cases where there were multiple reports of the same event or speech, no single publication is cited. The Irish Newspapers Archive website, which provides access to the *Irish Independent*, *Freeman's Journal* and *Cork Examiner* newspapers among many others, the *Irish Times* digital archive and the online archive of the London *Times* are extensively relied upon.

Unless otherwise indicated, accounts of meetings attended and correspondence engaged in by John Redmond are taken from his personal papers held at the National Library in Dublin. Where there is specific reliance on the David Lloyd George and Bonar Law papers, both held at the Parliamentary Archives office at Westminster, this is clearly expressed.

Debates in the House of Commons are largely taken from the digitised editions of Hansard, the official report of debates in parliament. Extensive use is also made of newspaper reports, in particular from the London *Times*, to add colour and detail.

A full list of publications and websites drawn on is provided in the bibliography but some merit special mention. Denis Gwynn's biography of John Redmond, *The Life of John Redmond* (1932), and Dermot Meleady's excellent *John Redmond: The National Leader* (2013) are both invaluable guides. The extract in Chapter 26 from Billie Redmond's letter from the Front in July 1916, which is part of a private collection, is taken from Meleady.

The references to Sinn Féin's rise to prominence rely heavily on Michael Laffan's *The Resurrection of Ireland* (1999). The descriptive account of the granting of the royal assent to the Government of Ireland Bill in Chapter 21 is largely based on the eyewitness account of the parliamentary reporter Michael MacDonagh in *The Home Rule Movement* (1920). The account of the murders of the archduke Franz Ferdinand and his wife in Sarajevo in the opening paragraphs of Chapter

18 draws on Christopher Clark's description in *The Sleepwalkers* (2013).

Patricia Jalland's *The Liberals and Ireland* (1993) is particularly good on the talks Herbert Asquith held with Bonar Law and Edward Carson, detailed in Chapter 10, and John Kendle's book *Walter Long, Ireland and the Union, 1905–1920* (1992) is equally so on the failure of the Lloyd George-brokered talks to secure a deal in the aftermath of the Easter Rising, discussed in Chapter 25. Both are very useful guides.

For the account of Willie Redmond's death in Chapter 26, acknowledgement is due to Terence Denman's *A Lonely Grave* (1995). Several biographies of Edward Carson are relied upon, in particular Ian Colvin's *Carson the Statesman* (1935) and H. Montgomery Hyde's *Carson* (1974). The insider account of the Ulster Unionist movement by Ronald McNeill, *Ulster's Stand for Union* (1922), and A.T.Q. Stewart's *The Ulster Crisis* (1997) are of enormous assistance in explaining the forces ranged against Redmond in the northern province. Also deserving of particular mention is H.H. Asquith's *Letters to Venetia Stanley* (1982), which is quoted from in several places – a terrific read on many levels.

BIBLIOGRAPHY

aan de Wiel, Jérôme . 'The "Irish factor" in the outbreak of war in 1914'. *History Ireland*. April 2011.

Andrews, C.S. *Dublin Made Me*. Lilliput Press, 2001.

Asquith, H.H. *Letters to Venetia Stanley*, eds Michael Brock and Eleanor Brock. Oxford University Press, 1982.

Bew, Paul. *John Redmond*. Dundalgan Press, 1996.

Brock, Michael and Eleanor Brock, *Margot Asquith's Great War Diary 1914–1916: The View from Downing Street*. Oxford University Press, 2014.

Calwell, C.E. *Field-Marshall Sir Henry Wilson: His Life and Diaries*. Cassell & Co. 1927.

Clark, Christopher. *The Sleepwalkers: How Europe Went to War in 1914*. Penguin, 2013.

Clarke, Peter. *Hope and Glory: Britain 1900–2000*. 2nd edn. Penguin, 2004.

Churchill, Winston S. *My Early Life: A Roving Commission*. Reprint Society, 1944.

Collins, Stephen. *People, Politics and Power: From O'Connell to Ahern*. O'Brien Press, 2007.

Colvin, Ian. *Carson the Statesman*. The Macmillan Company, 1935.

Crawford, Fred H. *Guns For Ulster*. Graham & Heslip, 1947.

Crowe, Catriona, ed. *Dublin 1911*. Prism, 2011.

Denman, Terence. *A Lonely Grave: The Life and Death of William Redmond*. Irish Academic Press, 1995.

Fanning, Ronan. *Fatal Path: British Government and Irish Revolution 1910–1922*. Faber & Faber, 2013.

Figgis, Darrell. *Recollections of the Irish War*. Doubleday, Doran & Co., 1928.

Gwynn, Denis. *The Life of John Redmond*. George G. Harrap & Co. 1932.

Gwynn, Stephen. *John Redmond's Last Years*. Edward Arnold, 1919.

Hobson, Bulmer. *A Short History of the Irish Volunteers*. Candle Press, 1918.

Horgan, John J. *Parnell to Pearse: Some Recollections and Reflections.* 1949. University College Dublin Press, 2009.

Jalland, Patricia. *The Liberals and Ireland: The Ulster Question in British Politics to 1914.* 1980. Gregg Revivals, 1993.

Kendle, John. *Walter Long, Ireland and the Union, 1905–1920.* McGill–Queen's University Press, 1992.

Laffan, Michael. *The Resurrection of Ireland: The Sinn Féin Party, 1916–1923.* Cambridge University Press, 1999.

Laffan, Michael. 'The Irish Revolution'. Podcast. *History Hub,* 2012. (http://historyhub.ie/theirishrevolution).

Lloyd George, David. *War Memoirs,* vols I and II. Nicholson & Watson, 1933.

Martin, F.X., ed. *The Irish Volunteers 1913–15: Recollections and Documents.* 1963. Merrion, 2013.

McConnel, James. *The Irish Parliamentary Party and the Third Home Rule Crisis.* Four Courts Press, 2013.

MacDonagh, Michael. *The Home Rule Movement.* Talbot Press, 1920.

McNeill, Ronald. *Ulster's Stand for Union.* John Murray, 1922.

Macready, Nevil. *Annals of an Active Life.* Hutchinson & Co. 1924.

Marjoribanks, Edward. *Carson the Advocate.* The Macmillan Company, 1932.

Meleady, Dermot. *John Redmond: The National Leader.* Merrion, 2013.

Montgomery Hyde, H. *Carson: The Life of Sir Edward Carson, Lord Carson of Duncairn.* Constable, 1974.

Privilege, John. *Michael Logue and the Catholic Church in Ireland, 1879–1925.* Manchester University Press, 2009.

Riddell, Lord George. *More Pages from My Diary, 1908–1914.* Country Life, 1934.

Ridley, Jane. *Bertie: A Life of Edward VII.* Vintage, 2013.

Stewart, A.T.Q. *Edward Carson.* Gill & Macmillan, 1981.

Stewart, A.T.Q. *The Ulster Crisis: Resistance to Home Rule 1912–1914.* 1967. Blackstaff Press, 1997.

Ulster Unionist Council, Belfast. 'The lesson of Craigavon: the voice of Ulster, "We will not have Home Rule"'. Belfast, 1911.

NEWSPAPERS

Cork Examiner
Freeman's Journal
Irish Independent
Irish Times
Skibbereen Eagle
Southern Star
The Times
Ulster Herald
Westmeath Examiner

PRIVATE PAPERS

John Redmond Papers, National Library, Dublin
John Dillon Papers, Trinity College, Dublin
Lloyd George Papers, Parliamentary Archives, Westminster
Bonar Law Papers, Parliamentary Archives, Westminster

WEBSITES

Historic Hansard (http://hansard.millbanksystems.com/)
History Hub (http://historyhub.ie/)
History Ireland (http://www.historyireland.com/)
Irish Newspaper Archives (https://www.irishnewsarchive.com/)
Irish Times digital archive (http://www.irishtimes.com/archive)
The Times digital archive (http://www.thetimes.co.uk/tto/archive/)

INDEX